STRATEGIC MANAGEMENT

Dr. T. P. Renuka Murty M.Com, MBA, Ph.D
Professor, Department of Management Studies & Research Center
GSSS Institute of Engineering & Technology for Women
Mysore

Mrs. Waseeha Firdose B.E, MBA, M.Phil, SLET, (Ph.D)
Asst. Prof., Department of Commerce & Management
Govt. R. C College of Commerce & Management
Bangaluru

MUMBAI • NEW DELHI • NAGPUR • BENGALURU • HYDERABAD • CHENNAI • PUNE • LUCKNOW • AHMEDABAD • ERNAKULAM • BHUBANESWAR • INDORE • KOLKATA • GUWAHATI

First Edition : 2013

Published by : Mrs. Meena Pandey for **Himalaya Publishing House Pvt. Ltd.,**
"Ramdoot", Dr. Bhalerao Marg, Girgaon, **Mumbai - 400 004.**
Phone: 022-23860170/23863863, Fax: 022-23877178
E-mail: himpub@vsnl.com; Website: www.himpub.com

Branch Offices :

New Delhi : "Pooja Apartments", 4-B, Murari Lal Street, Ansari Road, Darya Ganj, New Delhi - 110 002. Phone: 011-23270392, 23278631; Fax: 011-23256286

Nagpur : Kundanlal Chandak Industrial Estate, Ghat Road, Nagpur - 440 018. Phone: 0712-2738731, 3296733; Telefax: 0712-2721215

Bengaluru : No. 16/1 (Old 12/1), 1st Floor, Next to Hotel Highlands, Madhava Nagar, Race Course Road, Bengaluru - 560 001. Phone: 080-32919385; Telefax: 080-22286611

Hyderabad : No. 3-4-184, Lingampally, Besides Raghavendra Swamy Matham, Kachiguda, Hyderabad - 500 027. Phone: 040-27560041, 27550139; Mobile: 09848130433

Chennai : 8/2 Madley 2nd street, T. Nagar, Chennai - 600 017. Phone: 044-32463737; Mobile: 09320490962

Pune : First Floor, "Laksha" Apartment, No. 527, Mehunpura, Shaniwarpeth (Near Prabhat Theatre), Pune - 411 030. Phone: 020-24496323/24496333

Lucknow : House No 731, Shekhupura Colony, Near B.D. Convent School, Aliganj, Lucknow - 226 022. Mobile: 09307501549

Ahmedabad : 114, "SHAIL", 1st Floor, Opp. Madhu Sudan House, C.G. Road, Navrang Pura, Ahmedabad - 380 009. Phone: 079-26560126; Mobile: 09327324149, 09314679413

Ernakulam : 39/104 A, Lakshmi Apartment, Karikkamuri Cross Rd., Ernakulam, Cochin - 622011, Kerala. Phone: 0484-2378012, 2378016; Mobile: 09344199799

Bhubaneswar : 5 Station Square, Bhubaneswar - 751 001 (Odisha). Phone: 0674-2532129, Mobile: 09861046007

Indore : Kesardeep Avenue Extension, 73, Narayan Bagh, Flat No. 302, IIIrd Floor, Near Humpty Dumpty School, Indore - 452 007 (M.P.). Mobile: 09301386468

Kolkata : 108/4, Beliaghata Main Road, Near ID Hospital, Opp. SBI Bank, Kolkata - 700 010, Phone: 033-32449649, Mobile: 09910440956

Guwahati : House No. 15, Behind Pragjyotish College, Near Sharma Printing Press, P.O. Bharalumukh, Guwahati - 781009, (Assam). Mobile: 09883055590, 09883055536

DTP by : *SPS,* Bengaluru

Printed at : **M/s. Roshan Printers**, Bengaluru on behalf of HPH.

Dedicated to

Late Prof. B. S. Pandit

Hon, Founder Secretary

Geetha Shishu Shikshana Sangha (R)

Mysore

Preface

Strategic management activities enable businesses to capitalize on competitive opportunities worldwide. Effective managers develop tools and techniques to analyze their business environment. Appreciation of the complexities of national institutions, multiple stakeholders and fluctuating demands, helps managers allocate resources efficiently to sustain and grow their businesses. Environmental influences like politics, economics, social trends, technology, environment and laws affect business strategies. Because these influences occur on a large, global scale, their impacts can be difficult to assess, predict and handle.

The purpose of this book is to provide knowledge of strategy and its role in promoting the companies' competitive advantage. This text draws from all functional areas of business and presents a solid strategic management model from a top- level strategic perspective. It is most useful for the students with backgrounds in related fields such as management, accounting, economics, finance.

A summary of the main features follows:

- Overview of strategic management
- Analyzing a company's external environment
- Strategy formulation
- Analyzing a company's resources and competitive position
- Generic competitive strategies
- Business planning in different environments
- Strategy implementation
- Strategic control

The book presents Indian flavors and subject of strategic management against contemporary corporate events in India. The text includes numerous carefully integrated examples of practices in real organizations clearly illustrate the concepts being discussed and each chapter included case studies and analysis of case studies. The subject matter has been presented in a simple and lucid manner, keeping the multifarious requirements of students in mind. Every attempt has been made to maintain easy readability and quick comprehension.

Finally, we express our sincere thank to *SPS*, Bangalore, their excellent computer typesetting work and the printing.

We offer our gratitude to Himalya Publishing House Pvt. Ltd, who is leader in Commerce and Management publications. Our sincere regards to Mr. Niraj Pandey and Vijay Pandey for interest shown, and for the best effort put forth by the matter of publication of this book.

Any suggestions regarding improvement and errors, if any, will be gratefully acknowledged.

Bengaluru **Authors**

Sep, 2013

Preface

Authors

Contents *Cum Syllabus*

Module-1

Introduction to Strategic Management

Unit

Syllabus

Meaning and Nature of Strategic Management, its importance and relevance. Characteristics of Strategic Management. The Strategic Management Process. Relationship between a Company's Strategy and its Business Model.

INTRODUCTION

Strategy is the overall plan or courses of action of the firm deploying its resources to establish a favorable position and compete in the global market. Strategy is playing a vital role in the modern business due to the business environment. A strategic approach which builds on its strengths and is a fit with the firm's internal and external environment . It basically supports firm to achieve competitive advantage and firms can perform long period in this competitive world. As business organizations began to build their presence around the world and develop their resources in the global scenario, strategic management also gained sufficient momentum in the company policies, plans and procedures.

Today's dynamic markets and technologies have called into question the sustainability of competitive advantage. Under pressure to improve productivity, quality, and speed, managers have embraced tools such as TQM, benchmarking, and reengineering. Dramatic operational improvements have resulted, but rarely have these gains translated into sustainable profitability. And gradually, strategy has replaced these tools. As managers push to improve on all fronts, they move further away from viable competitive positions. Michael Porter argues that operational effectiveness, although necessary to superior performance, is not sufficient, because its techniques are easy to imitate. In contrast, the essence of strategy is choosing a unique and valuable position rooted in systems of activities that are much more difficult to match several organizations.

MEANING OF STRATEGY

The word "strategy" is derived from the Greek word "stratcgos"; stratus (meaning army) and "ago" (meaning leading/moving).

It defines the overall mission, vision and direction of an organization. The objective of a strategy is to maximize an organization's strengths and minimize impact of the strengths of the competitors.

The term strategy has expanded far beyond its original meaning. Strategy is used in all areas where there is a long vision, competition, the use of resources and objective to realise the goals. Strategy is a set of key decisions made to meet the corporate's objectives. It consists of thoughts, ideas, insights, experiences, goals, memories, perceptions and expectations that provides general guidance for specific actions.

Strategy, in short, bridges the gap between:

1. Where we are?
2. Where we want to be?

3. Where should we go?

4. Where can we go?

Strategy is an action that managers take to attain one or more of the organization's goals. Strategy can also be defined as "A general direction set for the company and its various components to achieve a desired state in the future. Strategy results from the detailed strategic planning process".

A strategy is all about integrating organizational activities and utilizing and allocating the scarce resources within the organizational environment so as to meet the present objectives. While planning a strategy it is essential to consider that decisions are not taken in a vacuum and that any act taken by a firm is likely to be met by a reaction from those affected, competitors, customers, employees or suppliers.

Strategy can also be defined as knowledge of the goals, the uncertainty of events and the need to take into consideration the likely or actual behavior of others. Strategy is the blueprint of decisions in an organization that shows its objectives and goals, reduces the key policies, and plans for achieving these goals, and defines the business, the company is to carry on, the type of economic and human organization it wants to be, and the contribution it plans to make to its shareholders, customers and society at large.

Clausewitz (1780-1831), a Prussian, was the first great study of strategy and the father of modern study of strategy. The contributions of Clausewitz to strategic thought are many and diverse. He was the first to explain the role of war both as an instrument of social development and as a political act. Clausewitz's definition of the strategy was " the art of the employment of battles as a means to gain the object of war". He also was the first to focus on the fact that strategy of war was a means to enforce policy and not an end in itself.

DEFINITION OF STRATEGY

Harvard's Alfred Chandler defined " Strategy is the determinate of the basic long-term goals of an enterprise and the adoption of courses of action and the allocation of resources necessary for carrying out these goals".

Learned stated that "Strategy is the pattern of objectives, purposes or goals and major policies or plans for achieving these goals, stated in such a way as to define what business the company is in or is to be in and the kind of business it is or is to be"

Kenneth Andrews, "Corporate strategy is the pattern of decisions in a company that determines and reveals its objectives, purposes, or goals, produces the principal policies and plans for achieving those goals, and defines the range of business the company is to pursue, the kind of economic and human organization it is or intends to be, and the nature of the economic and non-economic contribution it intends to make to its shareholders, employees, customers, and communities.

Kepner-Tregoe, "The framework which guides those choices that determine the nature and direction of an organization."

James B. Quinn has define strategy as "a unified, comprehensive and integrated plan designed to ensure that the basic objectives of the enterprise are achieved.

NEED FOR STRATEGY

1. ***To guide the search for new opportunities:*** Strategy management analyzes the business environment, when formulating strategy and find the opportunities for the growth of the business.

2. ***To take high quality project decisions:*** Decision Quality is a framework, process, tool set, and set of principles for making high quality decisions. In other words, decision quality is both something we do, and something we want. Strategic management is taking quality project decisions on the basis of the environmental scanning report which provide accurate information .

3. ***To measure a particular opportunity:*** It uses the measurement tool for identifying the opportunity like SWOT analysis, TOWS Matrix, PEST analysis, Critical Success Factors, Porter's Four corners Model, Mckinsey 7s framework etc.

4. ***To allocate resources efficiently:*** Resource allocation decisions must be based first on strategic priorities & with clear guidance from senior leadership on those priorities. It is those priorities that then drive allocation of resources. When decisions are made to reallocate resources, there are methods that can minimize the impact of resource reallocation and in fact leave an organization much healthier than when it started the activity.

5. ***To develop the internal ability to anticipate change:*** Strategic leadership is the capability to anticipate change, and create direction, alignment, commitment and results in complex environments. To do so, leaders think and work in a strategic way to discover the future and make it happen.

6. ***To save time, money and executive talent:*** Strategic management always focuses on ROIs which will reduce the time, money while emphasizing on effective use of HR talent.

SIGNIFICANCE OF STRATEGY

1. Strategy is significant because it is not possible to foresee the future. With uncertainty staring, the firms must be ready to deal with the uncertain events which constitute the business environment.
2. Strategy deals with long term developments rather than routine operations, i.e. it deals with probabilities of innovations or new products, new methods of productions, or new markets to be developed in future.
3. Strategy is created to take into account the probable behavior of customers and competitors. Strategies dealing with employees will predict the employee behavior.

The significance of strategy evaluation lies in its capacity to coordinate the task performed by managers, groups, departments etc., through control of performance. Strategic Evaluation is significant because of various factors such as - developing inputs for new strategic planning, the urge for feedback, appraisal and reward, development of the strategic management process, judging the validity of strategic choice, etc.

LEVELS OF STRATEGY

1. Corporate level Strategy

Corporate level strategy occupies the highest level of strategic decision-making and covers actions dealing with the objective of the firm, acquisition and allocation of resources and coordination of strategies of various SBUs for optimal performance. Top management of the organization makes such decisions. The nature of strategic decisions tends to be value-oriented, conceptual and less concrete than decisions at the business or functional level.

2. Business-Level Strategy

Business-level strategy is related in those organizations, which have different businesses- and each business is treated as strategic business unit (SBU). The fundamental concept in SBU is to identify the discrete independent product/market segments served by an organization. Since each product/market segment has a distinct environment, a SBU is created for each such segment. For example, Reliance Industries Limited operates in textile fabrics, yarns, fibers, and a variety of petrochemical products. For each product group, the nature of market in terms of customers, competition, and marketing channel differs.

Therefore, it requires different strategies for its different product groups. Thus, where the SBU concept is applied, each SBU sets its own strategies to make the best use of its resources , given the environment it faces. At such a level, strategy is a comprehensive plan providing objectives for SBUs, allocation of resources among functional areas and coordination between them for making an optimal contribution to the achievement of corporate-level objectives. Such strategies operate within the overall strategies of the organization. The corporate strategy sets the long-term objectives of the firm and the broader constraints and policies within which an SBU operates. The corporate level will help the SBU define its scope of operations and also limits or enhance the SBUs operations by the resources the corporate level assigns to it. There is a difference between corporate-level and business-level strategies.

3. Functional-Level Strategy

Functional strategy relates to a single functional operation and the activities involved therein. Decisions at this level within the organization are often described as tactical. Such decisions are guided and constrained by some overall strategic considerations. Functional strategy deals with the relatively restricted plan providing objectives for specific function, allocation of resources among different operations within that functional area and coordination between them for the optimal contribution to the achievement of the SBU and corporate-level objectives. Below the functional-level strategy, there may be operations level strategies as each function may be dividend into several sub functions. For example, marketing strategy, a functional strategy, can be subdivided into promotion, sales, distribution, pricing strategies with each sub - function strategy contributing to functional strategy.

4. Operating Strategy

Companies and organizations making products and delivering, be it for profit or not for profit rely on a handful of processes to get their products manufactured properly and delivered on time. Each of the process acts as an operation of the company. To the company this is essential. That is why managers find operations management more appealing. We begin this section by looking at what operations actually are. Operating strategy is to provide an overall direction that serves the framework for carrying out all the organization's functions.

STRATEGIC MANAGEMENT

The meaning of Strategic Management is all about identification and description of the strategies that managers can carry so as to achieve better performance and a competitive advantage for their organization. An organization is said to have a competitive advantage if its profitability is higher than the average profitability for all companies in its industry.

Strategic management can be used to determine mission, vision, values, goals, objectives, roles and responsibilities, timelines, etc.

Strategic management is a field that deals with the major intended and emergent initiatives taken by general managers on behalf of owners, involving utilization of resources, to enhance the performance of firms in their external environments. It entails specifying the organization's mission, vision and objectives, developing policies and plans, often in terms of projects and programs, which are designed to achieve these objectives, and then allocating resources to implement the policies and plans, projects and programs. A balanced scorecard is often used to evaluate the overall performance of the business and its progress towards objectives. Recent studies and leading management theorists have advocated that strategy needs to start with stakeholder expectations and use a modified balanced scorecard which includes all stakeholders.

Strategic management concentrates on monitoring and evaluation of external opportunities and threats based on company's strengths and weakness. It is a field of study of incorporating the integrative efforts of business by emphasizing more on the environment. Strategic Management on the whole is a study of integrating proper efforts of business with that of environment.

Strategic management is a level of managerial activity under setting goals and over Tactics. Strategic management provides overall direction to the enterprise and is closely related to the field of Organization Studies. In the field of business administration it is useful to talk about "strategic alignment" between the organization and its environment or "strategic consistency." According to Arieu (2007), "there is strategic consistency when the actions of an organization are consistent with the expectations of management, and these in turn are with the market and the context." Strategic management includes not only the management team but can also include the Board of Directors and other stakeholders of the organization. It depends on the organizational structure.

"Strategic management is an ongoing process that evaluates and controls the business and the industries in which the company is involved; assesses its competitors and sets goals and strategies to meet all existing and potential competitors; and then reassesses each strategy annually or quarterly [i.e. regularly] to determine how it has been implemented and whether it has succeeded or needs replacement by a new strategy to meet changing circumstances, new technology, new competitors, a new economic environment., or a new social, financial, or political environment".

Meaning of Strategic Management

Strategic management is the art and science of formulating, implementing and evaluating all functional decisions that enable on organisation, to achieve is objectives. It is focusing for the integration of the activities marketing, finance, accounting, production, researches and development and computer information systems to achieve organisational success. The term is used to refer strategy formulation, implementation and evaluation. The purpose is to exploit and create new and different opportunities for tomorrow's long range planning, and to optimise today's trends for tomorrow's success.

NEED FOR STRATEGIC MANAGEMENT

Strategic management is becoming an increasingly important way to keep track of economic developments and position of the company for long term competitive advantage. Every company needs to adopt strategic management techniques for its success. Company needs to be rational and to respond effectively to the challenges of the 21st century. It should study its external and internal environment to identify its opportunities and threads and to determine the usage of core competencies in the pursuit of the desired strategic outcomes. Therefore the firm has to adopt strategic plan so that it can balance its resources, capabilities and core competencies to win competition in the global economy.

Strategic competitiveness will be achieved only when a firm develops and implements a value added strategy. The challenges that are responsible for making effective strategic decisions to adopt a new mind set of learning the changing environments that produce disorder and uncertainty in the business. Film needs to adopt strategy to fulfil the following objectives :

a) To improve the financial performance in terms of profit and growth.

b) To encourage the activities of subordinates for to reward for their success.

c) To accept changes with minimum resistance.

d) To chose a particular option and a line of selecting the best among the alternatives

e) For the better understanding of the responsibilities of individuals and groups.

f) For the improved quality of decision making.

g) For the better understanding of the priorities and operations of the reward systems.

CHARACTERISTICS OF STRATEGIC MANAGEMENT

1. ***Future Orientation:*** Strategic management deals with future-oriented non-routine situation. Managers are unaware business environment of tomorrow and about the consequences of their present decisions.

2. ***Complex:*** Uncertainity brings complex business management problems and issues. Managers face an environment which is difficult to comprehend. External and internal

environment require careful analysis. Strategic management approaches try to address these problems and issues.

3. ***Organization wide:*** Strategic management has organization wide implication. It is not operation specific. It is a systems approach. It involves strategic choice.

4. ***Fundamental:*** Strategic management is fundamental to improving the long-term performance of the organization.

5. ***Long-term implication:*** Strategic management is not concerned with the day-to-day operation, decisions connected with these as also study long-term implications. It deals with vision, mission and objective.

6. ***Implication:*** Strategic management ensures that strategy is put into action, implementation is done through action plans. Develop a means to follow up to ensure continuity of management decisions and actions.

IMPORTANCE OF STRATEGIC MANAGEMENT

1. A rapidly changing environment in organizations requires a greater awareness of changes and their impact on the organization. Hence strategic management plays an important role in an organization.
2. Strategic management helps in building a stable organization.
3. Strategic management controls the crisis that arises due to rapid change in an organization.
4. Strategic management considers the opportunities and threats as also the strengths and weaknesses of the organization in the crucial environment for survival in a competitive market.
5. Strategic management helps the top level management to examine the relevant factors before deciding their course of action that needs to be implemented in a changing environment and thus aids them to better cope with uncertain situations.
6. Changes rapidly happen in large organizations. Hence strategic management becomes necessary to develop appropriate responses to anticipate changes.
7. The implementation of clear strategy enhances corporate harmony in the organization. The employees will be able to analyze the organization's ethics and rules and can tailor their contribution accordingly.
8. Systematically formulated business activities help in providing consistent financial performance in the organization.

9. A well designed global strategy helps the organization to gain competitive advantages. It increases the economies of scale in the global market, exploits other countries resources, broadens learning opportunities, and provides reputation and brand identification.

PROCESS OF STRATEGIC MANAGEMENT

The process are the steps by which management converts a firm's mission, objectives and goals into a workable strategy. The process involves the preparation of the best ways to respond to the circumstances of the organisations environment. It involves the anticipation of future environment and taking decisions based on its changes.

The strategic management process can be classified into five different parts:

1) Selections of the corporate mission and goals.
2) Analysis of the organisation's external competitive environment and to identify opportunities and threats.
3) Analysis of organisations internal operating environment and to identify the organisation's strength and weaknesses.
4) Selection of strategies to build the organisation's strengths and to correct its weaknesses.
5) To design an appropriate organisation structures and control systems.

EFFECTIVE STRATEGIES FOR LONG-TERM GROWTH

Air travel has become a regular part of life for many people, but managing the processes surrounding it is far from simple. During the summer of 2012 the UK welcomed around 200,000 more air passengers through Heathrow and Gatwick airports than in a non-Olympic year.

Over 3,000 extra flight slots were needed for the visitors and athletes for the London Olympic Games. Making sure all flights have a safe landing and take-off is part of the responsibilities of NATS.

History of NATS

Air traffic control for commercial flights in the UK started in 1920. Croydon was first used as London's air terminal, but all the controller could do was to give the pilot a red or green light for take-off and acknowledge position reports sent by radio.

After the war, ATC became the responsibility of the Ministry of Civil Aviation, and the network of air routes we use today began to develop in the 1950s.

NATS and the CAA

Our forerunner, National Air Traffic Control Services (NATCS), was established in December 1962. It covered civil ATC but liaised with the MoD (RAF) in areas where military traffic needed to cross civilian routes. When the Civil Aviation Authority (CAA) was established in April 1972, NATCS became part of it and shortened its name to NATS.

In 1992 it was recognised that as a service provider NATS should be operated at a distance from its regulator, the CAA. With that in mind, NATS was re-organised into a Companies Act in April 1996 and became a wholly owned subsidiary of the CAA.

NATS is a global air navigation provider. The organisation was originally established in 1962 as a government body but in 2001 it became a private entity (Public/Private Partnership (PPP)). The PPP model of ownership meant that private funding could be invested into NATS services and infrastructure. Over £123 million has been since invested.

NATS manages the world's busiest section of airspace as well as the busiest single and dual runway airports in Europe and the Middle East. Its systems and people manage over 6,000 flights a day through UK airspace – over 2 million a year – safely and efficiently. NATS-managed flights experienced delays of just 7.3 seconds per flight in 2011, around 1/10 of the European average. The majority of delays to flights in and out of the UK are caused by factors outside NATS' control.

Rate of growth

NATS has grown phenomenally in the last year. Its strategies have taken it from operating in just UK and Gibraltar to offering the full range of its services in 28 countries, with contracts of different sizes and values. NATS offers and operates a range of services. Main function is to manage runways and airspace through Air Traffic Control (ATC). Other roles include providing consultancy and developing solutions for operational, economic and environmental issues, engineering infrastructure and software, defence services and training. Its customers include airports, airlines and aviation authorities.

As well as managing 15 of the UK's busiest airports, NATS projects currently include air traffic controller training and redesigning airspace in Hong Kong; providing start-up training for ATC and safety management in Slovakia; providing and integrating all ATC equipment for the new control tower at Manchester airport.

NATS recognises that its people are a cornerstone of its strategy and essential to its future development. NATS offers a broad mix of challenging and exciting job roles which are open to men and women equally. These include the essential ATC role, scientists, marketing, business development, IT, finance, HR, safety, quality and business processing. With its expansion, NATS is moving from a national to international employer. This means future recruits will have a world of job opportunities to choose from.

This case study explores the strategies NATS is employing to achieve its vision of being a global provider of air traffic solutions.

Aims and vision

An organisation's vision describes where the business wants to be in an ideal world. A vision is aspirational and can be inspirational for employees and stakeholders. Aims describe what the business intends to do in the long term and help to deliver the vision. Examples of aims might be to increase profit or to improve the business' impact on the environment.

The aviation sector as a whole is experiencing significant change with air traffic management services now being a global market. NATS needs to be able to respond to economic pressures and meet efficiency and environmental targets. It also has to be able to meet the challenge of increasing numbers of competitors bidding for global contracts.

NATS' vision

NATS' vision is: To be acknowledged as a global leader in innovative air traffic solutions and airport performance. In order to achieve its vision, NATS has established several key aims:

- Continuous growth for the business, both organic and inorganic with a view of achieving and sustaining turnover of over £1bn by 2015.

- Reducing safety risks across the business – NATS handled 2.1 million flights in 2011. For the fourth year running, there were no incidents where the distance between aircraft under NATS air traffic control was compromised. In an industry where safety is of the greatest importance, NATS has also developed safety innovations such as a GPS-based device to help private pilots avoid controlled airspace, as well as a system to track helicopter flights between oil platforms in the North Sea.

- Engaging with and focusing on its customers' needs – this includes implementing technical developments that will deliver fuel savings for airlines, improve efficiency and ensure continued punctuality and reduced operating costs for airports.

• Increasing efficiency and effectiveness of internal operations – for example, NATS efficiency in purchasing has been recognised with the award of the Gold certificate from CIPS (the Chartered Institute of Purchasing and Supply). This has resulted in cost savings and established best practice for all parts of the business.

• Reducing carbon emissions – for example NATS made over 100 operational and procedural changes in air traffic flows. These have saved an estimated 115,000 tonnes of CO2 emissions since 2009 – a fuel saving worth £22 million.

Objectives

Objectives set out the outcomes the business needs in order to achieve its aims and may relate to functions or the whole business.

SMART objectives

The use of SMART objectives helps a business to ensure that its progress towards achieving its objectives can be measured.

Specific – so that everyone knows exactly what is to be achieved.

Measurable – sets out the level to be achieved.

Agreed – relevant staff are involved in setting the objectives and are committed to keeping them.

Relevant – to the organisation's overall purpose.

Time-framed – to ensure that it will fit within the organisation's overall plans.

Examples of SMART objectives set by NATS include:

• To reduce the level of safety risk across the business by 40% over a period of four years.

• To reduce carbon-di-oxide (CO2) emissions related to air traffic management by an average of 10% per flight by 2020, from a 2006 baseline. The interim target is to achieve an average of 4% per flight reduction by 2015.

Airlines bear significant costs, for example of fuel, fees for airport slots or in maintaining safety. Delays or flight inefficiency adds to these costs. In response to its customers' needs, NATS helps to limit delays by effective air traffic control and improves use of fuel by providing more efficient flight routes.

As an example, at Gatwick airport, which is the busiest single runway airport in Europe, 53 planes are scheduled to take off or land each hour and NATS has even managed up to 60 planes on the runway in peak hours. NATS is aiming to increase this scheduled capacity to 55 by the summer of 2014 through use of new technology and by improving the design of airspace and runway usage.

Strategy

A strategy is the plan by which the aims and objectives will be put into action. NATS' strategies centre around three key areas:

- Innovation – developing new and creative products and services to retain market position and grow the business.
- Partnerships – creating alliances to strengthen its position and open up new markets.
- People – enhancing the organisation's skills and competencies so it has the resources to meet challenges.
- Innovation

NATS is moving from a UK-focused business to a global one. For example, new contracts for consultancy services in the USA, Middle East and Asia-Pacific have contributed to forward orders worth £495 million. NATS' strengths in innovation are helping to deliver ground-breaking products and solutions. These will help it compete and establish the business as a market player in other countries, ensuring continued growth and expansion. For example, the 'Heathrow Dashboard' now provides live, real-time data on arrival and departure delays to help air traffic control operators make decisions.

Partnerships

Working with and through partners to deliver new solutions is helping NATS to expand its reach into global markets. For example, NATS has established a relationship in Spain with Ferroser, a private investor in transportation infrastructures. The joint venture (known as FerroNATS) enabled NATS to win a bid for running airport tower operations in Spain.

People

NATS' services are dependent on the expertise and innovation that its people can deliver. NATS' Human Resource Management strategy is focused not just on attracting but also retaining people with high levels of skill. NATS needs people with scientific or engineering backgrounds, as well as wider business skills such as finance, administration, intelligence gathering or sales. With its increasingly global markets, NATS people have the opportunity to work around the world. NATS training and development schemes enable the organisation to continue to develop the competencies which give it competitive edge and drive its vision forwards. People may join NATS at all levels – from school or college as air traffic controllers or engineering technicians or as graduates on its science or engineering graduate schemes.

In addition, NATS also offers industrial placement schemes, where students can include a year working with NATS as part of their degree courses to develop skills and learn about the industry. NATS employees have opportunities to develop their abilities, for example, through secondments.

Evaluation

Effective strategies require careful assessment of the progress made during the time scale of the strategies being set. The monitoring of the changes is summarized in the final section of the case study.

Tactics

Tactics are specific programmes of work or activities which help to achieve objectives. They may be customer-focused or operationally based.

Around 26,000 flights a day cross the European airspace – at different heights and along different routes. NATS solutions which support its strategy of innovation focus on making the most efficient use of this space.

3Di- a world "first"

For example, NATS delivered a world 'first' by developing an entirely new way of measuring the environmental performance of the airspace network above the UK. The flight efficiency metric, known as 3Di, will help air traffic control to route flight paths as close to the environmental optimum as possible. NATS' regulator, the Civil Aviation Authority, estimates that it will deliver 600,000 tonnes of CO2 savings over the next three years, worth up to £120 million.

'Perfect flight' test

NATS was also involved with British Airways in developing the 'Perfect Flight'. The programme, a UK 'first', involved measuring a trial flight under optimum conditions and flight plan in order to establish the potential for carbon savings. The trial proved that more than 10% of emissions could be saved. NATS is now investigating how it could make this possible for every flight.

Management of data

Timely and accurate management of data and information is vital for airports, airlines and air traffic control services. NATS is implementing a virtual and secure 'cloud'-based infrastructure for all its desktop IT services. This will reduce IT costs by £9 million over four years and allow better use of information for NATS 6,000 staff, as well as improved collaboration between NATS and its business partners.

Single European Sky initiative

NATS and the Irish Aviation Authority (IAA) are working in partnership as part of the Single European Sky (SES) initiative. This initiative organises airspace into Functional Airspace Blocks (FABs) according to traffic flows rather than to national borders. This aims to improve efficiency and reduce costs. Achievements between NATS and IAA so far have included establishing night time routes to save fuel. These have resulted in savings of around •24 million (mostly from fuel efficiency) against costs of just •2 million.

Developing people

In line with its HR strategy, NATS opened a new training centre in 2011. This specialised centre of excellence for training engineers and air traffic controllers has delivered cost savings and improved the training environment through the use of innovative simulation technology. NATS recognises that its people are a valuable asset and has therefore also introduced a new performance management and career development programme to enable it to manage and reward its talented people appropriately.

Conclusion

NATS has grown from a UK-only to an international air traffic management provider. Its range of services and wealth of expertise help to deliver efficient and effective solutions to the challenges its customers in the aviation industry face. Its strategies for continued growth rely on its innovation, partnerships and people. Statistical appraisal has shown that the strategies have helped to generate new business in the UK and 20 other countries worth over £495 million in 2011/12. At a time of global economic recession, NATS has delivered ways to help its customers add value, reduce emissions and save fuel. In 2011, by implementing operational and procedural changes from the air traffic control centres, NATS enabled fuel savings of over 19,000 tonnes. This was worth almost £13 million and saved 60,000 tonnes of CO2 emissions.

BENEFITS OF STRATEGIC MANAGEMENT

- It allows identification and exploitation of opportunities through the scanning of the environment.
- It provides an objective view of management problems,
- It represents a framework for improved coordination and control of activities,
- It minimizes the effects of adverse conditions and changes,
- It allows major decisions to better support, established objectives,
- It allows more effective allocation time and resources to identify opportunities,
- It creates a framework for internal communication among personnels,
- It helps to integrate the behaviors of individuals into a total effort,
- It provides a basis for the clarification of individual opportunities,

LIMITATIONS OF STRATEGIC MANAGEMENT

- It is based on certain premises and if the premises do not hold valid, the strategy based on that theory will not be realistic or effective,
- If SWOT analysis is not right, the strategy based on it will be wrong and further SWOT analysis requires a lot of experience and information,
- It makes organizations over ambitious and failure to reach goals will cause frustration,
- Several opportunities may be lost as strategic management makes the future vision tunneled,
- It may fail due to ineffective implementation due to ineffective resource allocation, wrong leadership and ineffective control
- It may fail due to lack of management commitment
- It may fail due to resistance to change
- It is a complex and difficult task which requires people with vision, expertise and commitment and an appropriate system
- It is a costly exercise
- Many people question the need for strategic management as many firms have failed after adopting it.

COMPONENTS OF STRATEGIC MANAGEMENT

1. Vision Statement

A vision statement is sometimes called a representation of your company in the future but it's so much more than that. Your vision statement is your inspiration, the framework for all your strategic planning. A vision statement may apply to an entire company or to a single division of that company. The vision statement answers the question, "Where do we want to go?" either all or part of an organization.

What you are doing when creating a vision statement is articulating your dreams and hopes for your business. It reminds you of what you are trying to build.

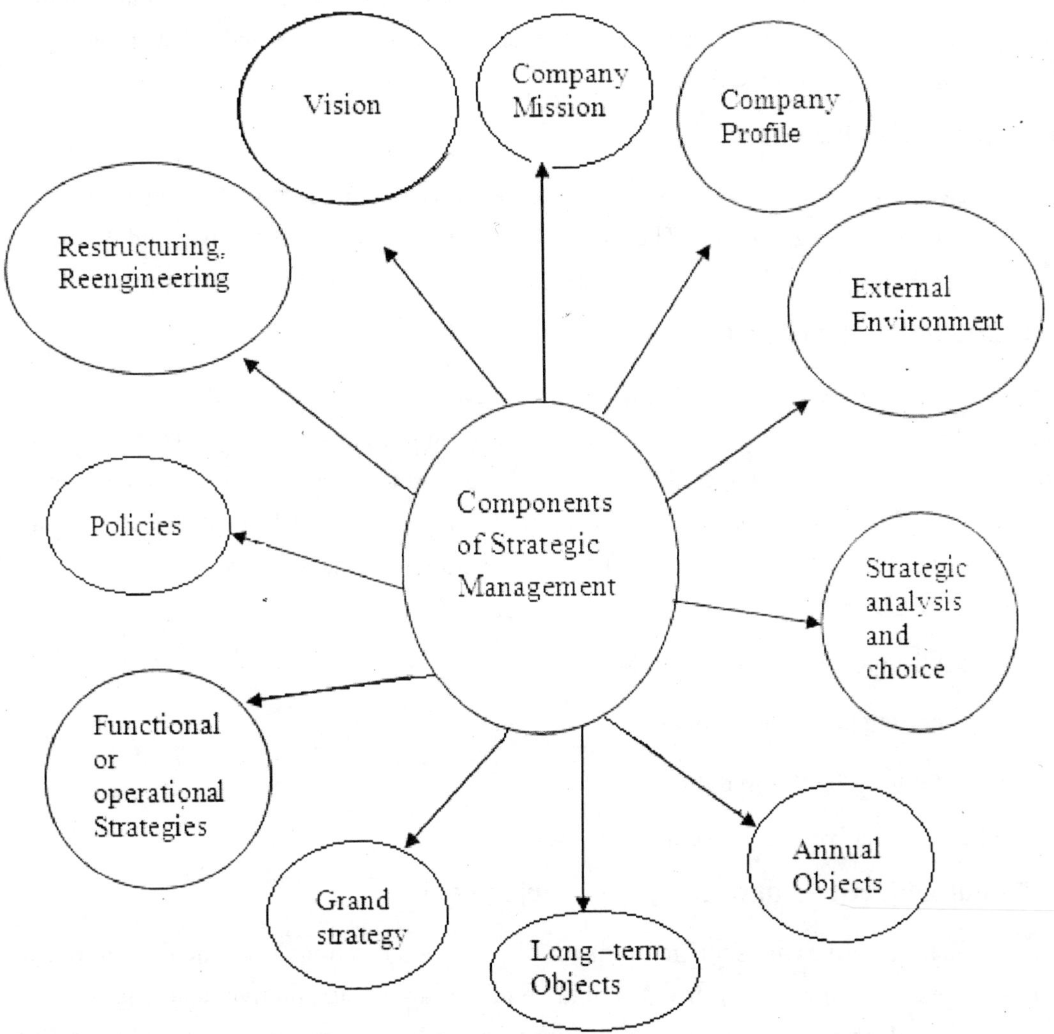

2. Mission Statement

A Mission statement is an enduring statement of purpose that distinguishes one business from other similar firms. A mission statement identifies that scope of a firm's operation in product and market terms. Mission statement describes the company's product, market, and technological areas of emphasis in the way that reflects the values and priorities of the strategic decision makers. Thus while vision sets out the aim, the mission shows the path that is traced to achieve the same.

3. Company Profile

The company profile consists of company information which includes (1) firm's history, (2) number and quality of its human, financial, and physical resources (3) organizational and management structure, (4) past, current and anticipated performance, and (5) its reputation, and the standing of its goods or services.

4. External Environment

External environment consists of all the conditions and forces that affect its business of the company and its strategic option. The external environment is how one's surroundings affect the area around them. Which includes businesses, human beings, and the external area around them.

5. Strategic analysis and Choice

Strategists never consider all feasible alternatives that could benefit the firm because there are an infinite number of possible actions and an infinite number of ways to implement those actions. Therefore, a manageable set of the most attractive, alternative strategies must be developed. The advantages, disadvantages, trade-offs, costs, and benefits of these strategies should be determined before going to the implementation of the strategy in the company. The following things should be considered

- Establishing long-term objectives
- Generating alternative strategies,
- Selecting strategies to pursue,
- Best alternative to achieve mission & objectives.

6. Annul Objectives and Long term Objectives

Annual objectives are short-term milestones that organizations must achieve to reach long – term objectives. Annual objectives should be measurable, quantitative, challenging, realistic, consistent, and prioritized. Annual objectives normally consists of a year which will work towards long term objectives of the company.

Long term objectives can be defined as specific results that an organization seeks to achieve in pursuing its basic mission. Long-term means more than one year . Objectives are essential for organizational success because they state direction, aid in evaluation, create synergy , reveal priorities, focus coordination and provide a basis for effective planning , organization, motivating and controlling activities.

7. Grand Strategy

Grand strategy is providing basic direction for strategic action. They are the basis of coordinated and sustained efforts directed towards achieving long-term business objectives. In other words Grand strategy is a general plan of major action by which a firm intends to achieve its long-term goals. Grand strategies are major, overarching strategies that shape the course of a business. Unlike tactics, they are focused on the long-term goals of the business. Running your own business means pondering grand strategies involving everything from product development to liquidation. Different strategies will, of course, fit different situations, so it is best to be familiar with different approaches.

8. Policies

Policies are guidelines, rules and procedures established to support efforts to achieve stated objectives. Policies are decision makers for address repetitive or recurring situations.

Business policies define business processes, industry practices, and the scope and characteristics of organization offerings. They are the central source and reference template for all allowed and supported practices within organizations.

The business policy definition may specify a set of parameters that are automatically fed into each invocation of any commands associated with the policy. A business policy command may specify additional parameters when it is invoked. Finally, a contract term and condition may proved extra parameters for a business command unique to the term and condition.

STRATEGIC MANAGEMENT PROCESS

I) Developing a Strategic Vision

This is first step involves in the strategic management process that the clarification of what the company is and who they do business for. At the very basic level, it defines what product, service or good is going to be offered. The vision of the company refers to the future of it's existence and serves the purpose to inspire and motivate members to work hard to achieve this vision. A Vision Statement takes into account the current status of the organization, and serves to point the direction of where the organization wishes to go. Vision Statement is a marketing tool and a business development tool because it announces your company's goals and future intent to your employees, suppliers, customers, vendors, and the media.

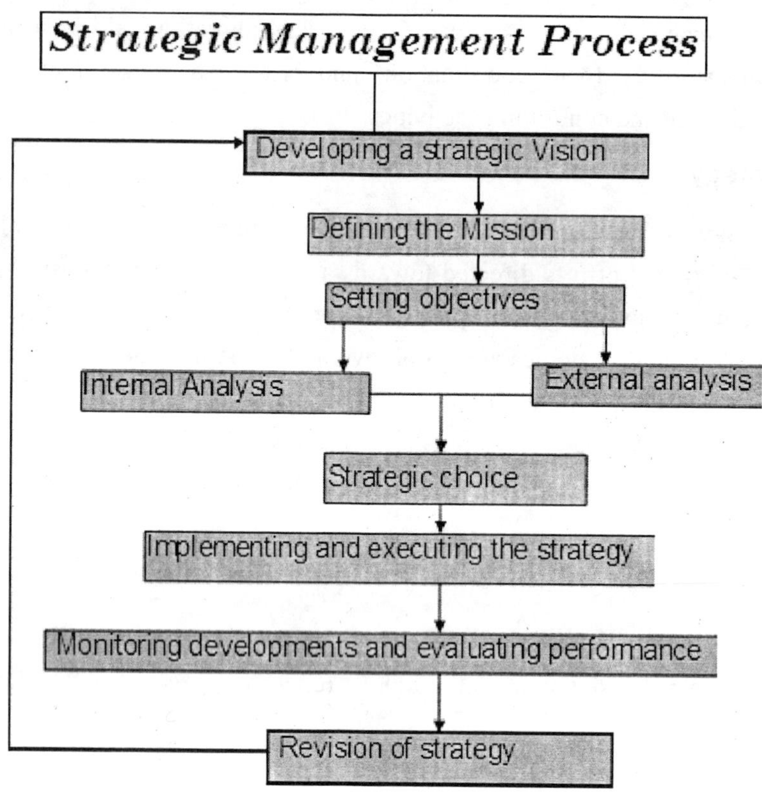

1. Define the mission statement

Mission statement is the statement of the role by which an organization intends to serve it's stakeholders. It describes why an organization is operating and thus provides a framework within which strategies are formulated. It describes what the organization does (i.e., present capabilities), who all it serves (i.e., stakeholders) and what makes an organization unique (i.e., reason for existence). A mission statement differentiates an organization from others by explaining its broad scope of activities, its products, and technologies it uses to achieve its goals and objectives.

2. Setting objectives

Setting objectives is a specific management tool that creates a target for business owners to achieve. Objectives can be company-wide goals, specific to the division or department and individual employee expectations. Business owners often use performance management to follow up on objectives and measure the company and company overall achievement effectiveness.

Internal and External environment analysis: The company finds the strength and weaknesses of the internal factors like financial, human, and physical resources which has influenced on the performance of the company and make its strengths for getting competitive advantages. A systematic internal factor analysis helps a firm find (i) where it stands of in its strengths and weakness (ii) find opportunities for business growth (iii) take steps to bridge any resource gaps.

External environment consists of all the conditions and external forces that affect its strategic decision and find its competitive advantages. The firms must develop requisite skills to identify opportunities and threats existing in that environment.

An external environmental analysis studies information about a business's industry, competition, and political and social environments. These factors affect the business but are out of its control, such as when a new political party takes office and change regulations, in turn requiring the business to invest in new equipment or modify its products. An external environmental analysis includes a list of factors in a business's external environment and their influence on the business. It further discusses opportunities the business can pursue and threats that could negatively impact it. The external environmental analysis concludes with a plan on how the business can take advantage of opportunities and either overcome or minimize its threats.

3. Strategic Choice

The primary purpose of a strategy is to provide the organization with a sustainable position of advantage within a competitive environment. In this regard we will determine the general strategic choices an organization can make, which is the first stage in defining the strategy it will ultimately follow. We will explore a number of different approaches including: (a) using the organizational purpose, vision and mission to make decisions about strategic choices, (b) focusing directly on achieving a competitive advantage, (c) competing by developing the organization's core competencies.

4. Implementing and executing Strategy

Execution is a fundamental component of strategy and must be the core element of the company’s culture. Execution is a systematic process of rigorously discussing how's and what, questioning tenaciously, following through and ensuring accountability. In its most fundamental sense, execution is a systematic way of exposing reality and acting on it.

In order to get a strategic plan to work effectively, it must be implemented and executed properly. Some of the ways that strategies tend to fail are because of miscommunication among different levels of the organization and losing clarity of the tasks at hand. Strategic tasks should be defined and the abilities of the organization should be determined. There should be a timetable/agenda created that outlines the implementation as well as a plan. There are many different types of strategies but some of the main ones to note are: corporate strategy, business strategy, low-cost strategy, differentiation strategy and functional strategies.

5. Monitoring developments and evaluating performance

After the strategy has been implemented, there needs to be a way to make sure that it is working. A control system should be put in place so that managers can evaluate the process. They need to be able to identify what's working and what isn't. The faster problems can be identified, the faster they can be resolved and improved. The firms must monitor and evaluate new strategy time to time which has already implemented in the firms and check the performance of the firms. In case, any changes are required, the films can modify and implement immediately,

II) Revision of Strategy

Revision of the strategy implementation is a continuous process in the business due to the business environment. The manager could review the performance of the business whether it is in the right path or not. After reviewing the performance of the firm, the manager may decide to continue the same strategy or not.

FAILURE OF STRATEGIC MANAGEMENT

A number of benefits can be recognised from the strategic management. But at the same time, there are many limitations to it. Many firms fail by adopting ineffective strategic management. The following are the reasons for the failure of strategic management.

(i) Adoptions of strategic management system is very expensive.

(ii) The top level management should devote their time and also to spend money for training managers.

(iii) Efficient strategic management depends on the mission and goals of the corporate enterprises. Over ambitions and unrealistic strategies may land companies in severe problems.

(iv) There is a risk of managers not participating effectively while making decisions and conclusion. Hence, the results of strategic decisions will depend on the performance achieved by the strategy manager and their subordinates.

(v) Strategic planning and decision making is a difficult task which requires expertise knowledge and commitment.

(vi) Failure of strategic decisions may due to non-fulfillment of subordinates expectations which leads to frustration and disappointment. Therefore managers are to be trained to anticipate disappointment, and to minimise the differences of opinion among the subordinates.

(vii) Another one more reason for failure of a strategy is ineffective implementation of decisions. Even a good strategy cannot produce effective results due to wrong implementation.

(viii) A good strategy can be criticised when there is a lack of modification and flexibility. Many organisations fail to adopt a good strategy because of not adopting changes for the unforeseen development.

(ix) Implementation of good strategy is based on certain assumptions. If the assumptions are not realistic, then leading to formulation of wrong or ineffective strategies.

(x) When someone has achieved status, privilege, or self esteem through effectively using an old system they often see a new plan as a threat. People may be uncertain of their abilities to learn new skills, their aptitude with new systems and their ability to take new roles.

RELATIONSHIP BETWEEN A COMPANY'S STRATEGY AND ITS BUSINESS MODEL

Starting a new business requires careful planning to maximize the chances of success. Many small businesses are unable to make profit and fail within the first few years of operation. The terms "business strategy" and "business model" describe related concepts that are key to the processes of planning and managing a business.

1. Business Strategy

The term "business strategy" describes the method a business uses to achieve its mission and objectives. A business' mission encompasses its overall purpose, core values and long-term goals. A grocery store might have the mission of making a profit while providing the best food to customers, minimizing its impact on the environment and promoting strength in the local economy. The company's strategy might involve buying products from local food producers, encouraging customers to bring their own grocery bags, advertising in local newspapers and buying recycled product packaging materials. A business strategy includes how it deals with the opportunities and threats it faces.

2. Business Model

A company's business model describes the basic means by which it creates value, delivers value to consumers and collects revenue from customers to make a profit. Business models can vary greatly from one company to another. A local grocery store's business model might involve buying food at wholesale prices and selling it to end consumers at a higher price to make profit. A website might have a business model based on providing video content to customers and generating revenue through advertisements placed on the site.

3. How they are Related

A company's business model is a part of its business overall strategy: It is the nuts and bolts behind how the company plans to achieve its goals, such as making a profit. A company can change its business model over time as a part of its profit-making strategy. For example, if a website does not make enough revenue from advertisements to make profit, managers might decide to implement a new business model, such as selling T-shirts and other goods though an online store, as a strategy to boost profits.

Business Strategy deals with a company's competitive initiatives and business approaches but Business Model Concerns whether revenues and costs flowing from the strategy demonstrate whether the business can be amply profitable and viable.

A business model addresses:

"How do we make money in this business?"

Is the strategy capable of delivering good bottom-line results?

Do the revenue-cost-profit economics of the strategy make good business sense?

STRATEGISTS AND THEIR ROLE IN STRATEGIC MANAGEMENT

Strategic decisions are the essence of strategic management. Strategies can be put into practice only after decisions. Strategic decisions by their nature are characterised by considerable task and uncertainty. They are future - oriented with long term objectives. Such decisions affect the organisation as a whole over long periods of time. Because strategic decisions have a tremendous impact on a firm, they require large commitment of company resources and can only be made by top managers in the organizational hierarchy.

The top management has to plan for new strategies, evaluate it, reviewing it and implementing it according to the plans. They have the power to recruit manager and to remove the existing managers. These people are the inside members directly involving in strategy formulation. They have the responsibility to discuss, to initiate, modify and communicate strategic plans.

Board of Directors play a vital role in corporate strategic management. They are responsible for producing wealth to the stock holders by ensuring the continuity of management and protecting the interests of the owner's resources. While representing the company with other organisations, the Board of Directors should have more initiative keeping in mind the corporate objectives. Approving major financial and operational decisions through the maintenance of corporate discipline.

In organisation, next to Board of Directors, the role of general managers is important in strategic management. They are responsible for the implementation of strategies formulated by top level management i.e. Board of Directors. The manager acts as a strategist and a builder to lead the firm. He should have his depth of commitment to support top level management at the time of strategy implementation. He should be a creative person to strengthen the firm as a whole by turning strategic thinking into a collective learning process.

Large organisations may establish a corporate planning division. It is one of the important staff function and the staff personnel are known as corporate planners. The planners should keep a track of economic developments and to exploit the opportunities in the market. They should supply inputs for the preparation of outputs necessary for the implementation of strategic management. They have to formulate various guidelines for preparing plan and these plans are to be co-oridnated to achieve corporate objectives.

It is a standard procedure for executives to brief the board members on important strategic moves and to submit the company's strategic plans to the board for official approval. Board of Directors typically meet once a month for six to eight hours. The task of directors is to be supportive and to be a critic, exercising their own judgment about whether proposals have been adequately analyzed or not. They also see to that whether the proposed strategic actions appear to have greater promise than available alternatives. However, if the company is experiencing gradual erosion of profits, market share, it is the duty of the members to express their concerns about the validity of the strategy. To rectify the situations, they involve in discussions with key executives and directly interven as a group to alter both the strategy and the company's executive leadership.

DIMENSIONS OF STRATEGIC DECISIONS

The major dimensions of strategic decisions are as follows:

1. Strategic issues require top-management decisions

Strategic issues involve thinking in totality of the organization's objectives in which a considerable amount of risk is involved. Hence, problems calling for strategic decisions require to be considered by the top management.

2. Strategic issues involve the allocation of large amounts of company resources

It may require either a huge financial investment to venture into a new area of business or the organization may require a huge amount of manpower with new skill sets.

3. Strategic issues are likely to have a significant impact on the long term prosperity of the firm

Generally the results of strategic implementation are seen on a long term basis and not on immediate terms.

4. Strategic issues are future oriented

Strategic thinking involves predicting the future environmental conditions and how to orient for the changed conditions.

5. Strategic issues usually have major multifunctional or multi- business consequences

As they involve the organization in totality they affect different sections of the organization with varying degree.

6. Strategic issues necessitate consideration of factors in the firm's external environment

Strategic focus in an organization involves orienting its internal environment to the changes of the external environment.

KEY TERMS IN STRATEGIC MANAGEMENT

Before discussing in detail about strategic management it is necessary to know the key terms in strategic management

Strategists

Strategists are individuals who are most responsible for the success or failure of an organisations. Strategists have various job titles, such as chief executive officer, president, owner, chair of the board executive, director, chancellor, deal or entrepreneur. Strategists help an organisation to gather, analyse and organise information. They forecast future industry and competitive trends and develop forecasting models and their talents to identify business threats and develop creative action plans. The *CEO* is the most visible and critical strategic management.

Strategists offer as much as organisations and these differences must be considered in the formulation, implementation and evaluation of strategies. Strategists differ in their attitudes, values, ethics, willingness to take risks, concern for short run vs. long run aims and management style.

Vision

Many organisations today develop a 'Vision statement which answer the questions of what do we want to become? Developing a vision is often considered the first step in strategic planning, preceding the development of a mission in the form of statement. Many vision statements are single sentence.

Mission

Mission is the description of an organisation's reason for existence, its fundamental purpose. It is the guiding principle that drives for goal and action formation. Mission should focus on long-range economic potentials, attitudes towards customer's product and service quality, employee relations and attitudes towards owners. It becomes the cornerstone for strategic management and around it all functions revolve.

External Opportunities and Threats

This refer to economic, social, cultural, demographic, environmental, political, legal, governmental technological and competitive trends that could significantly benefit or harm an organisation in the future. These are largely beyond the control of an organisation. The computer evolution, biotechnology, population, changing work values, attitudes, space exploration, recyclable packages, competition are the examples of opportunities or threats for companies.

Internal Strengths and Weaknesses

Internal strengths and weaknesses are an organisation's controllable activities that are performed for its efficiency or inefficiency. They arise in the management, marketing, finance, production, research, etc. Identification and evolution of strengths and weaknesses in the functional areas of a business is an essential activity of strategic management.

Long term objectives

Objectives can be defined as the specific results which an organisation wants to achieve in pursuing its basic mission. Objective are essential for its success because they state direction, evaluation, create synergy, reveal priorities, focus co-ordination and provide a basis for effective planning, organising, motivating and controlling activities. It should be challenging, measurable, consistent, reasonable and clear. It should be established for the overall objectives of the company.

Strategies

Strategies are the means by which long term objectives will be achieved. Business strategies may include geographic expansion, diversification, acquisition, product development, market penetration, retrenchment, liquidation, etc. These are potential actions that require top management decisions and require large amount of firms resources. Strategies affect an organisation's long term prosperity typically for at least five years.

Policies

Policies are the means by which annual objectives will be achieved. Policies include guidelines, rules and procedures established to support efforts to achieve stated objectives. Policies are guides to decision making and to address repetitive or recurring situations. It can be established at the corporate level, divisional level, functional level or to a particular operational activity or department. Policies allow consistency and coordination with in and between organisational departments.

CASE -1

SO, WHAT 'S COOKING IN YOUR COMPANY?

M/s TTK Prestige Limited, the largest provider of kitchen appliances in the country has registered a third quarter sales of Rs.149.20 Crores as against 127.81 crores for the corresponding quarter in the previous year. The company registered a pre tax profit of Rs.22.12 Crores as compared to Rs.8.79 Crores in the corresponding quarter of the previous year, thus registering a profit growth of 151% over the corresponding quarter of the previous year. The profit after tax for the quarter is Rs.15.33 crores as compared to Rs.6.52 crores in the corresponding quarter of the previous year, thus registering a growth of 135%. For the cumulative 9 months ending 31.12.2009 the turnover amounts to Rs. 391.38 crores as against Rs. 329.87 crores in the corresponding period of the previous year.

Several years ago, M/s TTK Prestige used to have a visible T V commercial with the line " jo biwi se kare pyar woh kaisa kare inkar?. It was one of those hard-working commercials showing a friendly dealer advising a young couple who is choosing from amongst various brands of pressure cookers. The bottom line was that if you really loved your wife you would buy her a prestige pressure cooker! Lots of South Indian houses had Prestige pressure cookers (though we do not have conlusive evidence that those husbands loved their wives) as the brand was dominant in this region. Notwithstanding the fact that the brand was well recognized and well patronized, it struggled for both top line and bottom line growth in the Nineties, and the turn of the century saw the company to into the red. The company, it seemed, was at the crossroads. Franklin D Roosevelt said, "One thing is sure. We have to do something. We have to do the best we know how at the moment... if it does not turn out right, we can modify it as we go along"

The company did something which turned out to be real smart. It came out with a line extension with a difference. It launched prestige Smart Kitchen. In hindsight, that could be called a defining moment in the brand's life. It was what could be described as "disruptive thinking" which, if not successful, could have sent the company furiously downhill. Today, with over a 100 franchised outlets and a growth of 30 percent consistently over the last few years, the now profitable company has just demonstrated that any one of 4 Ps- product, price, promotion and place- can guide your brand into winning ways. And the unlikely hero? The 4th P or distribution! Not glamorous advertising. Not mind boggling price-offs. Not amazing product innovations. But the often unrecognized and largely ignored retail outlet where the consumer bought her pressure cooker.

Questions:

1. What is your observation of this case study?
2. Is it possible to improve growth percentage from 30 percentage & above? Which strategy do you prefer?

CASE -2

About Us - The Amul Model

The Birth of Amul

- It all began when milk became a symbol of protest
- Founded in 1946 to stop the exploitation by middlemen
- Inspired by the freedom movement

The seeds of this unusual saga were sown more than 65 years back in Anand, a small town in the state of Gujarat in western India. The exploitative trade practices followed by the local trade cartel triggered off the cooperative movement. Angered by unfair and manipulative practices followed by the trade, the farmers of the district approached the great Indian patriot Sardar Vallabhbhai Patel for a solution. He advised them to get rid of middlemen and form their own co-operative, which would have procurement, processing and marketing under their control.

In 1946, the farmers of this area went on a milk strike refusing to be cowed down by the cartel. Under the inspiration of Sardar Patel, and the guidance of leaders like Morarji Desai and Tribhuvandas Patel, they formed their own cooperative in 1946.

This co-operative, the Kaira District Co-operative Milk Producers Union Ltd. began with just two village dairy co-operative societies and 247 litres of milk and is today better known as Amul Dairy. Amul grew from strength to strength thanks to the inspired leadership of Tribhuvandas Patel, the founder Chairman and the committed professionalism of Dr Verghese Kurien,who was entrusted the task of running the dairy from 1950.

The then Prime Minister of India, Lal Bahadur Shastri decided that the same approach should become the basis of a National Dairy Development policy. He understood that the success of Amul could be attributed to four important factors. The farmers owned the dairy, their elected representatives managed the village societies and the district union,Â they employed professionals to operate the dairy and manage its business. Most importantly, the co-operatives were sensitive to the needs of farmers and responsive to their demands.

At his instance in 1965 the National Dairy Development Board was set up with the basic objective of replicating the Amul model. Dr. Kurien was chosen to head the institution as its Chairman and asked to replicate this model throughout the country.

The Amul Model

The Amul Model of dairy development is a three-tiered structure with the dairy cooperative societies at the village level federated under a milk union at the district level and a federation of member unions at the state level.

- Establishment of a direct linkage between milk producers and consumers by eliminating middlemen
- Milk Producers (farmers) control procurement, processing and marketing.
- Professional management.

The Amul model has helped India to emerge as the largest milk producer in the world. More than 15 million milk producers pour their milk in 1,44,246 dairy cooperative societies across the country. Their milk is processed in 177 District Co-operative Unions and marketed by 22 State Marketing Federations, ensuring a better life for millions.

REVIEW QUESTIONS

Conceptual Type

1. What do you mean by strategy?
2. What are the three levels of strategy? ***(VTU, MBA, Dec-2011)***
3. What is strategic management? ***(VTU, MBA, Dec-2010)***
4. Explain the difference between strategy and business model. ***(VTU, MBA, June-2010)***

Analytical Type

1. Explain the need for strategy.
2. Explain the significance of strategy.
3. Discuss the levels of strategy.
4. Explain the characteristics of strategic management. ***(VTU, MBA, Dec-2012, 2010)***
5. Explain the need for strategic management.
6. Explain the seven criteria used in preparing long term objectives. ***(VTU, MBA, Dec-2011)***
7. Explain the importance of strategic management.
8. What are the various benefits of strategic management? ***(VTU, MBA, July-2006)***
9. What are the limitation of strategic management?

Descriptive Type

1. Discus the various components of strategic management model. ***(VTU, MBA, July-2006)***
2. With the help of the strategic management model, briefly explain the steps in the strategic management process. ***(VTU, MBA, Dec-2011)***
3. Explain the strategic management process.
4. Discus the various key terms in strategic management.

******

Module-2

Strategy Formulation

Unit

Syllabus

Strategy Formulation – Developing Strategic Vision and Mission for a Company – Setting Objectives – Strategic Objectives and Financial Objectives – Balanced Scorecard. Company Goals and Company Philosophy. The hierarchy of Strategic Intent – Merging the Strategic Vision, Objectives and Strategy into a Strategic Plan.

INTRODUCTION

It is useful to consider strategy formulation as part of a strategic management process that comprises three phases: diagnosis, formulation, and implementation. Strategic management is an ongoing process to develop and revise future-oriented strategies that allow an organization to achieve its objectives, considering its capabilities, constraints, and the environment in which it operates.

The formulation, the second phase in the strategic management process, produces a clear set of recommendations, with supporting justification, that revise as necessary the mission and objectives of the organization, and supply the strategies for accomplishing them. In formulation, we are trying to modify the current objectives and strategies in ways to make the organization more successful.

VISION STATEMENT

Vision is the clear picture about the firms which is focus on future intent of the firms. A strategic vision is a road map showing the route a company intends to take in developing and strengthening its business. It paints a picture of a company's destination and provides a rationale for going there Objectives, expressed as strategic intent, should lead to an end; otherwise they would just be strongholds in the air. That end is the vision of an organization or an individual. Ultimately, What is the aim in the future of the firm or individual . For instance, some of you, say in 10 years, or may be even earlier, would like to become general managers managing an SBU in a large, diversified multinational corporation. Or some others among you would like to believe that you will be an entrepreneur in 1016 years owning your own company dealing with IT services and employing cutting edge technology to serve a global clientele. A firm thinks like that too. Witness what Tata Steel says about its vision: "Tata Steel enters the new millennium with the confidence of a learning, knowledge based and happy organization. We will establish ourselves as a supplier of choice by delighting our customers with our service and our products. In the coming decade, we will become the most cost competitive steel plant and so serve the community and the nation." A vision, therefore, articulates the position that a firm would like to attain in the distant future. Seen from this perspective, the vision encapsulates the basic strategic intent.

"A vision statement is sometimes called a picture of your company in the future but it's so much more than that. Your vision statement is your inspiration, the framework for all your strategic planning".

The vision statement is a guide to implementing strategy. Vision is about feelings, beliefs, emotions and pictures.

DEFINITION

Kotter (1990) defines it as a "description of something (an organization, corporate culture, a business, a technology, an activity) in the future". ElNamaki (1992) considers it as a "mental perception of the kind of environment an individual, or an organization, aspires to create within a broad time horizon and the underlying conditions for the actualization of this perception". Miller and Dess (1996) view it simply as the "category of intentions that are broad, all inclusive, and forward thinking". The common strand of thought evident in these definitions and several others available in strategic management literature relates to 'vision' being future aspirations that lead to an inspiration to be the best in one's field of activity

When you are formulating vision statement for your company, you have to consider the following points:

1. It should be clarity and understandable.
2. It should be reachable and achievable.
3. It should be shortness and very simple.
4. It should be reality.

BENEFITS OF VISION

Parikh and Neubauer (1993) point out the several benefits accruing to an, organization having a vision. Here is what they say:

1. Good visions are inspiring and exhilarating
2. Visions represent a discontinuity, a step function and a jump ahead so that the company knows what it is to be
3. Good visions help in the creation of a common identity and a shared sense purpose
4. Good visions are competitive, original and unique. They make sense in the market place, as they are practical
5. Good visions foster risk taking and experimentation
6. Good visions foster longterm thinking.
7. Good visions represent integrity; they are truly genuine and can be used for the benefit of people.

GENERAL MOTORS VISION STATEMENT

GM's vision is to be the world leader in transportation products and related services. We will earn our customers' enthusiasm through continuous improvement driven by the integrity, teamwork, and innovation of GM people

Nike

"To be the number one athletic company in the world"

Infosys

Vision 2050: The New Agenda for Business' provides a pathway leading to sustainability by 2050, requiring fundamental changes in governance structures, economic frameworks, business, and human behavior.

Hindustan Lever Ltd

We work to create a better future every day. We help people feel good, look good and get more out of life with brands and Services that are good for them and good for others. We will inspire people to take small everyday actions that can add up to a big difference for the world.

We will develop new ways of doing business that will allow us to double the size of our company while reducing our environmental impact.

MISSION STATEMENT

The mission statement is a permanent statement of purpose that distinguishes one business from other similar business. It finds the scope of its operations in product and market terms. Mission statement focuses on why does the organization exist? What's its function? What its value addition? What business is it in?

A mission statement helps the organization to link its activities to the needs of the society and legitimize its existence Bharat Heavy Electricals Ltd Mission statement is " To achieve and maintain a leading position as suppliers of quality equipment, systems and service to serve the national and international market in the field of energy. The areas of interest would be the conversion, transmission utilization and conservation of energy for applications in the power, industrial and transportation fields, to strive for technological excellence and market leadership in these areas". The above Mission clearly indicate the exits, intent, distinguishes of the Bharat Heavy Electricals Ltd.

A mission statement is a brief description of a company's fundamental purpose. It answers the question, "Why do we exist?"

The mission statement articulates the company's purpose both for those in the organization and for the public.

DEFINING MISSION

Thompson (1997) defines mission as the "essential purpose of the organization, concerning particularly why it is in existence, the nature of the businesses it is in, and the customers it seeks to serve and satisfy"

Hunger and Wheelen (1999) say that mission is the "purpose or reason for the organization's existence". Now there is not much difference of opinion about the definition of mission. Yet, you find instances of organizations confusing mission with vision or objectives. In strategic management literature, mission occupies a definite place as a part of strategic intent.

COMPONENTS OF A MISSION STATEMENT

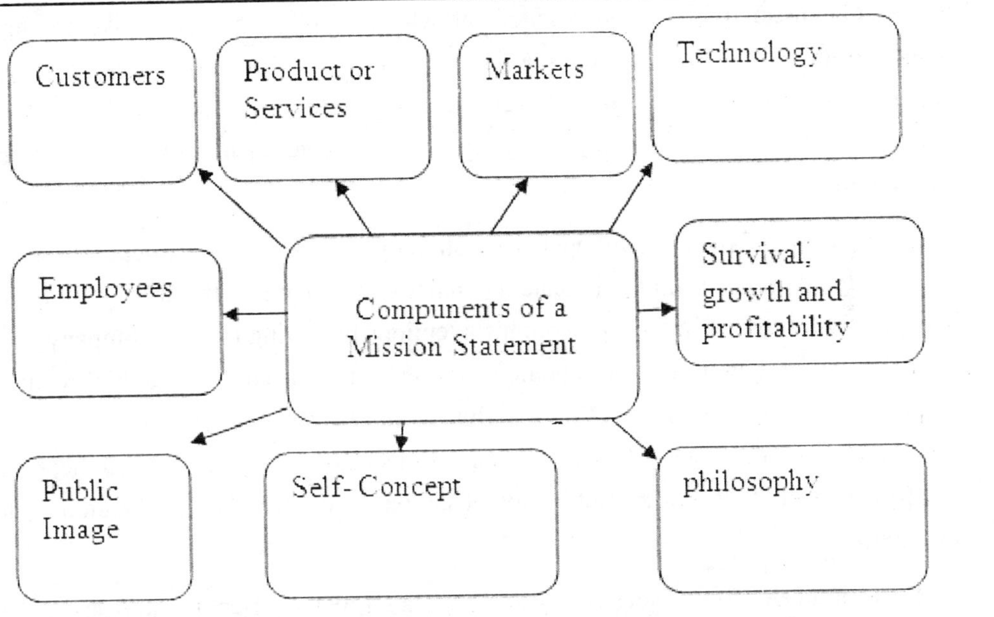

CHARACTERISTICS OF A MISSION STATEMENT

A mission statement defines the basic reason for the existence of that organization. Such a statement reflects the corporate philosophy, identity, character, and image of an organization. It may be defined explicitly or could be deduced from the management's actions, decisions, or the chief executive's press statements. When explicitly defined it provides enlightenment to the insiders and outsiders on what the organization stand for. In order to be effective, a mission statement should possess the following seven characteristics.

1. It should be feasible. A mission should always aim high but it should not be an impossible statement. It should be realistic and achievable its followers must find it to be credible. But feasibility depends on the resources available to work towards a mission.

2. It should be precise. A mission statement should not be so narrow as to restrict the organization's activities nor should it be too broad to make itself meaningless. It should be very specific about the firm activities.

3. It should be clear. A mission should be clear and understandable to lead to action. It should not be a high sounding set of platitudes meant for publicity purposes

4. It should be motivating. A mission statement should be motivating for members of the organization and of society, and they should feel it worthwhile working for such an organization or being its customers.

5. It should be distinctive. A mission statement, which is indiscriminate, is likely to have little impact. If all scooter manufacturers defined their mission in a similar fashion, there would not be much of a difference among them. But if one defines it as providing scooters that would provide 'value for money, for years' it will create an important distinction in the public mind.

6. It should indicate major components of strategy. A mission statement along with the organizational purpose should indicate the major components of the strategy to be adopted. The chief executive of Indal expressed his intentions by saying that his company "begins its fifth decade of committed entrepreneurship with the promise of a highly diversified company retaining aluminum as its mainline business, but with an active presence in the chemical, electronics and industrial equipment business". This statement indicates that the company is likely to follow a combination of stability, growth and diversification strategies in the future.

7. It should indicate how objectives are to be accomplished. Besides indicating the broad strategies to be adopted, a mission statement should also provide clues regarding the manner in which the objectives are to be accomplished.

FEATURES OF A GOOD MISSION STATEMENT

1. The mission should be clear, both in terms of intentions and words used;
2. It should be feasible, neither too high to be unachievable, nor too low to demotivate the people for work.
3. It should be precise but self-explanatory, neither too narrow so as to restrict the organization's activities, nor too broad to make itself meaningless.
4. It should be distinctive, both in terms of the organization's contributions to the society and how these contributions can be made.

FORMULATION OF MISSION STATEMENT

While the preparation of mission statement, you can keep below the question and its answers:

1. Who our team serves?
2. Why we serve these people?
3. The specific client needs our team strives to meet?
4. The specific ways in which we serve our clients?
5. How we communicate our mission to the community and our clients:
6. How we measure how well we're fulfilling our mission:

A few examples of mission statement are as follows:

India Today " The complete new magazine"

Bajaj Auto, "Value for Money for Years"

HCL, " To be a world class Competitor"

HMT, "Timekeepers of the Nation"

OBJECTIVES

Objective works towards the mission statement of the company. The objective is indicating the end results or end point of the firm's seeks to achieve over a specified period. "Objectives are aims, or purposes that organizations wish over varying periods of time." It is determining the scope of the future events. They provide the highlight on the routes over which activities are organized.

It can define objective as the intended end result that an organization desires to achieve over varying periods of fame. Because of time variation, objectives may be specified in different ways in which long-term objectives are supported by short-term objectives.

FEATURES OF OBJECTIVES

1. Each organization, has some objectives. In fact, organizations are created basically for certain objectives. Members in the organization try to achieve these objectives.

2. Objectives may be broad and specifically mentioned. They may pertain to a wide or narrow part of the organization. They may be set either for the long term or for the short term.

   For example, the basic objective of a business organization may be to earn profit. General, objectives may be translated into operational objectives to provide definite action.

3. Objectives may be clearly defined and have to be interpreted by organizational members, particularly those at the top level. However, clearly defined objectives provide clear direction for managerial action.

4. Objectives have a hierarchy. At the top level, it may be broad organizational purpose which can be broken into specific objectives at the departmental level. From departmental objectives, units of the department may derive their own objectives. This is possible because combining people into sections, departments, divisions, etc create organization. All of them try to achieve organizational objectives and, at each level a unit may contribute to the fulfillment of tasks assigned to it. Thus, a hierarchy of objectives is created.

5. Organizational objectives have social sanction, that is, they are created within the social norms. Since organizations are social units, their objectives must confirm to the general needs of the society. Various restrictions on organizational objectives are put through social norms, rules and customs.

6. An organization may have multiple objectives. For example, Hindustan Lever Limited, under the chairmanship of T. Thomas (during 1973-80) formulated the following objectives:

   i. To expand and diversify in the area of chemicals;

   ii. To continue to control costs and improve productivity very rigorously;

   iii. To build up management skills for future growth; etc.

7. Organizational objectives can be changed; new ones may replace old objectives. It is possible because organizations are free to set their objectives within the overall social norms. Since objectives are formulated keeping in view the environmental factors and internal conditions, any change in these may result into change.

GUIDELINES FOR OBJECTIVE SETTING

1. Objectives must be clearly specified and maintained.
2. It must be set taking into account the various factors affecting their achievement.
3. It should be consistent with the organizational mission.
4. Objectives should be rational and realistic rather than idealistic.
5. Objectives should be achievable but must provide a challenge to those responsible for achieving.
6. Objectives should yield specific results when achieved.
7. It should be desirable for those who are responsible for the achievement.
8. Objectives should start with the word 'to' and be followed by an action verb.
9. It should be consistent over the period of time.
10. Objectives should be periodically reviewed.

SEVEN CRITERIA USED IN PREPARING LONG-TERM OBJECTIVES

1. ***Acceptable:*** Managers are most likely to pursue objectives that are consistent with their preferences. They may ignore or even obstruct the achievement of objectives that offend them (e.g., promoting a non-nutritional food product) or that they believe to be inappropriate or; unfair (e.g., reducing spoilage to offset a disproportionate allocation of fixed overhead). In addition, long-term corporate objectives are frequently designed to be acceptable to groups external to the firm. An example is efforts to abate air pollution that are undertaken at the insistence of the Environmental Protection Agency.

2. ***Flexible:*** Objectives should be adaptable to unforeseen or extraordinary changes in the firm's competitive or environmental forecasts. However, such flexibility usually increased at the expense of specificity. Moreover, employee confidence may be tempered because adjustment of flexible objectives may affect their jobs. One way of providing flexibility while minimizing its negative effects is to allow for adjustments in the level, rather than in the nature of objectives. For example, the personnel department objective of providing managerial development training for 15 supervisors per year over the next five-year period might be adjusted by changing the number of people to be trained. In contrast, changing the personnel department's objective of assisting production supervisors in reducing job-related injuries by 10 percent per year after three months had gone by would understandably create dissatisfaction.

3. ***Measurable:*** Objectives must clearly and concretely state what will be achieved and when it will be achieved. Thus, objectives should be measurable over time. For example, the objective of "substantially improving our return on investment" would be better stated as "increasing the return on investment on our line of paper products by a minimum of percent a year and a total of 5 percent over the next three years."

4. ***Motivating:*** Studies have shown that people are most productive when objectives are set at a motivating level-one high enough to challenge but not so high as to frustrate or so low as to be easily attained. The problem is that individuals and groups differ in their perceptions of what is high enough. A broad objective that challenges one group frustrates another and minimally interests a third. One valuable recommendation is that objectives be tailored to specific groups. Developing such objectives requires time and effort, but objectives of this kind are more likely to motivate.

5. ***Suitable:*** Objectives must be suited to the broad aims of the firm, which are expressed in its mission statement. Each objective should be a step toward the attainment of overall goals. In fact, objectives that do not coincide with the company mission can subvert the firm's aims. For example, if the mission is growth oriented, the objective of reducing the debt-to- equity ratio to 1.00 would probably be unsuitable and counterproductive.

6. ***Understandable:*** Strategic managers at all levels must understand what is to be achieved. They also must understand the major criteria by which their performance will be evaluated. Thus, objectives must be so stated that they are as understandable to the recipient as they are to the giver. Consider the misunderstandings that might arise over the objective of "increasing the productivity of the credit card department by 20 percent within five years." What does this objective mean? Increase the number of outstanding cards? Increase the use of outstanding cards? Increase the employee workload? Make productivity gains each year? Or hope that the new computer-assisted system, which should improve productivity, is approved by year 5? As this simple example illustrates, objectives must be clear, meaningful, and unambiguous.

7. ***Achievable:*** Finally, objectives must be possible to achieve. This is easier said than done. Turbulence in the remote and operating environments affects a firm's internal operations, creating uncertainty, and limiting the accuracy of the objectives set by strategic management. To illustrate, the wildly fluctuating prime interest rates in 1980 made objective setting extremely difficult for the years 1982 to 1985, particularly in such areas as sales projections for producers of consumer durable goods like General Motors and General Electric.

CLASSIFICATION OF OBJECTIVES

Long-term Objectives

Objectives can be defined as specific results that an organization seeks to achieve in pursuing its basic mission. Long-term means more than one year objectives are essential for organizational success because they state direction, aid in evaluation, create synergy, reveal priorities, focus coordination and provide a basis for effective planning, organization, motivating and controlling activities.

Strategic objectives

Strategies are the means by which long term objectives will be achieved . Business strategies may include geographic expansion, diversification, acquisition, product development , market penetration, retrenchment, divestiture, liquidation and joint ventur

Annual Objectives

Annual objectives are short-term milestones that organizations must achieve to reach long – term objectives. Like long term objectives annual objectives should be measurable, quantitative, challenging, realistic, consistent, and prioritized

Financial objectives

Financial strategy examines the financial implication at corporate and business levels to identify the best financial course of action, this can provide competitive advantage through lower cost of funds and flexibility to raise capital This strategy normally helps in maximizing the financial value

Operations strategy

Operations strategy answers vital questions of manufacturing, concerning where to produce, vertical integration, deployment of resources, relationship with suppliers, technology to be used and levels of quality to be achieved.

OBJECTIVES AND GOALS A COMPARISON

Objectives and goals are the end results which an organization strives for. Since there may be different ways in expressing end results like market leadership (a qualitative measurement), or a certain percentage of increase in sales in a particular year (a quanti-tative measurement), the question is: for which result the term objectives should be used and for which result the term goal should be used. This problem arises because these two terms are used in variety of ways; many of them are conflicting. First, these terms are used interchangeably meaning one and the same thing. Therefore, there is no difference between the two. To make a distinction between long-term and short-term orientations, these prefixes are used either with objectives or goals. Second, some authors use goals as the long-term results, which an organization seeks to achieve, and objectives as the short-term results. Third, some writers reverse the usage referring to objectives as the desired long-term results and goals as the desired short-term results. This latter view is, however, more prevalent and we will take this view in our discussion. From this point of view, Ackoff has defined both the terms as follows:

"Desired states or outcomes are objectives. Goals are objectives that are scheduled for attainment during planned period. Thus, objectives and goals defined in this way convey two different concepts. The distinction between these two concepts is important because management needs both

DISTINCTION BETWEEN OBJECTIVES AND GOALS OF NATIONAL THERMAL POWER CORPORATION LTD.

Objective	Goals
1. To add generating capacity by installing thermal power plants including gas based power plants as per the prescribed time schedule costs and reliability levels.	1. The Corporation would make efforts to commission one unit of 210 MW at the National Thermal Power Project, Dadri and one unit of 131 MW at the Dadri Gas Project also during 1990-91.
2. To manage the financial operation of the Corporation in accordance with sound commercial practices to enable generation of adequate internal resources in order to be able to contribute in the National Power Development Programme.	2. The NTPC will generate a total of 46,475 million units during the year from its various power stations representing an increase of about 15% over the generation of 40,892 million units the previous year. The Corporation will achieve a total sale of Rs. 2429.72 crore during the year, based on the existing tariff. The Corporation will earn a total profit before tax of Rs. 257.13 crore during the year, based on existing tariff rates. The net internal resources available for plan schemes during the year would be Rs. 309.27 crore.

3. To develop and implement a well-knit Human Resource Development Policy, result oriented personnel development program and an organizational culture, which motives employees to contribute their best towards achievement of organizational objectives.	3. To review on a continuous basis, the Human Resources Development Systems/subsystems, to make them more responsive to the changing organizational requirements and employees aspirations, and in particular, to review during the year Performance Appraisal System and Promotion Policy so as to promote merit, promote excellence and serve as an objective measure of performance and to enthuse the executives for effective performance.
4. To strengthen in-house technical and managerial capabilities not only to be self-reliant to cater to the needs for setting up of its projects/transmission systems and their operation but also for providing consultancy services to the organizations within the countryand abroad.	4. The corporation will strive to increase its role in consultancy through the consultancy wing established by it, by serving and executing consultancy assignments in the area of power development and power management in India and abroad.

BALANCED SCORECARD

The Balanced Scorecard is a management tool that provides stakeholders with a comprehensive measure of how the organization is progressing towards the achievement of its strategic goals.

R.S. Kaplan and D.P. Norton the balanced scorecard in the early 90's linking corporate goals with strategic actions undertaken in the business unit, departmental and individual level. The Balanced Scorecard is a set of measures that gives top managers a quick but comprehensive view of the business.

Kaplan and Norton suggested that organizations should focus their efforts on a limited number of specific, critical performance measures which reflect stakeholders key success factors.

1. Financial Perspective

Kaplan and Norton do not disregard the traditional need for financial data.

Timely and accurate funding data will always be a priority, and managers will do whatever necessary to provide it.

There is perhaps a need to include additional financial-related data, such as risk assessment and cost-benefit data, in this category.

2. Customer Perspective

Recent management philosophy has shown an increasing realization of the importance of customer focus and customer satisfaction in any business.

These are leading indicators: if customers are not satisfied, they will eventually find other suppliers that will meet their needs.

Poor performance from this perspective is thus a leading indicator of future decline, even though the current financial picture may look good.

3. Business Process Perspective

This perspective refers to internal business processes. Metrics based on this perspective allow the managers to know how well their business is running, and whether its products and services conform to customer requirements (the mission).

In addition to the strategic management process, two kinds of business processes may be identified:

a) Mission-oriented processes, and

b) Support processes.

Mission-oriented processes are the special functions of government offices, and many unique problems are encountered in these processes.

The support processes are more repetitive in nature, and hence easier to measure and benchmark using generic metrics.

4. The Learning and Growth Perspective

This perspective includes employee training and corporate cultural attitudes related to both individual and corporate self-improvement.

Kaplan and Norton emphasize that learning is more than training; it also includes things like mentors and tutors within the organization, as well as that ease of communication among workers that allows them to readily get help on a problem when it is needed. It also includes technological tools; what the Baldrige criteria call high performance work systems.

BENEFITS OF BALANCED SCORECARD

- Helps companies focus on what has to be done in order to create breakthrough performance
- Acts as an integrating device for a variety of corporate programmers
- Makes strategy operational by translating it into performance measures and targets
- Helps break down corporate level measures so that local managers and employees can see what they need to do well if they want to improve organizational effectiveness
- Provides a comprehensive view that overturns the traditional idea of the organization as a collection of isolated, independent functions and departments.

STRATEGIC INTENT

The strategic intent refers to the purposes the organization strives for. These may be expressed in terms of a hierarchy of strategic intent. Broadly stated, these could be in the form of a vision and mission statement for the organization as a corporate whole. At the business level of a firm these could be expressed as the business definition. When stated in precise terms, as an expression of the aims to be achieved operationally, these may be the goals and 'objectives. Here you take the position that strategic intent lays down the framework within which firms would operate, adopt a predetermined direction, and attempt to achieve their goals. But the term strategic intent has a definite meaning in strategic management. Let's first see the meaning and some associated concepts before you learn about the hierarchy of strategic intent.

Understanding strategic Intent lets discuss who coined strategic intent?

Hamel and Prahalad coined the term 'strategic intent' which they believe is an obsession with an organization and obsession with having ambitions that may even be out of proportion to their resources and capabilities. This obsession is to win at all levels of the organization while sustaining that obsession in the quest for global leadership. They explain the term 'strategic intent' like this: "On the one hand, strategic intent envisions a desired leadership position and establishes the criterion the organization will use to chart its progress. At the same time, strategic intent is more than simply unfettered ambition. The concept also encompasses an active management process that includes:

Focusing the organization's attention on the essence of winning, motivating people by communicating the value of the target, leaving room for individual and team contributions, sustaining enthusiasm by providing new operational definitions as circumstances change and using intent consistently to guide resource allocations.

Hamel and Prahalad quote several examples of global firms, almost all of American and Japanese origin, to support their view. In fact, the concept of strategic intentas evident from their path-breaking article, published in 1989 in the Harvard Business Review seems to have been proposed by them to explain the lead taken by Japanese firms over their American and European counterparts.

THE HIERARCHY OF STRATEGIC INTENT

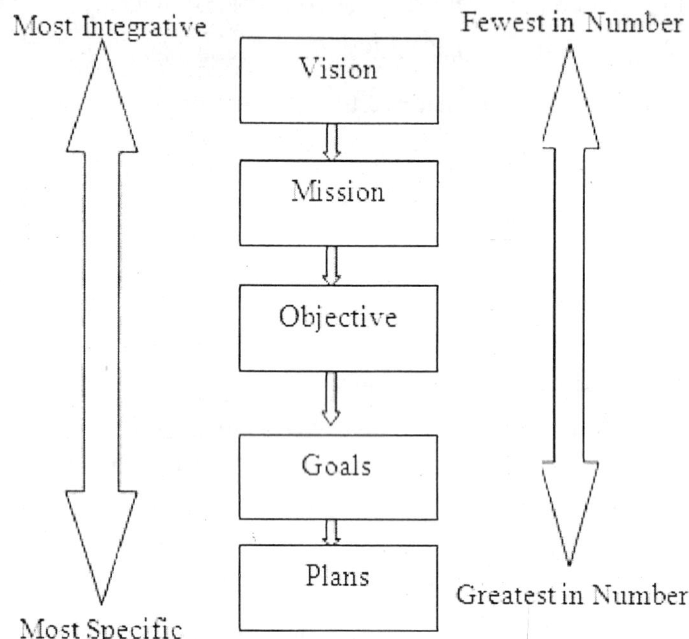

The foundation for the strategic management is laid by the hierarchy of strategic intent. The concept of strategic intent makes clear What An Organisation Stands For Harvard Business Review, 1989 described the concept in its infancy Hamel and Prahalad coined the term strategic intent. A few aspects about strategic intent are as follows:

- It is an obsession with an organization.
- This obsession may even be out of proportion to their resources and capabilities.
- It envisions a derived leadership position and establishes the criterion; the organization will use to chart its progress.

It involves the following:

- Creating and Communicating a vision
- Designing a mission statement

- Defining the business
- Setting objectives

Vision serves the purpose of stating what an organization wishes to achieve in the long run.

Mission relates an organization to society.

Business explains the business of an organization in terms of customer needs, customer groups and alternative technologies.

Objectives state what is to be achieved in a given time period.

- The strategic intent concept also encompasses an active management process that includes focusing the organization's attention on the essence of winning.
- The concept of stretch and leverage is relevant in this context.

Important: Stretch is a misfit between resources and aspirations. Leverage concentrates, accumulates, conserves and recovers resources so that a meager resource base can be stretched.Leverage reduces the stretch and focuses mainly on efficient utilization of resources.

- The strategic fit matches organizational resources and environment. This positions the firm by assessing organizational capabilities and environmental opportunities.
- Under fit, the strategic intent would seem to be more realistic.
- It is hierarchy of intentions ranging from a board vision through mission and purpose down to specific objectives.

Vision: It is at the top in the hierarchy of strategic intent. It is what the firm would ultimately like to become. A few definitions are as follows:

KOTTER: Description of something (an organization, corporate culture, a business, a technology, an activity) in the future. The definition itself is comprehensive and states clearly the futurist position.

Core Ideology will remain unchanged. It has the enduring character. It consists of core values and core purpose. Core values are essential tenets of an organization. Core purpose is related to the reasoning of the existence of organization.

Envisioned Future will basically deal with following:

- The long term objectives of the organization.
- Clear description of articulated future.

Goals denote a broad category of financial and non-financial issues that a firm sets for itself.

Objectives are the ends that state specifically how the goals shall be achieved. It is to be noted that objectives are the manifestation of goals whether specifically stated or not.

Difference between objectives and goals

The points of difference between the two are as follows:

- The goals are broad while objectives are specific.
- The goals are set for a relatively longer period of time.
- Goals are more influenced by external environment.
- Goals are not quantified while objectives are quantified.

MERGING THE STRATEGIC VISION, OBJECTIVES AND STRATEGY INTO A STRATEGIC PLAN

The steps of strategy planning involves stating the mission, vision, SWOT analysis, strategy implementation and control measures.Since the strategic vision explains about the future dream of the organization and mission clearly states the purpose of the existence of the current business and also objectives are the end result of objectives.

Strategy planning involves establishing goals, analyzing the business environment, specifying the period, finalizing the action plan, developing and implementing the plan and finally setting control measures.

Merging the vision, objectives and strategy results in effective situational analysis, generating feasible goals, alternate plans, SMART goals. Also merging of these concepts helps to effectively evaluate the stated goals and mode of achievement.. Hence for effective strategy planning it is necessary to synchronize the effective vision, objectives, mission and strategy into strategy planning.

The Balanced Scorecard Today: Tesco PLC

Tesco was founded in 1919 by Jack Cohen when he began selling surplus groceries from a stall in the East End of London (Tesco 2009). In 1932, Tesco Stores Limited became a private limited company (Tesco 2009). Tesco floated on the stock exchange for the first time in 1947 with an initial share price of 25p (Tesco 2009). Tesco introduced the Clubcard in 1995, which is a loyalty card for customers (Tesco 2009). This card has helped Tesco evaluate its customers.

"Tesco is the UK's leading food retailer in an extremely competitive market" (Vignali 2001). For this reason it decided to expand operations across Europe, which also included expanding to Ireland. According to Vignali (2001), Tesco entered the Irish food retail market by choosing to purchase all Quinnsworth, Crazy Prices and Stewart's stores in Ireland.

Tesco plc currently employs over 470,000 people across 14 countries (Tesco 2009). In 2009, Tesco's turnover exceeded £1 billion per week over the 12-month period (Microsoft, 2010). The current share price is 427.55p, which exceeds its leading competitors share price of 332.40p (Tesco 2009). The company's major shareholder is Legal & General Assurance (Pensions Management Limited) (Tesco 2009). Tesco floats on the London Stock Exchange under the symbol TSCO and it also floats on the Irish Stock Exchange as TESCO PLC.

While most people call their strategic planning and management systems a balanced scorecard (Witcher and Chau, 2008), Tesco call it the Steering Wheel (Tesco 2009). This organisational tool centers their business on the delivery of their core purpose (Tesco 2009). The only difference is that there are five perspectives instead of four; the fifth perspective being community (Tesco 2009). The editors of Strategic Direction (2009) found that at Tesco "performance is reported quarterly to the board, and a summary report sent to the top 2,000 managers to cascade to staff" (p.5). The salary of senior management is created by the KPIs, with bonuses established on a descending scale according to the level of success on the steering wheel (Editors of Strategic Direction 2009)

However, according to ICMR (2005), Tesco's 'Steering Wheel' was so successful in fulfilling the company's strategic objectives that the company forgot about HR policies and procurement policies when the company began to grow rapidly. This resulted in Tesco paying unduly low wages and having a high absenteeism rate. The balanced scorecard does appear to have been a great success for Tesco as it is the largest British retailer.

Financial Perspective

"The Financial Perspective covers the financial objectives of an organisation and allows managers to track the financial success of a company for example how wealth is created for shareholders" (Advanced Performance Institute 2010). However, despite the need to provide a balanced approach to performance measurement, companies remain focused on traditional financial measures (gross revenue, profit before tax, and cost reduction) and often forget about intangible assets (Chia, Goh and Hum 2009). According to Valiris, Chytas and Glykas, (2005) financial measures remain an important dimension within the balanced scorecard. The Financial perspective measures whether a company's strategy, implementation, and execution are contributing to bottom-line improvement (Valiris et al. 2005). The financial perspective focuses on traditional return-based efficiency and effectiveness metrics (Punniyamoorthy and Murrali 2008).

In order for Tesco to meet its target profits in 2009 it decided to charge elevated prices in its Irish stores at the beginning of the year (Cullen 2009). Cullen (2009) also found that Tesco then lowered their prices from March on 11 Border stores in preparation for a price war against competitors. For Tesco to achieve its profit targets for 2009 it had to make up to 100 employees redundant at its Irish headquarters in Dún Laoghaire (Cullen 2009). In 2008, Tesco had a profit margin of 9.3 per cent in Ireland, while its profits were •248 million and 2009 profits were projected to rise to •255 million (Cullen 2009). Tesco have reduced their costs in order to increase sales revenue. These figures may look great to the shareholders in times of economic downturn but for Tesco to cut their prices they put pressure on their suppliers (especially Irish suppliers) to reduce their prices. This in effect can put some suppliers out of business. Tesco have also reduced their direct expenses by cutting employee hours and introducing self service scan tills into most of their stores. This may have benefited Tesco's bottom line but it has made its employees threaten strike action.

Tesco's main competitor in the UK is Sainsbury's. Tesco is appealing to shareholders as it achieving a return on capital employed of 15%, while its competitor (Sainsbury's) is achieving a return on capital employed of 9% (Appendix1). The absolute difference between these returns on capital employed is 6%, which means that Tesco is the more profitable company. The relative difference is 66%, which indicates that Tesco are 66% more profitable than Sainsbury's. Tesco paid out a final dividend of 8.39p (Tesco 2009) to its shareholders at the end of 2009, while its competitor Sainsbury plc paid out a dividend of 9.6p (Sainsbury plc 2009). Tesco has a policy of not paying their trade creditors for 54 days, which in turn puts pressure on their suppliers. Tesco's group sales have increased by 7,000 since 2008 (Tesco 2009), while Sainsbury's increased by 1,000 from 2008 (Sainsbury plc 2009). Tesco should be given credit for their increased sales during tough economic times but to achieve these sales they have had to cut prices, which means that they would have also undercut their suppliers. Tesco's net profit percentage has an absolute difference of 3% when compared to Sainsbury's (Appendix3). The relative difference is 88%, which signifies that management in Tesco are controlling their costs more efficiently than Sainsbury's. This is evident in that Tesco have cut wages, which would increase Tesco's net profit.

Customer Perspective

"In the customer perspective of the Balanced Scorecard, managers identify the customer and market segments in which the business unit will compete and the measures of the business unit's performance in these targeted segments" (Kaplan and Nortan 1996, p26). According to

Kaplan and Norton (1996) the customer perspective, if implemented correctly, should have successful outcomes such as customer satisfaction, customer retention, customer profitability, new customer acquisition and market share in targeted segments. It also enables companies to measure and identify the value propositions (unique mix of product, price, service, relationship etc., offered to customers) that they will deliver to targeted customers and market segments (Kaplan and Norton 1996). For this to work, businesses must identify the market segments in their existing and possible customer populations and then they must identify which segment they are going to compete in (Kaplan and Norton 1996). However, for many companies this may be difficult to implement but for Tesco it is easier as they have a value clubcard, which enables them to identify what their customers want.

According to Liptrot (2005) Tesco attracts 15 million customers per week. When Tesco implemented the 'Steering Wheel' they appealed to all segments of the market instead of focusing on certain segments (Liptrot 2005). Tesco wanted to gain customer satisfaction and in order to do this; they decided to cater for all incomes. Tesco offer three distinct ranges of own-brand products to satisfy all their customers (Tesco 2009).

It is far cheaper for Tesco to keep its customers than it is for it to gain new ones. Tesco launched a Loyalty Clubcard in 1995 (Tesco 2009). The information gained by Tesco from its customers using the Clubcard allows them to understand their customers and offer them a variety of coupons to suit their needs (Tesco 2009). It was also found by Turner and Wilson (2006) that there was a positive moderate relationship between the Clubcard returns and customer loyalty. In May, Tesco offered a Double Up scheme, giving card holders a chance to turn vouchers into twice their face value, this incentive drew 500,000 extra shoppers (Mirror 2009).

Tesco also retain customers by marketing online grocery shopping as a convenience to its customers (Delaney-Klinger et al. 2003). This allows shoppers to shop from the comfort of their home and have their purchases delivered to their door. According to Rowley (2003) Tesco online (tesco.com) has developed a sophisticated and extended shopping experience which sets new standards for retailing. If a customer has signed up for online shopping then they will receive offers on a regular basis. For example, they may receive free delivery codes to encourage people to shop with them.

In the three months to November 2009, Tesco's market share rose to 30.7% from 30.6% in the same period in 2008 (Finch 2009). Tesco's sales increased in 2009 with a growth rate of 4.7% compared with a market growth of 4.4% (Finch 2009), which indicates that they acquired a great deal of new customers in 2009. Tesco took on board the fact that families were experiencing financial difficulties due to the current economic climate and targeted those areas which dually increased their market share.

Internal Business Process Perspective

In the internal business process perspective, managers identify the important internal processes that the business must succeed in, in order to implement its strategy (Drury 2004). Metrics based on this perspective let managers measure how successful their organisation is doing and whether its goods and services conform to customer needs (Papenhausen 2006). The internal business process measures should focus on the internal processes, which the organisation will need to achieve its customer and financial objectives (Drury 2004). According to Chavan (2009) a "well-oiled machinery" of internal processes is important in any business, and may not always correlate with external perceptions. Internal business processes are identified by three principal processes which are: innovation processes, operation processes and post-service processes (Drury 2004).

Innovation

The product development manager for Tesco is Seaneed O' Neill (bbc news 2002). Seaneed O'Neil is constantly on the lookout for the latest trends regarding the food market so that it can be developed into a new line in Tesco (bbc news 2002). The latest range that Tesco have delved into is the healthy eating market with its finest range. The design and development of these new products can be timely for the organisation as they have to source suppliers and conduct market research (bbc news 2002). The company then has to measure the payback period of the new product and the sales from the new product (Drury 2004).

Operations Process

Traditionally, the operations process has been the major focus of an organisation's performance measurement system (Drury 2004). Tesco needs to manage its transport better as it has 2,000 trucks (Tesco 2009). They identified issues with their drivers and fleets so they decided to start up a 'Managing Transport Better' project to reduce the cost of transport and to have one standard way across their depots (Tesco 2009). According to Tesco (2009), it saved millions of pounds on this project as it improved the efficiency of its systems by trailing the improvements over three months. Tesco then rolled out the new routines across the depots.

Supplier Processes

"However, the fact that a handful of supermarkets control access to consumers means that they are increasingly in a position to exercise buyer power" (Fearne, Duffy and Hornibrook 2005). According to Irish Times journalist Cullen (2010), Tesco has been demanding millions from Irish suppliers in return for the sustained stocking of their items on Irish shelves. Tesco are putting great pressure on their suppliers, which may in turn push Irish suppliers out of the market (Cullen 2010). Cullen (2010) also found that if suppliers did not pay the sum demanded by Tesco then the space allocated to the supplier's products in store would be significantly reduced. According to Cullen (2010), suppliers have suggested the demands by Tesco may have something to do with improving its figures as Tesco's financial year runs to the end of february which has made suppliers believe the demands by Tesco are a move to improve its figures before the year end. It has been a difficult trading year for Tesco as the retail market is down by 7 percent and profits have tight due to the price war (Cullen 2009).

Learning and Growth Perspective

The learning and growth perspective includes employee training and employees learning from within the organization so that the company will continue to please customers in the future (Drury 2004). According to the Balanced Scorecard Institute (2010), learning and growth metrics can be put into place to guide mangers in centering training funds where they can help the most in the organisation. Kettunen (2005) presented in his research paper that the learning and growth perspective included three principles: "the capability for R&D", "environmental scanning and customer knowledge" and "quality and assessment capabilities, and in-house training".

Tesco employs staff from a multitude of different backgrounds and all employees are given the opportunity to develop in tandem with the company. The majority of companies fail to measure the outcomes of learning and growth but Tesco are different as it regularly measures the performance of its staff. Employees are able to apply for training through yearly appraisals to improve their knowledge and skills (Thetimes100 2010). However, it has been noted that training is not one of Tesco's primary focuses.

According to Tesco (2009), training is tailor to its employees. They treat their employees like they treat their customers as persons with their own specific requirements (Tesco 2009). Tesco (2009) have a off-the-job training and development program known as 'Options'. Options is an accommodating program that is tailored to the employees needs, which can last between 6 months to 2 years (Tesco 2009). This program aims to develop a combination of broad skills, leadership and operating skills through off the job experiences and a clear procedure that is designed to provide clear feedback and schooling (Tesco 2009).

Tesco also offer their staff on-the-job training (Thetimes100). On-the-job training techniques would include shadowing, coaching, mentoring and job rotation (Thetimes100). The method of shadowing is used for many reasons but it is mainly used for the training of cashier staff and aisle staff. The trainee employee is shadowed by a more experienced employee until they are competent in their new role. On-the-job training is directly related to the employees work and is usually favoured over off-the-job training as it is cheaper for Tesco to implement (Thetimes100). The researchers Van Der Klink and Streumer (2002) found that from a study of on-the-job training, the results of the study were only partially successful in realising training goals. On-the-job training may not be a great success as more experienced employees often see it as a way to reduce their work load.

Hayman and Lorman (2004) found that most graduates entered companies directly from further education and had a solid academic background. They found that training made sure graduates were prepared with a working knowledge to complete their job role (Hayman and Lorman 2004). Tesco offer graduate programmes where the employees training depends on its graduate programme (Tesco 2009). Tesco (2009) also provide training in specialised areas for example in Finance they offer to pay for the employees CIMA qualification.

Conclusion

"Although there are some criticisms concerning the balanced scorecard approach, many of these seem to represent problems of practical application rather than fundamental flaws" (Atkinson 2006).

The 'Steering Wheel' strategy has assisted Tesco in accomplishing big goals by breaking them down into smaller, more achievable goals. While Tesco have achieved their targets for 2009, the manner in which they have done so can be considered to be slightly furtive, including demanding money from suppliers for shelf space in their shops.

Even though Tesco's employee training programmes are held in high regard, training is not their primary concern. Instead Tesco adopt a more customer-oriented focus, with the intention of getting customers into their store in any conceivable way. The fact that Tesco have delved into new markets, e.g. healthy eating, in order to satisfy their customers needs, exemplifies the above statement. In general, the balanced scorecard has proven to be an effective and successful tool, in the achievement of Tesco's respective goals.

CASE STUDY

CELEBRITIES WORTH –WATCHING

M/s Titan Industries Limited is engaged in manufacturing of watches/accessories, jewelry, precision engineering and Eyewear. The Company has four divisions: watches/accessories, jewellery, precision engineering and eyewear. As of March 31, 2012, the Company had 332 World of Titan stores. As of March 31, 2012, the Company had over three business units in Bangalore, India, a manufacturing unit at Hosur and three assembly plants located in the north of India. The brands under the watches/accessories division include: Titan, Sonata, Fastrack, Xylys and others.

India is a great country for celebrities. They seem to come in all sizes, hues, shapes, interests and prices! Advertisers and advertising agencies seem to love them as well and often end up using them indiscriminately. In the Nineties, Sachin was King and a few years ago it was Amitabh. It is decisions like these that throw up the very question of the efficacy of using celebrities as a strategy into sharp focus.

All too often signing on celebrities seems to be done too mechanically and smacks of lazy thinking. One company seems to have got its celebrity and brand strategies right and that is a company that several people in the business including us admire. That is Titan Industries Ltd., a company that has changed the way watches have been made, looked at and sold in this country. The same company uses Amari Khan for Titan, Rani Mukherjee for Titan Raga, Mahendra singh Dhoni for Sonata and John Abraham for Fastrack eye gear. And the results are there for consumers to see as advertising that cuts clean through the clutter, and for the investors to see in terms of the brand's dominant market share and improved top line and bottom lines.

Questions:

1. What is Titan doing right?
2. What are the learning's for other companies which are already using celebrities or are contemplating their usage?

REVIEW QUESTIONS

Conceptual Type

1. What is vision?
2. What do you mean by strategic vision?
3. What is mission statement?
4. Differentiate between a mission statement and vision statement. ***(VTU, MBA, Dec-2011)***
5. What is objectives?
6. What is balanced scorecard?
7. What is strategic intent?
8. What do you mean by innovation?

Analytical Type

1. Explain the benefits of vision.
2. Discuss the characteristics of an effective vision statement. ***(VTU, MBA, Dec-2011)***
3. Explain the components of a company's mission statement. ***(VTU, MBA, Dec-2011)***
4. Explain the seven criteria used in preparing long term objectives. ***(VTU, MBA, Dec-2011)***
5. Explain the features of objectives.
6. Discuss the various classification of objectives.
7. Explain the balanced score card approach. ***(VTU, MBA, Dec-2010)***
8. What is company Mission? How do you formulate a mission? ***(VTU, MBA, July-2006)***

Descreptive Type

1. "Balance score card is an approach to measure the company's performance". ***(VTU, MBA, Dec-2011)***
2. Explain vision and mission of an organization with an example. ***(VTU, MBA, June-2010)***

*****

Module-3

Analyzing a Company's External Environment

Unit

Syllabus

Analyzing a Company's External Environment – The Strategically relevant components of a Company's External Environment – Industry Analysis – Industry Analysis – Porter's dominant economic features – Competitive Environment Analysis – Porter's Five Forces model – Industry diving forces – Key Success Factors – concept and implementation.

INTRODUCTION

Environment analysis is an important aspect in strategic management. It gives accurate information about the current trends of the local and the global level market. Companies find opportunities for expanding locally as also think of extending their business at the global. It enables to determine the strengths and weaknesses of the firm as also that of the competitors when formulating strategy. A firm must be aware of the business environment (both internal and external) only then it is possible to formulate effective business strategy. Today, without business strategy no firm can move its product or service in the market.

Environmental analysis, also known as environmental scanning or appraisal, is the process through which an organization monitors various environmental factors and determines the opportunities and threats that are provided by these factors. Thus, these two aspects involved in environmental analysis:

1. Monitoring the environment, i.e. environmental search and
2. Identifying opportunities and threats based on environmental monitoring.

Environmental analysis must be a continuous process rather than being an intermittent scanning system. In this process, there is continuous scanning of the environment to pick up the new signals or triggers in the overall pattern of developing trends.

INTERNAL AND EXTERNAL ENVIRONMENT

Internal and External business environments indicate how forces act on the company and what, as a Manager you need to establish the effect of each environment force. As the name suggests, "internal" business environment refers to internal factors and resources that affect the running of the business. This primarily includes the workforce, our company standing orders, rules & regulations, etc. The employees play a vital role in affecting the company's performance. If you have well trained, motivated employees, you are more likely to get good output from them. However, if you have employees with low morale or who don't work hard or dig in their heels when a new plan is proposed, it will definitely affect company's production levels.

Another factor is the company's assets and facilities available, such as plant and machinery, motor vehicles, and such other equipment used in production. If have adequate assets in good condition, production will be better than if you don't. Yet another component of the internal business environment is available finances. This includes working capital, if just starting out, it is all the more important. In an established business, this includes all the money available to facilitate the day-to-day running of the business.

The external business environments include factors such as political, technological, economical, legal, demographic and socio-cultural issues etc. These factors may not have an immediate direct effect on your business, but they will play a role in shaping your business with passage of time. For instance, if your country faces economic hardships, your business may not do so well. The market's spending habits will change accordingly, raw materials costs will also change, and it may end up reducing production and letting go of some of the employees. Retrenchment is one of the biggest negative impacts of economic problems.

ENVIRONMENT

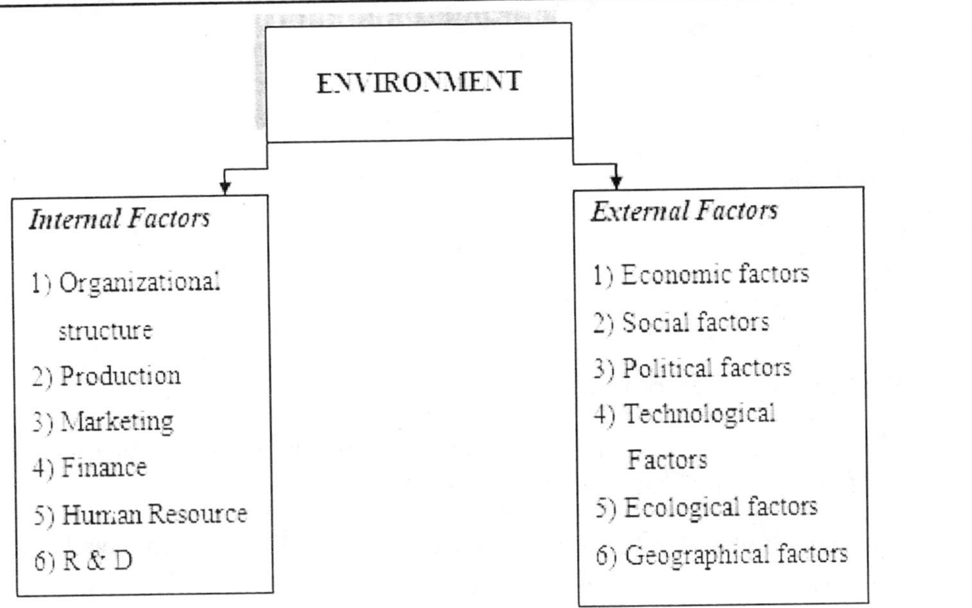

EXTERNAL ENVIRONMENT

1. Economic Environment

Economic environment is the most important environmental factor which the business organizations first take into account. In fact, a business organisation is an economic unit of operation. Since the measurement of organizational performance is mostly in the form of financial terms, often managers concentrate more on economic factors. Economic environment covers nature of economic system, general economic conditions, various economic policies, and various production factors which give shape and form to the development of economic activities. From analytical point of view various economic factors can be divided into two broad categories: general economic conditions and market factor. The discussion of these factors will bring out the nature of total economic environment. The following are example of economic environment:

- Industrial Policy
- Industrial Licensing
- Foreign Investment
- Foreign Technology Agreements
- Public Sector
- Monopolies Of Restrictive Trade Practices.
- Foreign Trade
- Privatization
- Small Scale Industries
- Financial Sector
- Infrastructure
- Income Level
- Five-Year Plans
- Agricultural Sector
- Consumers

2. Political-Legal Environment

Politico-legalforces allocate power and provide laws and regulation that may constrain or protect the business. The factors to be considered are:

- The political system and its features like nature of the political system, ideological forces of the political parties and sentries of power.
- The political structure, its goals and stability.
- Political process like party systems, elections, funding of elections and legislation in economic and industrial matters and regulations.
- Political philosophy, role of government in business and its policy approach towards economic and business development. With the developments on the political front affecting the economy all the time, the economic environment often becomes a byproduct of the political environment. Legislations regulating the business are the byproduct of the political configuration. In addition to government and legislative measures, media, social and religious organizations and lobbies of various kinds are also a part of the political environment. They collectively exercise a huge influence on the conduct of business in a country.

The constitutional framework, directive principles, fundamental rights and divisions of legislative power between central and state government.

- Policies related to licensing, monopolies, foreign investments and financing to industries
- Policies related to distribution and pricing and their control
- Policies related to imports and exports

Other policies related to PSU, SSI, sick industries, and development of backward areas and control of environmental pollution.

Businesses have to operate within the framework of the prevailing legal environment. They have to understand the general legal aspects and those particular to the industry the company is in. Businesses have to understand the implication of such legislations and adapt themselves accordingly.

3. Technological Environment

Technological environment is playing important role in the business as it affects the type of conversion process that businesses adopt for its purpose. The technological environment refers to the sum total of knowledge providing ways to do things. It may include inventions and techniques, which affect the ways of doing things, that is designing, producing, and distributing products. A given technology affects an organisation in the way it is organised and faces competition. From strategic management point of view, technology has following implications:

1. Technology is a major source of productivity increase. Though human beings are primarily responsible for handling technology, their efficiency is determined by the type of technology being used.
2. Various jobs in an organisation being performed by individuals are determined by the technology being used. If there is a change in technology, the jobs are changed because technology determines the level of skills required.
3. Technology influences the social situation, that is, the size of groups, membership of group, patterns of interpersonal interactions, opportunity to control activities are influenced in a variety of ways by technology.
4. As organizations become more secure by developing efficiency through the adoption of efficient technology. However, as 'the technology becomes more complex, it becomes relatively more difficult for new organizations to enter the field.

The organization will have some sort of monopolistic advantages. Petrov has analyzed the strategic implication of technological environment as follows:

1. It can change relative competitive cost position within a business;
2. It can create new markets and new business segments; and
3. It can collapse or merge previously independent businesses by reducing or eliminating their segment cost barriers. The following are example of Technological factors:

Influence of technology on business:

- Rise and decline of products
- Increase in quality and use of products
- Demand for more capital
- Rise in productivity
- More emphasis on R&D
- Demand for more skilled employees
- Organization structure becomes a techno- structure.
- Increase in professionalism
- Social change
- Regulation and opposition
- Changes in business combinations.

4. Socio Cultural Environment

The socio-cultural environment of business can be defined as follows: Social and cultural environment consists of attitudes, beliefs, desires, expectations; education and customs of the society at a given point of time. Thus, social and cultural environment, in its broad sense, includes many - aspects of society and its various -constituents. From the business organization's point of view, it may include: (i) expectations of the society from the business; (ii) attitudes of society towards business and its management; (iii) views towards achievement of work; (iv) views towards authority structure, responsibility and organizational positions, (v) views towards customs, traditions, and conventions; (vi) class structure and labor mobility; and (vii) level of education. The various elements of the social and cultural environment affect the working of the organizations mainly in three ways: organizational objective setting, organizational processes and the products to be offered by the organization.

5. Ecological Factors

The term ecology refers to the relationships among human beings and other living things and the air, soil, and water that support them. Threats to our life-supporting ecology caused principally by human activities in an industrial society are commonly referred to as pollution. Specific concerns include global warming, loss of habitat and biodiversity, as well as air, water, and land pollution are the issues involved here. Stringent laws are designed to thwart any anti-nature businesses. Not only the laws of the land, even environmentalists and their movement do form part of this factor.

6. Geographic and Competitive Factors

Geographic and competitive factors are also playing an important role in the organizational activities which will affect on overall progress and performance of an organization. Besides the following points too are considered:

1. Efficiency of transport system.
2. Proximity of site to export markets.
3. State of marketing and distribution system.
4. Profit margin on operations.
5. Competitive situation in the industry.

INDUSTRY ANALYSIS

Effective industry analyses are very important due to globalization, international markets and rivalry must be included in the company's analyses; in fact, research shows international variables may have more impact on strategic competitiveness than domestic ones. An industry is a group of companies producing products that are close substitutes for each other. As they compete for market share, the strategies implemented by these companies influence each other and include a broad mix of competitive strategies as each company pursues strategic competitiveness and above average returns. It should be noted that, unlike the general environment, which has an indirect effect on strategic competitiveness and company profitability the effect of the industry environment is direct. Industry, and individual company, profitability and the intensity of competition in an industry are a function of the five competitive forces as presented in Michael Porter's Five Forces Model of Competition indicates that these five forces interact to determine the intensity or strength of competition, which ultimately determines the profitability of the industry.

In order to have a better understanding of the external environment, analyzing the industry in detail is critical. In conducting an industry analysis manager need to analyze seven aspects carefully:

1. General features and basic conditions of the industry

General features/basic conditions of the industry include factors such as the current size of the industry, product categories/sub categories, their relative volumes, the performance of the industry in recent years, etc.

2. Industry environment

Industries can be classified based on their settings/environment. Porter classified industries as fragmented, emerging, matured, declining and global industries.

3. Industry structure

Industry structure essentially means the underlying fundamental economic and technical forces of an industry. Each company will have its own key structural features such as number of players, market size, the relative shares of the player, nature of the competition,differentiation practiced by the various players in the industry, the cost structure of the players etc. These features determine the strength of competitive forces operating in the industry and thereby serve as direct indicators to the attractiveness or the profitability of the industry.

4. Industry attractiveness

The various determinants of industry attractiveness are industry potential, industry growth, industry profitability, future pattern of the industry barriers and forces shaping the competition in the industry.

5. Industry performance

Industry performance entails looking at production, sales, profitability and technological development.

6. Industry practices

Industry practices refer to what a majority of the players do in the industry with respect to essential aspects of the business such as distribution, pricing, promotion, methods of selling, service field support, R&D and legal tactics.

7. Emerging trends and likely future

The emerging trends/likely future pattern of the industry can be discerned by analyzing issues such as the product life cycle, stage of the industry, rate of growth, changes of buyer needs, innovation in product/process, entry and exit of firms and emerging changes in the regulatory environment governing the industry.

PORTER'S DOMINANT ECONOMIC FEATURES

Identification of dominant economic features is very important because the company could understand about competitive environment. It helps the orgnisations to know the different kinds of strategic moves that industry members are likely to employ, some of the dominant economic features are given below:

1. ***Market Size and Growth rate:*** Market size indicates the number of firms in the industry. It is also important to know whether the industry is growing or declining. It depends upon the position of an industry in the business life cycle.

2. ***Number of Rivals:*** The Organizations also aware of small rivals or dominated by a few large firms. Similarly they should also know about the various developments in the industry such as merger and acquisitions etc.

3. ***Scope of competitive rivalry:*** Scope of competitive rivalry is an important factor for the organization to know the level of competition. Industry number must know about the nature of future competition.

4. ***Buyer need and Requirement:*** Industry members must take into consideration the need and taste of female buyers as well as the middlemen. Basically organization has to do a lot of periodic research in order to know the major shifts in buyers needs requirements, and they should affect consumer behavior.

5. ***Degree of Product Differentiation:*** Product differentiation is another important factor in analyzing the overall industry situation. If all the products of industry are not fully differentiated than it will increase competition among the members of the industry. In such case price of the products will be low and the new entrants will find it difficult to complete with the existing firms.

6 ***Technological change:*** If the industry is characterized by repaid pace of technological change then the art of the state technology is imperative for the success of organizations; for example, industry of mobile phones requires repaid changes in the technology in order to meet the changing consumer demands.

7. ***Vertical Integration:*** It is important to know whether the competitors in the industry are partially or fully integrated, similarly the competitive advantages and disadvantage of fully partially and non integrated firms should be taken into consideration. Vertical integration can cause the potential cost of production differences.

8. ***Economies of Scale:*** The organization must also know about the different economics of scale in purchasing, manufacturing, and other activities. They should analyse whether the companies with higher scale operations has any cost advantage or not. Any reduction in the cost of production leads to higher competitiveness which ultimately results higher profits.

9. ***Product Innovation:*** Product innovation can be used as a measure to know the dominate industry future. If the industry is characterized by rapid product innovation and short product life cycle than the research and development is very important for the success of an organization. In such cases, members of the industry must come up with new products to compete effectively

COMPETITIVE ENVIRONMENT ANALYSIS

Competitor analysis represents a necessary adjunct in performing an industry analysis. An industry analysis provides information regarding potential sources of competition (including the possible strategic actions and reactions and effects on profitability for all companies competing in an industry). However, a structured competitor analysis enables a company to focus its attention on those companies with which it will directly compete and is especially important when a company faces a few powerful competitors. Competitor analysis is ultimately interested in developing a profile on how competitors might be expected to react in response to a company's strategic moves. As illustrated in the process involves developing answers to a series of questions regarding the company's and its competitors future objectives, current strategy, assumptions, capabilities, and response

Through the competitive analysis, you can understand the:

1. What are the major competitor's strengths?
2. What are the major competitor's weaknesses?
3. What are the major competitor's objectives and strategies?
4. How will the major competitors most likely respond to current economic, social, cultural, demographic, geographic, political, governmental, technological, and competitive trends affecting our industry?
5. How vulnerable are the major competitors to our alternative company strategies?
6. How vulnerable are our alternative strategies to success. Counter attack by our major competitors?
7. How are our products or services positioned relative to major competitors?

8. To what extent are new companies entering and old companies leaving this industry.
9. What key factors have resulted in our present competitive position in this industry?
10. How have the sales and profit rankings of major competitors in the industry changed over recent years? Why have these rankings changed that way?
11. What is the nature of supplier and distributor relationships in this industry?

COMPETITOR ANALYSIS COMPONENTS

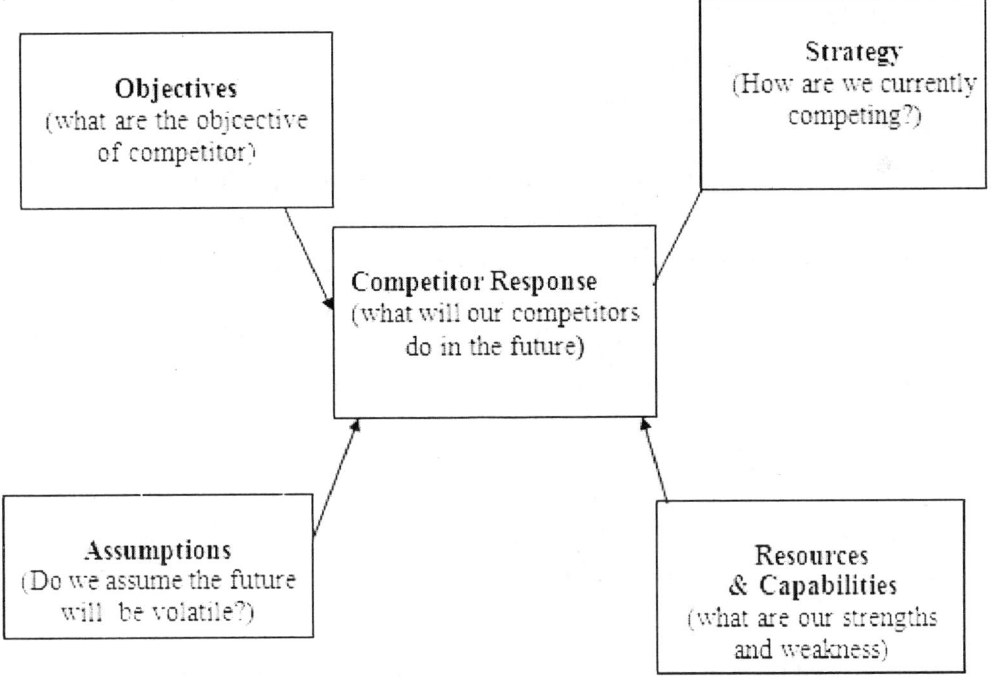

Information about these four issues helps the firm prepare an anticipated response profile for each competitor. The information obtained through competitor analysis often helps a firm, understand, interpret and predict its competitors' actions and initiatives.

a) Competitor's Current Strategy

The two main sources of information about a competitor's strategy is what the competitor says and what it does. What a competitor is saying about its strategy is revealed in:

- Annual shareholder reports
- Interviews with analysts
- Statements by managers
- Press releases

However, this stated strategy often differs from what the competitor actually is doing. What the competitor is doing is evident in where its cash flow is directed, such as in the following tangible actions:

- hiring activity
- R & D projects
- Capital investments
- Promotional campaigns
- Strategic partnerships
- Mergers and acquisitions

b) Competitor's Objectives

Knowledge of a competitor's objectives facilitates a better prediction of the competitor's reaction to different competitive moves. For example, a competitor that is focused on reaching short-term financial goals might not be willing to spend much money responding to a competitive attack. Rather, such a competitor might favor focusing on the products that hold positions that better can be defended. On the other hand, a company that has no short term profitability objectives might be willing to participate in destructive price competition in which neither firm earns a profit.

Competitor objectives may be financial or other types. Some examples include growth rate, market share, and technology leadership. Goals may be associated with each hierarchical level of strategy-corporate, business unit, and functional level.

The competitor's organizational structure provides clues as to which functions of the company are deemed to be the more important. For example, those functions that report directly to the legal or contractual restrictions, and any additional corporate-level goals that may influence the competing business unit. Whether the competitor is meeting its objectives provides an indication of how likely it is to change its strategy.

c) Competitor's Assumptions

The assumptions that a competitor's managers hold about their firm and their industry help to define the moves that they will consider. For example, if in the past the industry introduced a new type of product that failed, the industry executives may assume that there is no market for the product. Such assumptions are not always accurate and if incorrect may present opportunities. For example, new entrants may have the opportunity to introduce a product similar to a previously unsuccessful one without retaliation because incumbant firms may not take their threat seriously. Honda was able to enter the U.S. motorcycle market with a small motorbike because U.S. manufacturers had assumed that there was no market for small bikes based on their past experience.A competitor's assumptions may be based on a number of factors, including any of the following:

Chief Executive officer are likely to be given priority over those that report to a senior vice president.

- Other aspects of the competitor that serve as indicators of its objectives include risk tolerance, management incentives, backgrounds of the executives, composition of the board of directors, beliefs about its competitive position
- Past experience with a product
- Regional factors
- Industry trends

A thorough competitor analysis also would include assumptions that a competitor makes about its own competitors, and whether that assessment is accurate.

d) Competitor's Resources and Capabilities

Knowledge of the competitor's assumptions, objectives, and current strategy is useful in understanding how the competitor might want to respond to a competitive attack. However, its resources and capabilities determine its ability to respond effectively.

A competitor's capabilities can be analyzed according to its strengths and weaknesses in various functional areas, as is done in a SWOT analysis. The competitor's strengths define its capabilities. The analysis can be taken further to evaluate the competitor's ability to increase its capabilities in certain areas. A financial analysis can be performed to reveal its sustainable growth rate.

Finally, since the competitive environment is dynamic, the competitor's ability to react swiftly to change should be evaluated. Some firms have heavy momentum and may continue for many years in the same direction before adapting. Others are able to mobilize and adapt very quickly. Factors that slow down a company include low cash reserves, large investments in fixed assets, and an organizational structure that hinders quick action.

e) Competitor Response Profile

Information from an analysis of the competitor's objectives, assumptions, strategy, and capabilities can be compiled into a response profile of possible moves that might be made by the competitor. This profile includes both potential offensive and defensive moves. The specific moves and their expected strength can be estimated using information gleaned from the analysis.

The result of the competitor analysis should be an improved ability to predict the competitor's behavior and even to influence that behavior to the firm's advantage.

MICHAEL PORTER'S FIVE FORCES MODEL

a) Threat of New Entrants

New entrants in an industry are important because, with new competitors, the intensity of competitive rivalry in an industry generally increases. This is because new competitors may bring substantial resources into the industry and may be interested in capturing a significant market share. If a new competitor brings additional capacity to the industry when product demand is not increasing, prices that can be charged to consumers generally will fall. One result may be a decline in sales revenues and lower returns for many companies in the industry.

The seriousness or extent of the threat of new entrants is affected by two factors: 1) Barriers to entry and 2) Expected reactions from, or the potential for retaliation by, incumbent companies in the industry.

1. Barriers To Entry

Barriers to entering an industry are present when entry is difficult or when it is too costly and places potential entrants at a competitive disadvantage there are seven barriers mainly .

i. ***Economies of Scale:*** Economies of scale indicates relationship between quantity produced and unit cost. As the quantity of a product produced during a given time period increases, the cost of manufacturing each unit declines. Economies of scale can serve as an entry barrier when existing companies in the industry have achieved these scale economies and a potential new entrant is only able to enter the industry on a small scale (and produce at a higher cost per unit).

ii. ***Product Differentiation:*** Customers may perceive that products offered by existing companies in the industry are unique as a result of service offered, effective advertising campaigns, or being first to offer a product or service to the market. If customers perceive a product or service as unique, they generally are loyal to that brand. Thus, new entrants may be required to spend a great deal of money over a long period of time to overcome customer loyalty to existing products.

iii. ***Capital Requirements:*** When you start a business which will require sufficient fund for establishment of infrastructure, working capital, product promotion, R&D, HR etc. the company has to maintainsufficient funds while starting a businesss.

iv. ***Switching Costs:*** Are the one time costs customers will incur when buying from a different supplier. These can include such explicit costs as retraining of employees or retooling of equipment as well as the psychological cost of changing relationships. In cumbent companies in the industry generally try to establish switching costs to offset new entrants that try to win customers with substantially lower prices or an improved (or, to some extent, different) product. For example, switching costs have to be borne by companies for switching from Microsoft's Windows to other operating systems creating entry barriers in the market for operating systems.

v. ***Access to Distribution Channels:*** Existing companies have developed effective channels for distributing products, these same channels may not be available to new companies entering an industry. Thus, access may serve as an effective barrier to entry.

vi. ***Cost Disadvantages Independent of Scale:*** Existing companies in an industry often are able to achieve cost advantages that cannot be costless duplicated by new entrants (other than those related to economies of scale and access to Distribution Channels). These can include proprietary process (or product) technology, more favourable access to or control of raw materials, the best locations, or favorable government subsidies. Potential entrants must find ways to overcome these disadvantages to be able to effectively compete in the industry.

vii. ***Government Policy:*** Governments are able to control entry into an industry through licensing and permit requirements one of the barriers of new entry.

viii ***Branding:*** Making your product or service synonymous with superior and consistent quality, whether or not a 'brand' in the conventional sense is used.

b) Bargaining Power of Buyers

While companies competing in an industry seek to maximize their return on invested capital, buyers are interested in purchasing products at the lowest possible price. To reduce cost or maximize value, customers bargain for higher quality or greater levels of service at the lowest possible price by encouraging competition among companies in the industry. Buyer groups are powerful relative to companies competing in the industry when:

- Buyers are important to sellers because they purchase a large portion of the supplier industry's total sales
- Supplier industry's products represent a significant portion of the buyers' costs
- Buyers are able to switch to another supplier's product at little cost, if any,

- Suppliers' products are undifferentiated and standardized
- Buyers represent a credible threat to integrate backwards into the supplier's industry because of resources or expertise.

c) The Threat of Substitute Products

All companies must recognize that they compete against companies producing substitute products, those products that are capable of satisfying similar customer needs but come from outside the industry and thus have different characteristics. In effect, prices charged for substitute products represent the upper limit on the prices that suppliers can charge for their products. The Threat of Substitute Products is greatest when:

- Buyers or customers face few, if any switching costs;
- Prices of the substitute products are lower;
- Quality and performance capabilities of substitutes are equal to or greater than those of the industry's products.

Companies can offset the attractiveness of substitute products by differentiating their products in ways that are perceived by customers as relevant. Viable strategies might include price, product quality, product features, location, or service level.

d) Bargaining Power of Suppliers

The bargaining power of suppliers depends on supplier's economic bargaining power relative to companies competing in the industry. Supplier's are powerful when company profitability is reduced by suppliers' actions. Suppliers can exert their power by raising prices or by restricting the quantity and/or quality of goods available for sale.

Suppliers are powerful relative to companies competing in the industry when:

- The supplier segment of the industry is dominated by a few large companies and is more concentrated than the industry to which it sells;
- Satisfactory substitute products are not available to buyers;
- Buyers are not a significant customer group for the supplier group;
- Suppliers goods are critical to buyers marketplace success;
- Effectiveness of suppliers' products has created high switching costs for buyers;
- Suppliers represent a credible threat to integrate forward into the buyers industry, especially when suppliers have substantial resources and provide highly differentiated products.

Intensity of Rivalry Among Competitors: The intensity of rivalry in an industry depends upon the extent to which companies in an industry compete with one another to achieve strategic competitiveness and earn above average returns because success is measured relative to other companies in the industry Competition can be based on price, quality, or innovation. Because of the interrelated nature of company's actions, action taken by one company generally will result in retaliation by competitors (also known as competitive actions and reactions).

FACTORS DRIVING INDUSTRY CHANGE

Industry conditions change because of important forces that are driving industry participants (competitor, customer, or suppliers) to alter their actions; the driving forces in an industry are the major underlying causes for the changes and competitive conditions. They have the biggest influence on how the industry landscape will be altered,some originate in the outer ring of the macro - environment and some originate from the inner ring.

Driving forces Analysis:

1. *Identifying:* what the driving forces are?
2. *Assessing:* whether the drivers of change are, on the whole, acting to make the industry more or less attractive
3. Determining what strategy changes are needed to prepare for the impact of the driving force

Identifying an Industry's Driving Forces:

1) ***Emerging new internet capabilities and applications:*** Internet usage is very important in the global business environment which open up all kinds of new business to business and business to consumer market opportunities and threats, sparks competition from new and entirely different breeds of enterprises and mandates fundamental changes in business practices.

2) ***Increasing globalization:*** Competition begins to shift from regional ,national to an international or global focus. Industry members begin seeking out customers in foreign market.

   Production activities begin to migrate to countries where costs are lowest. Global competition really starts when one or more ambitious companies precipitate a race for worldwide market leadership.

Globalization happens:

- Blossoming of customer and demand in more and more countries.
- Action on Govt to reduce the trade barrier.
- Significant difference in labor cost, locate plant e.g. China, India, Singapore, Maxico and Brazil ¼ of those in US, Germany and Japan.

3) ***Changes in an industry long term growth rate:*** Shift in industry growth or down are driving force for industry change, affecting the balance between industry supply and buyer demand, entry and exit of the firms and the character and strength of competition.

4) ***Changes in who buys the product and how they use it:*** Shift in buyer demographics and new ways of using the product can alter the state of competition by forcing adjustments in customer service offerings, opening the way to market the industry's product through a different mix of dealers and retail outlets and prompting producers to broaden or narrow their product-lines, bringing different sales and promotion approaches into play.

5) ***Product innovation:*** Rivals racing to be first to introduce the new product or product enhancement after another.Competition changes are attracting more first time buyers , rejuvenating industry growth, creating wider or narrow product differentiation among rival sellers. Successful new product introductions strengthen the market positions of the innovating companies, usually at the expense of companies that stick with their old products or are slow to follow with their own versions of the new product. Eg. Digital Cameras, Golf Club, Video games, Toys and Prescription Drugs.

6) ***Technological change:*** Advances in the technology can dramatically alter an industry's landscape, making it possible to produce new and better products at lower cost and opening up whole new industry frontiers. Technological developments can also produce a competitively significant change in capital requirements, minimum efficient plant distribution channels and distribution logistics, and learning or experience curve effects.

- Internet based phones are stealing a large number of customers from using traditional telephone to world wide high cost technology, hard wired connections via overheads and underground telephone lines.
- Flat screen technology is killing CRT monitors.
- LCD and Plasma screen tech are driving CRT tech further.
- Digital tech driving huge change in camera and the film industry.
- MP3 technology is transforming how people listen to music.

7) ***Marketing innovation:*** Successful in introducing new ways to market their products, they can

- Spark a burst in buyer interest
- Widen industry demand
- Increase product differentiation
- Lower unit cost-any or all of which can alter the competitive position of rival firms. Eg. Online marketing of Electronics goods. Music artist marketing their own website V/s contract with recording studios.

8) ***Entry or exit of major firms:*** Entry of one or more foreign companies into a geographic market once dominated by domestic firms nearly always shakes-up competitive conditions. Likewise, when an established domestic firm from another industry attempts entry either by acquisition or by launching its own start-up venture, it usually applies its skills and resources in some innovative fashion that pushes competition in new directions.

9) ***Diffusion of technical know how across more companies and more countries:*** As knowledge about how to perform a particular activity or execute a particular manufacturing technology spreads, any technically based competitive advantage held by firms originally possessing this know-how erodes. The diffusion of such knowledge can occur through scientific journals, trade publication, on site plant tours, word-of mouth among suppliers and customers and the hiring away of knowledgeable employees. It can also occur when those possessing technological know-how license others to use it for a royalty fee or team up with a company interested in turning the technology into a new business venture.

10) ***Change in cost and efficiency:*** Widening or shrinking differences in the costs among key competitors tend to dramatically alter the state of competition. Low cost fax and email put mounting pressure on the inefficiency and high cost operation of Postal Dept. Shrinking the cost differences in producing multifeatured mobiles is turning the mobile phone market into commodity business and making more buyers to base Price as their Purchase decision

11) ***Growing buyer preferences*** for differentiated products instead of a commodity product when buyers taste and preferences start to diverge, sellers can win a loyal following by providing different variants and taste then the competitors. Eg. Beer and Automobile

12) ***Reduction in uncertainty and business risk:*** An emerging industry is typically characterized by much uncertainty and risk in terms of time and efforts required to cover up with the investments.

Emerging industries tend to attract only risk-taking entrepreneurial companies. over time how ever, if the business model of industry pioneers proves profitable and market demand for the product appears durable, more conservative firms are usually enticed to enter the market. Often the later entrants are large and financially strong looking to invest into attractive growth industry.

Low biz risk and less industry uncertainty also affect competition in international market. In the early stage the company. enters foreign market with a conservative approach with less risky strategies like exporting, licensing, joint marketing agreement and Joint venture with local companies.

As time goes and the company accumulates experience, it starts moving boldly and independently making acquisitions, constructing their own plants, putting their own sales and market capabilities to build strong competitive position.

13) ***Regulatory influence and government poliy changes:*** Govt regulatory actions can often force significant changes in industry practices and strategic approaches. Deregulation has proved to be a potent pro competitive force in the airline, banking, natural gas, telecommunications, and electric utility industries. Govt efforts to reform Medicare and health Insurance have become potent driving forces in the health care industry.

COMMON KEY SUCCESS FACTORS

The following are the Key success factors of the industy:

- Scale economies
- Distributors
- Breadth of product line and selection
- A talented workforce
- Costs that meet the expectations of customers
- Technological expertise
- Ability to improve production processes
- Quality control
- High labor productivity
- Low costs
- Ability to make products customized to buyer specifications

- Direct sales capabilities
- Well-known and well-respected brand
- Fast, accurate technical assistance
- Design expertise
- Excellent customer service
- Effective advertising
- Patent protection
- Convenient location
- Supply chain management capabilities.

CASE STUDY-1

Tangy spices Ltd

Tangy spices Ltd, the countries' biggest spices marketer has decided to launch a hostile bid for Italy's major spice marketer Chilliano. This is a rare case of an Indian company making an unsolicited hostile bid for a foreign company. The Tangy Spices Ltd. has competencies in Indian spices. The major destination markets for the Tangy spices Ltd. exports have been the Europe and America. The competencies of Chilliano lie in Italian herbs and spices. The Indian company with the takeover wishes to synergies its operations in the world market. It also wants to take advantage of the reach enjoyed by the Italian company in several countries where its products are not being sold presently.

The move of hostile takeover follows Chilliano's rejection to an agreement entered a year back. At that time Chilliano was suffering losses and it offered majority shares at a price of Euro 2.25. A total of 20% shares were transferred at that time. In one year Chilliano was able to turnaround its operations and the company made handsome profits in the last quarter. The promoters who have residual holding of 35% in the company are reluctant to transfer the shares now. They have rejected the agreement with a plea that the earlier offer price was not sufficient.

Tangy spices Ltd has revised its offer to Euro 2.95. By this lucrative offer some of the large shareholders of Chilliano reveal their interest for selling their stakes. On the other hand, promoters maintained their position on this matter. Through the process of buying of shares in the market the Tangy spices Ltd. gradually consolidated its holding in Chilliano to 45%. Being a major shareholder they were ready for a takeover. At the same time, Tangy spices Ltd. was trying hard to improve their position so that they do not leave any space for Chilliano's promoters in future.

Questions:

(1) What strategic alternative is followed by Tangy spices Ltd?

(2) Is the hostile takeover by an Indian company appropriate?

(3) Why the Tangy Spices Ltd. is interested in this takeover?

(4) Why the promoters are reluctant to transfer the shares after the agreement?

CASE -2

Competing within a changing world

A Rolls-Royce case study

No business today operates in a complete vacuum unaffected by market forces. By their very nature business activities are competitive. Within a dynamic, rapidly changing business environment producers are constantly entering and leaving the market. At the same time, changing customer preferences provide signals for businesses to develop new strategies with different products and services. Some businesses will succeed by responding to and meeting market needs, while others may not perform quite so well.

Few markets have changed in recent years as much as civil aerospace. Ten years ago 950 million people travelled by air; five years ago they numbered 1.1 billion and the total is set to climb to 2.5 billion by 2009. The aviation industry provides more than 24 million jobs worldwide, while its contribution to the world economy is estimated to rise to $1,800 billion by 2009. Today, one-third of the world's manufactured exports are transported by air. Twenty years ago the proportion was just one-tenth.

Growth in civil aviation markets has stimulated the competition between the businesses that operate in it such as the airlines. This has a knock-on effect on their suppliers - the aeroplane manufacturers - and in turn on their suppliers - the engine manufacturers.

Rolls-Royce is one of only three engine manufacturers in the world that has a proven capability to design, develop and produce large gas turbine aero-engines. In recent years the company has faced many challenges that have affected its position in the aero-engine industry.

By providing an analysis of the competitive environment affecting Rolls-Royce, this case study illustrates how such information is being used by the company as it works towards its vision of becoming the world's first choice for power solutions for the new century.

The market

Rolls-Royce has not made motor cars since 1971. Rolls-Royce and Bentley Motor Cars Limited is owned by Volkswagen but exclusive rights to use the Rolls-Royce name for motor vehicles will pass to BMW in 2003.

The Rolls-Royce group is a global business with customers in 135 countries and production facilities in 14 countries. It employs around 40,000 people focused upon the present and future requirements of civil aerospace, defence, marine and energy markets. It has 56,000 aero engines in service with 300 airlines, 2,400 corporate and utility operators and supplies more than 100 armed forces.

The engines are used in all sizes of commercial aircraft from business jets to the largest modern airlines made by the two main aeroplane manufacturers Airbus Industrie and Boeing. As one of the most powerful brands in the world, Rolls-Royce symbolises a promise to deliver reliability, integrity and innovation to buyers and users.

The changing external environment

The commercial aero-engine business of Rolls-Royce operates within two distinct market sectors. These are:

- new engine sales to the two manufacturers such as Airbus Industrie and Boeing, as well as airlines;
- engine parts sales to airlines that service and maintain aircraft.

Competitors in this secondary market include specialist maintenance companies. The new engine market is the primary market, which provides access to the secondary market for the sales of engine parts.

During the 1970s, Rolls-Royce controlled less than 10% of the civil aerospace market. The sector was characterised by intense commercial and technical competition from General Electric and Pratt & Whitney of the USA.

Market share could only be increased by major investment in new engines, and developing an improved range of services for customers. This required the company to become focused on service rather than products with services such as information management, inventory management and on- and off-wing maintenance.

Improving service

The aero-engine market is vertical with a limited number of buyers. The customers of Rolls-Royce need to satisfy both their future and present needs. In the past, decisions about aero-engines were largely based upon cost and efficiency.

However, in today's more competitive environment, Rolls-Royce's customers look for a much more complete service. Buying an aero-engine is a long-term decision. In this very competitive environment, a key element is relationship marketing. Through this process, Rolls-Royce and its staff have learned to develop activities and services that build good relationships with its customers.

Customers are increasingly looking for a much more complete service. Although the product will always be important, customers expect higher levels of service such as the shipping of parts, after care service and total customer care. Where total customer care is successfully provided alongside efficient products, occasional customers become regular customers and then regular customers become advocates.

The Rolls-Royce share of the competitive secondary engine parts market has been growing. An emphasis upon total care is at the heart of the growth strategy. Rolls-Royce provides parts and a service for its customers that extends through the operational product life-cycle.

Porter's Five Forces model

One way in which staff within Rolls- Royce have focused their actions for responding to the changing role of the business, has been to use Porter's 'Five Forces' model of industry competition. Five Forces analysis gives an improved understanding of the degree of competition within the business environment. It has helped them to develop a better understanding of the business environment so that business opportunities could be analysed. The model identifies one force within the industry – competitive rivalry - as well as four forces outside the industry:

- potential entrants and the threat of entrants
- power of buyers
- power of suppliers
- threat of substitutes

Competitive rivalry

As described above three dominant players operate in this oligopolistic global industry. The industry is capital intensive and there is a requirement for high investment in advanced technology and research and development. No single manufacturer dominates the industry, so balance fuels the rivalry.

Competition in the primary market for aero-engines is intensified by the link to the secondary market for engine part sales and services. Access to the secondary market is dependent on achieving the original sale of new engines. In recent years the intensity of competition has increased as each manufacturer has tried to improve its volumes and market share. Rivalry has also intensified because gas turbine engines are now essentially a mature product and the potential for technological differential advantage has been reduced.

Power of buyers

The numbers of potential buyers of new aircraft are low. Buyers of aircraft engines are therefore essentially price makers, with the market price for new engines being largely set by the buyer. The power of buyers has further increased in recent years as many airlines have become 'global carriers'.

The decision to purchase a particular aircraft or engine combination is a long-term one. This means that failure to secure an order may prevent an engine manufacturer trading with a particular airline for more than a decade. The selection of one engine type can lead to a domino effect, with other competing buyers following the same selection. Airlines are increasingly seeking lifetime cost of ownership guarantees, and reduced repair costs.

Power of suppliers

The suppliers to the aero-engine manufacturer have limited power. There are many hundreds of different suppliers to the aero-engine industry. They supply all nature of components, from nuts and bolts to state-of-the-art electronic control systems costing hundreds of thousands of pounds. The power of many of the smaller companies, which represent most of the supplier base, has been reduced. This is due to engine manufacturers adopting dual sourcing strategies, using a range of alternative sources of supply. The most powerful suppliers are those involved in the supply of high specification electronic control equipment.

Threat of entry

Although not unknown, entry to the aero-engine industry is extremely difficult. The highly specialised advanced nature of aero-engine design combined with the costs of research and development as well as the confidence of customers represent significant barriers to entry. New engines also need extensive testing before gaining airworthiness approval from the authorities. The market is also sensitive to the reputation of the engine manufacturer, where names such as Rolls-Royce represent a range of proven high-technology products.

Threat of substitutes

There is no substitute for an aero engine and the threat of substitutes for air transport itself is minor. However, it is thought that the development of video conferencing capability will reduce some business travel and the growth of high speed train travel (e.g. Eurostar) will affect some travel decisions. However, both of these developments are taking place at a time when the demand for air travel is increasing.

This analysis shows that the commercial aero-engine business is highly competitive, with the buyer possessing and exerting a very powerful influence upon organisations. The high barriers to entry and the low threat of substitutes indicate that existing competitors will continue to share the business between them. However, a slow down in industry growth and the increasing maturity of products will intensify the degree of rivalry between the engine manufacturers.

Conclusion

In response to changes within its business environment, Rolls-Royce has developed its orientation from that of engineering to become more business- and service-focused. The organisation has had to become much more proactive, dealing with new ideas to create more services and customer focus. In the past, change was rare and slow, the company tended to follow the market trend. The structure of the organisation has been realigned to meet the needs of the new way of operating.

Organisational structures define important relationships within the business and create a mechanism for meeting business objectives. At the same time, it has been important to create a new business culture within Rolls-Royce. A culture exists within the minds and hearts of the people of an organisation and contributes to the way they make decisions and develop business strategies. As an organisation changes from a product-focused organisation towards becoming a service-orientated culture, this requires more involvement of its people, with greater empowerment and rapid decision-taking.

The corporate identity is the sum of the culture and its expression in behaviour and physical terms. Rolls-Royce has defined the identity that it needs to encourage, building on its past reputation and achievements for continuing success. As these changes take place, the organisation is also realigning its financial reporting framework and corporate governance. This will change how the whole business shapes its purposes and priorities.

REVIEW QUESTIONS

Conceptual Type

1. What do you mean by environment?
2. What is external environment?
3. What is economic environment?
4. What do you mean by political environment?
5. What is legal environment?
6. What is technological environment?
7. What is socio cultural environment?

Analytical Type

1. Discuss how remote environmental factors influence running of a business.

   (VTU, MBA, Dec-2012)
2. Discuss the economic and political environment.
3. What are the technological, geographic and competitive factors of environment?

Descriptive Type

1. Disucss the various factors of external environment.
2. Explain Porters five force model. ***(VTU, MBA, Dec-2012)***
3. Disucss the complexities of multinational business environment. ***(VTU, MBA, Dec-2012)***
4. Explain the Porter five forces model. How can it be assessed whether the collective strength of the five competitive forces promotes profitability. ***(VTU, MBA, Dec-2012)***
5. Explain Michael E Porter's five forces model and its implication on the soft drinks industry.
6. Explain the impact of environmental factors on the performance of the company.

   (VTU, MBA, Dec-2012)

*****

Module-4

Analyzing a Company's Resources & Competitive Position

Unit

Syllabus

Analyzing a company's resources and competitive position – Analysis of a Company's present strategies – SWOT analysis – Value Chain Analysis – Benchmarking.

ANALYSING A COMPANY'S RESOURCES AND COMPETITIVE POSITION

We described how to use the tools of industry and competitive analysis to assess a company's external environment and lay the groundwork for matching a company's strategy to its external situation. In this chapter we discuss the techniques of evaluating a company's internal situation, including its collection of valuable resources and capabilities, its relative cost position, and its competitive strength versus its rivals. The analytical spotlight will be trained on five questions:

1. How well is the company's strategy working?
2. What are the company's competitively important resources and capabilities?
3. Is the company competitively stronger or weaker than key rivals?
4. Are the company's prices and costs competitive?
5. What strategic issues and problems merit front-burner managerial attention?

The answers to these five questions complete management's understanding of " Where are we now" and position the company for a good strategic situation fit required of the "Three Tests of a Winning Strategy".

1. How Well Is the Company's present Strategy Working?

The two best indicators of how well a company's strategy is working are:

(1) Whether the company is achieving its stated financial and strategic objectives and

(2) Whether the company is an above-average industry performer. Persistent shortfalls in meeting company performance targets and weak performance relative to rivals are reliable warning signs that the company suffers from poor strategy making, less-than-competent strategy execution, or both. Other indicators of how well a company's strategy is working include:

- Trends in the company's sales and earnings growth.
- Trends in the company's stock price.
- The company's overall financial strength.
- The company's customer retention rate.
- The rate at which new customers are acquired.
- Changes in the company's image and reputation with customers.

- Evidence of improvement in internal processes such as defect rate, order fulfillment, delivery times, days of inventory, and employee productivity. The stronger a company's current overall performance, the less likely the need for radical changes in strategy. The weaker a company's financial performance and market standing, the more its current strategy must be questioned.

The first thing to pin down is the company's competitive approach. Is the company striving to be a low-cost leader or stressing ways to differentiate its product offering from rivals? It is concentrating its efforts on serving a broad spectrum of customers or a narrow market niche? Another strategy- defining consideration is the firm's competitive scope within the industry – what its geographic market coverage is and whether it operates in just a single stage of the industry's production/ distribution chain or is vertically integrated across several stages.

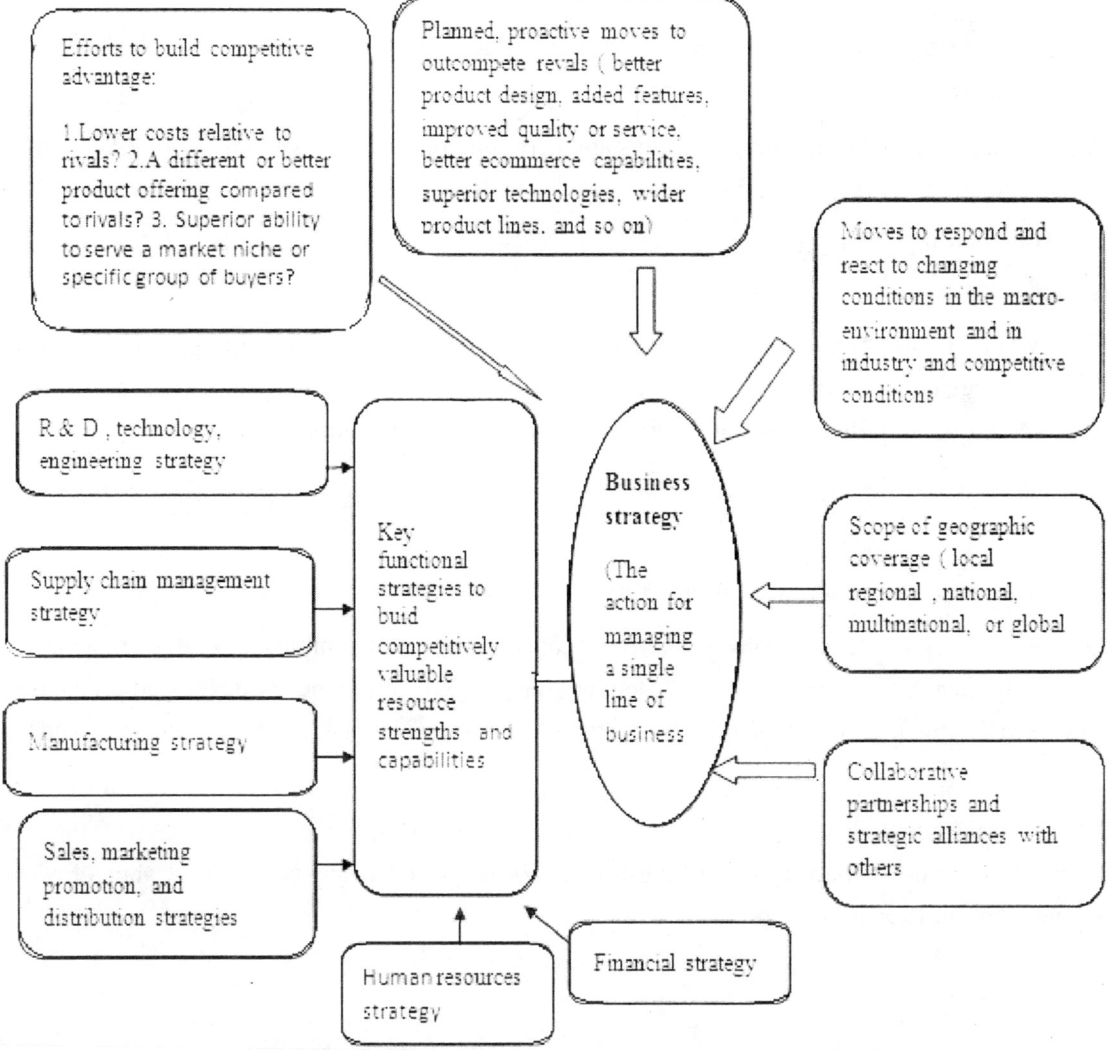

Fig: *Components of a Single-Business Company's Strategy*

Another good indication of the company's functional strategies is whether the company has made moves recently to improve its competitive position and performance – for instance, by cutting prices, improving design, stepping up advertising, entering a new geographic market or merging with a competitor, The company's functional strategies in R&D, production, marketing , finance, human resources, information technology, and so on further characterize the company strategy.

The indicators of how well a company's strategy is working include:

1. Whether the firm's sales are growing faster, going down , or about the same pace as the market as a whole, thus resulting in a rising, eroding, or a stable market share.
2. Whether the company is acquiring new customers at an attractive rate as well as retaining existing customers.
3. Whether the firm's profit margins are increasing or decreasing and show good margins compared to its rival'S firms margins.
4. Trends in the firms net profit margins are increasing or decreasing and how well its margins compare to rival firm's margins
5. Whether the company's overall financial strength and credit rating are improving or on the decline.
6. Whether the company can demonstrate continuous improvement in such internal performance measures as days of inventory, employee productivity, unit cost, defect rate, scrap rate, misfiled orders, delivery times, warranty costs and so on.
7. How shareholders view the company based on trends in the company's stock price and shareholder value
8. The firms image and reputation with its customers
9. How well is the company stacks up against rivals on technology, product innovation, customer service, product quality, delivery time , price, getting newly developed products to market quickly and other relevant factors on which buyers base their choice of brands .

The stronger a company's current overall performance, the less likely the need for radical changes in strategy. The weaker a company's financial performance and market standing, the more its current strategy must be questioned. Weak performance is almost a sign of weak strategy, weak execution or both.

2. The Company's Competitively Important Resources and Capabilities

A company's business model and strategy must be well-matched to its collection of resources and capabilities. An attempt by management to create and deliver customer value in a manner that depends on resources or capabilities that are deficient and cannot be readily acquired is unwise and positions the company for failure. A company's competitive approach requires a tight fit with a company's internal situation and is strengthened when it exploits resources that are competitively valuable, rare, hard to copy, and not easily trumped by rivals' equivalent substitute resources. In fact, many companies pursue research-based strategies that attempt to exploit company resources in a manner that offers value to customers in ways rivals are unable to match.

Identifying Competitively Important Resources and Capabilities:

Common types of valuable resources and competitive capabilities that management should consider when crafting strategy includes:

- A skill, specialized expertise, or competitively important capability - examples include skills in low-cost operations, proven capabilities in creating and introducing innovative products, cutting-edge supply chain management capabilities, expertise in getting new products to market quickly, and expertise in providing consistently good customer service.
- Valuable physical assets-such as state of the art plants and equipment, attractive real estate locations, or ownership of valuable natural resource deposits.
- Valuable human assets and intellectual capital - an experienced and capable workforce, talented employees in key areas, collective learning embedded in the organization, or proven managerial know-how.
- Valuable organizational assets - proven quality control systems, proprietary technology, key patents, and a strong network of distributors or retail dealers.
- Valuable intangible assets - a powerful or well-known brand name or strong buyer loyalty.
- Competitively valuable alliances or cooperative ventures - alliances or joint ventures that provide access to valuable technologies, specialized know-how, or geographic markets.

3. What Is the Company's Competitive Strength Relatively to it's Key Rivals?

An additional component of evaluating a company's situation is developing a comprehensive assessment of the company's overall competitive strength. Making this determination requires answers to two questions:

1. How does the company rank itself relatively to it's competitors on each of the important factors that determine market success?
2. All things considered, does the company have a net competitive advantage or disadvantage versus major competitors?

SWOT ANALYSIS

SWOT analysis is a strategic planning tool which is useful to understand the organizational strengths, weaknesses , opportunities and threat and is based on the assumption that if managers carefully review internal strengths and weaknesses and external threat and opportunities, a useful strategy for ensuring organizational success can be formulated. It is a simple technique for getting a quick overview of a strategic situation so that such strategies can be formulated as to produce a good Product /Services between the company's internal competencies (strength and weaknesses) and environment (opportunities and threats).

Strengths and Weaknesses

A "strength" is a positive sign that gives a company's capability. It is an important resource which enhances a company, competitive position. Some of the internal strengths of an organization are:

- Distinctive competence in key areas
- Manufacturing/Service efficiency
- Skilled workforce, Adequate financial resources and Superior Image and Reputation
- Economies of scale
- Superior technological skills
- Insulation from strong competitive pressures
- Product or service differentiation
- Proprietary technology.

A "weakness" is a limitation, which puts the company at difficulty. Weaknesses adds to the competitive pressures of the company . These are competitive liabilities and strategic managers must evaluate their impact on the organization's strategic position when formulating strategic policies and plans. Weaknesses require a close scrutiny because some of them can prove to be fatal. Some of the weaknesses to be reviewed are:

- No clear strategic direction
- Outdated facilities
- Lack of innovation is Complacency
- Poor research and developmental programs
- Lack of management vision, depth and skills
- Inability to raise capital
- Weaker distribution network
- Obsolete technology
- Low employee morale
- Poor track record in implementing strategy
- Too narrow a product line
- Poor market image
- Higher overall unit costs relative to competition.

Opportunities and Threats

An "opportunity" is considered as a favorable circumstance to the organization, which can be utilized for the growth of the company. It is offered by outside environment and the management can decide as to how to make the best use of it. Such an opportunity may be the result of a positive change in any one or more of the elements that constitute the external environment. It may also be created by a proactive approach by the management in molding the environment to its own benefit. Some of the opportunities are:

- Strong economy
- Possible new markets
- Emerging new technologies
- Complacency among competing organizations
- Vertical or horizontal integration
- Expansion of product line to meet broader range of customer needs
- Falling trade barriers in attractive foreign markets

A "threat" is a characteristic of the external environment, which is hostile to the organisation. Management should anticipate such possible threats and prepare its strategies in such a manner that any such threat is neutralized. Some of the elements that can pose a threat are:

- Entry of lower cost foreign competitors cheaper technology adopted by rivals
- Rising sales of substitute products
- Shortages of resources
- Changing buyer needs and preferences
- Recession in economy
- Adverse shifts in trade policies of foreign governments
- Adverse demographic changes

SWOT analysis involves evaluating a company's internal environment in terms of strengths and weaknesses and the external environment in terms of opportunities and threats and formulating strategies that take advantage of all these factors. Such analysis is an essential component of thinking strategically about a company's situation.

Are the Company's Costs and Prices Competitive?

Company managers are often stunned when a competitor cuts its prices to "unbelievably low" levels or when a new market entrant comes on strong with a very low price. The competitor may not, however, be buying its way into the market with super-low prices that are below its costs-it may simply have substantially lower costs. One of the most telling signs of whether a company's business position is strong or precarious is whether its prices and costs are competitive with industry rivals. Price and cost comparisons are especially critical in industries where price competition is typically the ruling market force. But even in industries where products are differentiated, rival companies have to keep their costs in line with rivals offering a similar mix of differentiating features. Two analytical tools are particularly useful in determining whether a company's prices and costs are competitive: value chain analysis and benchmarking

VALUE CHAIN ANALYSIS

Value chain analysis is an analytical tool which brings in cost improvement and improve value creation. The companies can use to identify and evaluate the ways in which their resources and capabilities can add value is value chain analysis. The value chain is useful because it enables companies to understand which part of their operations or activities create value by segmenting the value chain into primary and secondary activities. The company can be separated into primary and secondary activities. Primary activities, shown vertically, represent traditional line activities such as inbound logistics, operations, outbound logistics, marketing and sales, and service. Support activities, shown horizontally, are represented by a company's staff activity and include its financial infrastructure, human resource management practices, technological development, and procurement activities.

The first step in value chain analysis is to carefully examine each of the company's primary activities to determine the potential for creating or adding value.

Primary Activities

Inbound Logistics: Examine all activities related to the receipt, control, warehousing, inventory, and distribution of raw materials or component parts into the production process.

Operations: Activities necessary to convert the inputs (raw materials or components) available as a result of inbound logistics into finished products. Examples, include machining, assembly, equipment maintenance, and packaging.

Outbound Logistics: The company's activities involved with the collection, storage, and physical distribution of products to customers. Examples include warehousing or storage of finished products, material handling, and order processing.

Marketing and Sales: Several marketing and sales activities must be completed to induce both customers to purchase products and ensure that products are available. Activities include Developing, Advertising and Promotion campaigns,selecting and developing distribution channels and selecting, training, developing, and supporting a sales force.

Service: These are the activities that a company offers to enhance or maintain a product's value, including installation, product use training, adjustment, repair, and warranty services.

Support activities

Procurement: Procurement activities that are completed to purchase the inputs needed to produce a company's products, including items consumed or used in the manufacturing process (such as raw materials or component parts), supplies, and fixed assets (machinery, equipment and facilities).

Technological Development: Technological development that improves quality of product and process. This includes basic research, process and equipment design, product design, and servicing procedures.

Human Resource Management: These is dealing with HR that are recruiting, hiring, training, developing, and compensating (including performance assessment and reward systems) of a company's employees.

Company Infrastructure: The firm infrastructure includes general management practices, planning, finance, accounting, legal, and government relations that are required to support the work of the entire value chain. By performing its infrastructure related activities, a company identifies external opportunities and threats, and internal strengths and weaknesses related to company resources and capabilities, and supports or nurtures its core competencies. Using the value chain framework enables managers to study the company's resources and capabilities in relationship to the primary and support activities performed to design, manufacture, and distribute products, and to assess them relative to competitors' capabilities.

PEST ANALYSIS

PEST analysis is a scan of the external macro-environment in which an organisation exists. It is a useful tool for understanding the political, economic, socio-cultural and technological environment that an organisation operates in. It can be used for evaluating market growth or decline, and as such the position, potential and direction for a business.

Political factors: These include government regulations such as employment laws, environmental regulations and tax policy. Other political factors are trade restrictions and political stability.

Economic factors: These affect the cost of capital and purchasing power of an organisation. Economic factors include economic growth, interest rates, inflation and currency exchange rates.

Social factors: These impact on the consumer's need and the potential market size for an organization's goods and services. Social factors include population growth, age demographics and attitudes towards health.

Technological factors: These influence barriers to entry, make or buy decisions and investment in innovation, such as automation, investment incentives and the rate of technological change. PEST factors can be classified as opportunities or threats in a SWOT analysis. It is often useful to complete a PEST analysis before completing a SWOT analysis.

STRENGTHS

1. *Hardware integration with many open source OS and software:* Samsung is focused on producing devices which can be integrated with most of the software and OS. This gives Samsung products an edge over Apple's (its arch rival) devices, especially as Android and other OS are gaining market share when iOS and OS X are losing it.

2. *Excellence in engineering and producing hardware parts and consumer electronics:* Samsung is the number 1 by market share in televisions and mobile phones sales and some of the hardware parts (processors, memory chips, etc.). This was largely achieved due to excellence in engineering and both efficient and effective production.

3. *Innovation and design:* In 2011, Samsung ranked second on the list of US top patent assignees. More patents strengthen Samsung position among its competitors. The firm also won many awards for the design of its products, proving the superior advantage over the competitors.

4. *Focus on environment:* Samsung focuses on producing environment friendly products that are free from PVC and BFRs (currently only MP3 and mobile phones). It also develops various recycling programs that are awarded for their success. Thus, Samsung's focus on environment gives it an edge over its competitors in the eyes of its customers.

5. *Low production costs:* The company has set up its production facilities in low cost countries. This allows producing goods with low production cost and benefit Samsung as it can offer lower price and earn higher margins.

6. *Largest share in mobile phones and 2 nd place in Smartphone sales in the world:* Samsung Electronics has achieved a large market share in many products they sell, especially in mobile phones, Smartphones, semiconductors and television sets. Large market share has its advantage, bargaining power, that Samsung can use to further reduce costs and demand for better contract conditions.

7. *Ability to market the brand:* Samsung is named as the top rising brand by Interbrand and is the 9th most valuable brand with value nearly $33 billion. It has raised by 40% from 2011 to 2012. This was mainly achieved due to a company's ability to market the brand in sporting events and social contributions.

WEAKNESSES

1. *Patent infringement:* Samsung is infringing Apple's and some other firms' patents, thus, damaging its reputation and having to pay a huge amount of money in damages.

2. *Too low profit margin:* Samsung Electronics is the largest technology business in the world in terms of revenues but it has a low gross profit and net profit margins. Although its smartphone business is quite profitable, Samsung's profit margin is low due to its semiconductors sales and aggressive price cuts.

3. *Main competitors are also largest buyers:* Apple, Sony, Dell, HP are the main buyers of Samsung Electronics products as well as the firm's main competitors. Such situation would

be favorable to Samsung (if competitors could not find complementary products and would form a relatively low share Samsung's revenues) because it could use its bargaining power over competitors. Due to reverse conditions (competitors can find complements and they form a relatively high share of firm's revenues) Samsung cannot use its bargaining power over competitors as it can easily lose its customers and sales.

4. *It lacks it's own OS and software:* Software and OS production has a high profit margin, can increase integration of company's products and brand loyalty. Without strong software and OS Samsung is at disadvantage over its competitors.

5. *Focus on too many products:* Samsung Electronics serves 4 different industries with many different products in them. Samsung is at disadvantage over its competitors because it loses a focus when competing in too many industries and too many products.

OPPORTUNITIES

1. Growing India's smartphone market. India's smartphone market is one of the least penetrated among Asia/Pacific countries. Samsung has a strong presence in India's market and could use this opportunity to expand its sales.

2. Growing mobile advertising industry. The company could develop advertising platform for its mobile devices and significantly benefit from this lucrative market.

3. Growing demand for quality application processors. Samsung is one of the key manufacturers of application processors for smartphones and tablets. The growing demand for these products requires best quality application processors ,which only Samsung provides.

4. Growth of tablets market. Tablets market is expected to grow in double digits over the next few years. Samsung business has a strong position in tablets market and could expand it by introducing newer, better quality tablet models, such as its current galaxy line.

5. Obtaining patents through acquisitions. The key to Samsung's competitive advantage is the large portfolio of patents. Patents can be discovered by engaging in costly R&D or through acquisitions of other firms.

THREATS

1. Saturated smartphone markets in developed countries. Smartphones market in the developed economies is saturated and the sales will not be growing at a high rate.

2. Rapid technological change. The serious threat that Samsung and the other tech companies are facing is a rapid technological change. Companies are under the pressure to release the

new products faster and faster. The one that cannot keep up with the competition soon fails. This is especially hard when the business wants to introduce something new, innovative and successful.

3. Declining margins on hardware production. Samsung is the second largest semiconductors producer where the profit margins are very thin, thus weakening the whole company's figures.
4. Breached patents. Samsung Electronics has many patents which are often used by its many competitors. Such situation makes it hard to find out which companies benefit from Samsung's technology but do not pay for the rights to use it.
5. Apple's iTV launch. Apple's iTV is the next big lunch from Apple, which may hurt Samsung's TV sales.
6. Price wars. Samsung has a very low gross margin on many of its products and is already selling some of them with significant price cuts. Competitors could follow price cutting strategy too and induce price wars, which would erode Samsung's profit margin to 0%!

BENCHMARKING

Benchmarking is another tool, which can be used to generate competitive advantage. It is a process of identifying in systematic ways of superior products, services, and processes & practices that can be adopted in an organization to reduce costs, decrease operation cycle time, and provide greater customer satisfaction. The concept of benchmarking has been derived from land surveying in which it indicates a reference point called benchmark, which is established as benchmark as "a survey's mark; previously determined position used as a reference point; standard by which something can be measured and judged." Sarah Cook has defined benchmarking as follows: "Benchmarking is a process of identifying, understanding, and adapting outstanding practices from within the same organization or from other businesses to help improve performance."

How it Began

The Japanese are given credit for inventing the concept of benchmarking through their practice of sending managers to visit other companies in order to improve their understanding of good business practices. However, Xerox is commonly associated with the development of the modern concept. In 1979 the Xerox Manufacturing Operations began a process of competitive benchmarking in order to combat increasing competition. The company compared their unit manufacturing costs of the copying machines with that of their competitors and used the data collected to identify performance gaps.

In undertaking this procedure Xerox gained a better understanding of their organisation. The Xerox success story encouraged others to consider the benchmarking process. Two important facets emerged:

1. Benchmarking could be used to better understand any organisation by the identification of common standards of measurement (metrics).
2. Rather than only concentrating on outcomes and products this approach looked at process issues, ie. how the product was produced. (Massheder & Finch, 1998).

FEATURES OF BENCHMARKING

1. Benchmarking is based on the theme "see what others do and try to improve upon that." Therefore, this implies some kind of measurement, which can be accomplished in two forms: internal and external. Both internal and external practices are compared and a statement of the significant differences is prepared to identify the gap which should be filled.
2. Benchmarking can be applied to all facets of a business; it includes products, services, processes, and methods. It goes beyond the traditional competitor analysis in the form of identifying strengths and weaknesses and includes a clear understanding of how the best practices are used.
3. Benchmarking is not aimed solely at direct product competitors but those organizations and businesses that are recognized as best or industry leaders.
4. Benchmarking is a continuous process and not just one shot action. It is continuous because industry practices constantly change and a continuous monitoring of these practices is required to bring suitable change in the organization.

Some common areas benchmarked by businesses are:

Sales, turnover and profitability

Products and services

Pricing structures, fees and overheads

Key performance indicators (KPIs)

Quality control processes

Customer service standards or the number of customers

Staff management and turnover.

What are the Strategic Issues and Problems that must be addressed by the Management?

The final and most important analytical step is to zero in on exactly what strategic issues company managers need to address. This step involves drawing on the results of both industry and competitive analysis and the evaluations of the company's internal situation. The task here is to get a clear fix on exactly what the industry and competitive challenges confront the company, which of the company's internal weaknesses need fixing, and what specific problems merit front-burner attention by company managers. Pinpointing the precise things that management needs to worry about ,sets the agenda for deciding what actions to be taken next to improve the company's performance and business outlook.

CASE STUDY

Meters Ltd

Meters Limited is a company engaged in the designing, manufacturing, and marketing of instruments like speed meters, oil pressure gauges, and so on, that are fitted into two and four wheelers. Their current investment in assets is around Rs. 5 crores and their last year turnover was Rs. 15 crores, just adequate enough to breakeven. The company has been witnessing over the last couple of years, a fall in their market share prices since many customers are switching over to a new range of electronic instruments from the ange of mechanical instruments that have been the mainstay of Meters Limited.

The Company has received a firm offer of cooperation from a competitor who is similarly placed in respect of product range. The offer implied the following:

(i) Transfer of the manufacturing line from the competitor to Meters Limited;

(ii) Manufacture of mechanical instruments by Meters Limited for the competitor to the latter's specifications and brand name; and (iii) marketing by the competitor.

The benefits that will accrue to Meters Limited will be better utilization of its installed capacity and appropriate financial ompensation for the manufacturing effort. The production manager of Meters Limited has welcomed the proposal and points out that it will enable the company to make profts. The sales manager is doubtful about the same since the demand for mechanical instruments in shrinking. The chief Executive is studying the offer.

Questions:

(1) What is divestment strategy? Do you see it being practised in the given case? Explain.

(2) What is stability strategy? Should Meters Limited adopt it?

(3) What is expansion strategy? What are the implications for Meters Limited in case it is adopted?

(4) What are your suggestions to the Chief Executive?

REVIEW QUESTIONS

Conceptual Type

1. What is competitive position?
2. What is SWOT analysis?
3. What is TOWS matrix?
4. What do you mean by "strengths?"
5. What do you mean by "weaknesses?"
6. Give the meaning of "opportunity?"
7. What is value chain?
8. What is Benchmarking? ***(VTU, MBA, Dec-2012)***

8\. State any three benefits of benchmarking.

Analytical Type

1. Explain company's resources and competitive position.
2. Write short note on Focused Strategy.
3. Write short notes on differentiation Strategy.
4. What are the strategic options for a company to enter and compete in the foreign markets ? Explain with examples.
5. Briefly describe the generic strategic alternatives given by Glueck and Jauch.
6. Write note on value chain analysis.
7. Explain the steps a corporate value chain goes through.
8. Why do Value Chains of rival Companies differ?
9. Write a short note on benchmarking in strategic audit.

Descriptive Type

1. Discuss the company's present strategies and how to analyse with an example.
2. What is the resources based view of a firm?
3. Explain SWOT analysis.
4. What are the strategic options for achieving cost competitiveness?

5. Compare and contrast SWOT analysis with portfolio analysis.

6. Explain the concept of a company value chain? ***(VTU, MBA, June-2010)***

7. Write a note on benchmarking.

8. Briefly describe the generic strategic alternatives given by Glueck and Jauch. Explain the value-chain approach for diagnosing a firm's key strengths and weaknesses.

(VTU, MBA, Dec-2012)

9. Explain the value chain approach for diagosising a firm's keep strengths and weaknesses. ***(VTU, MBA, Dec-2012)***

10. Discuss the process of conducting value chain analysis. ***(VTU, MBA, Dec-2012)***

*****

Module-5

Strategy and Competitive Advantage

Unit

Syllabus

Generic Competitive Strategies – Low cost provider Strategy – Differentiation Strategy – Best cost provider Strategy – Focused Strategy – Strategic Alliances and Collaborative Partnerships – Mergers and Acquisition Strategies – Outsourcing Strategies –International Business level Strategies.

INTRODUCTION

A competitive advantage is an advantage gained over competitors by offering customers greater value, either through lower prices or by providing additional benefits and service that justify similar, or possibly higher, prices. For growers and producers involved in niche marketing, finding and nurturing a competitive advantage can mean increased profits and a venture that is sustainable and successful over the long term. This fact sheet looks at what defines competitive advantage and discusses strategies to consider when building a competitive advantage, as well as ways to assess the competitive advantage of a venture.

The Essence of Competitive Advantage

To begin, it may be helpful to take a more in-depth look at what it means to have a competitive advantage: an edge over the competition. Essentially a competitive advantage answers the question, "Why should the customer purchase from this operation rather than the competition?". For some ventures, particularly those in markets where the products or services are less differentiated, answering this question can be difficult. A key point to understand is that a venture that has customers, has customers for a reason. Successfully growing a business is often dependent upon a strong competitive edge that gradually builds a core of loyal customers, which can be expanded over time. Producers and suppliers familiar with farming and ranching may know that successful ventures in the agricultural industry have typically operated in a commoditized, price-driven market, where all parties to produce essentially the same product. Such conditions imply that the ultimate "winners" are the most cost-efficient producers, meaning that agricultural producers have historically relied on strategies that focused on lower costs and higher volumes (i.e. a bushel of hard red winter wheat is assumed to be of similar quality across the entire high plains region, meaning each bushel is assumed to be of the same value; so there is an incentive for producers keep prices low and volume high). With the advent of product differentiation and niche and direct marketing, that reality has changed, and now there are niche markets in which both individual and wholesale buyers are looking for products with very specific characteristics or special services. These characteristics often use strategies that don't focus on costs and volumes exclusively; rather the product or service may be of premium quality, be differentiated from other products and services available in the market (such as organic, natural, or humane production), or have a value-added component (i.e. flavored meats, pre-washed salad mixes, etc.). Successful ventures perform a combination of business activities well, including marketing, production, distribution, finance, customer service, and/or other activities important to the enterprise. However, a competitive advantage is often a single key element that gives an edge to a business beyond what the competition has or does.

PORTER'S GENERIC COMPETITIVE STRATEGIES

A firm's relative position within its industry determines whether a firm's profitability is above or below the industry average. The fundamental basis of above average profitability in the long run is sustainable competitive advantage. There are two basic types of competitive advantage a firm can possess: low cost or differentiation. The two basic types of competitive advantage combined with the scope of activities for which a firm seeks to achieve them, lead to three generic strategies for achieving above average performance in an industry cost leadership, differentiation, and focus. The focus strategy has two variants, cost focus and differentiation focus.

1. Cost Leadership

Cost leadership is a strategy that is finding ways to lower the cost structure. The company pursuing a cost leadership strategy seeks to achieve a competitive advantage and higher profit. The firm sells its products either at average industry prices to earn a profit higher than that of rivals, or below the average industry prices to gain market share. In the event of a price war, the firm can maintain some profitability while the competitor suffers losses. Even without a price war, as the industry matures and prices decline, the firms that can produce more cheaply will remain profitable for a long period of time. The cost leadership strategy usually targets a broad market.

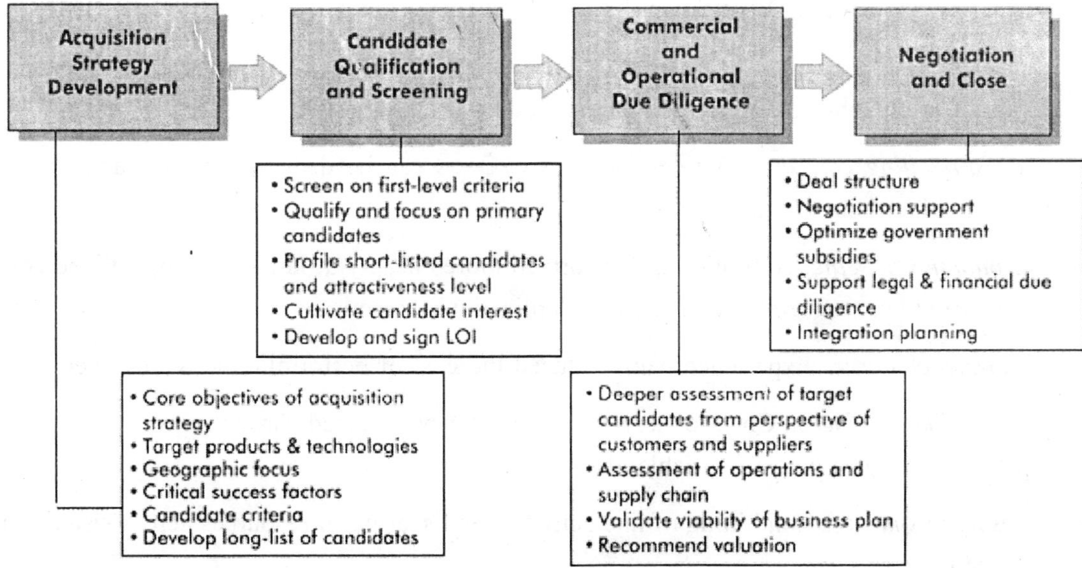

Some of the ways that firms acquire cost advantages are by improving process efficiencies, gaining unique access to a large source of lower cost materials, making optimal outsourcing and vertical integration decisions, or avoiding some costs altogether. If competing firms are unable to lower their costs by a similar amount, the firm may be able to sustain a competitive advantage based on cost leadership.

Porter points out that cost leadership requires;

1. Aggressive construction of efficient scale facilities,
2. Vigorous pursuit of cost reduction from experience,
3. Tight cost and overhead control,
4. Avoidance of marginal customer accounts,
5. Cost minimization in areas like R&D, services, sales force, advertising and so on.

Porter also observes that the low cost firm "has a broad scope and serves many industry segments and may even operate in related industries and the firm's breadth is often important to its cost advantage". Low cost leadership means low overall costs. Low costs mean lower prices. This strategy aims to achieve low costs relative to competitors. The organization becomes the industry's lowest cost provider of products. It finds ways to drive costs out of business by reducing waste. This strategy appeals to a broad segment of price sensitive buyers. It elicits quick response.

Cost can be reduced in two ways:

1. Control cost drivers: Drive down the costs of value chain activities by doing a better job than competitors.
2. Revamp value chain: By-pass some cost producing activities.

a. Controlling cost drivers to reduce costs: Costs can be driven down in each activity segment of value chain through.

- *Economies of scale:* Activities are performed more cheaply at larger volumes. Fixed costs are spread out over grater volume. Standardization is practice.
- *Experience curve:* Experience helps reduced the cost of performing activities over time.
- *Cost of key reduces:* Costs of key resources can be reduced through strong bargaining power of buyer. Location variable also reduce costs.
- *Resource sharing:* Combining of like activities and sharing of resources across sister units to reduce cost.
- *Outsourcing:* It involves purchasing some activities from outside specialists who can perform them cheaply. Vertical integration also reduces costs.

- *Capacity utilization:* Higher rates of capacity utilization reduce costs.
- *First mover advantage:* Being first in the market in introducing a new product provides cost advantage.
- *Operating decision:* They can outperform competitors in controlling costs.

b. Revamping value chain to reduce costs: Costs can be driven by revamping value chain through:

- *Shifting to E-business technology:* Use of Internet for doing business can reduce costs.
- *Direct marketing:* Marketing products directly from producer to buyers reduces costs. Channel costs are saved.
- *Simplify product design:* Simplified produced design reduced cost by simplifying the value chain. For example, using standardized parts and components.
- *No-frills offers:* Offering only basic product cuts costs. There are no multiple features and options.
- *By pass high cost materials:* New low cost materials reduce costs.
- *Relocate facilities:* Move plants closer to supplier or customer or both.
- *Re engineering:* Core business processes can be re-engineered to cut out low value added activities.

Low-cost position yields the form above average returns in the industry. This may enable the firm to reinvest and improve further its position in the industry

Cost leadership, however, has several risks:

- Other firms may imitate the cost leader so that the cost leadership is lost
- Technological changes may result in the firm losing cost leadership
- Cost foci may achieve even lower cost in segments
- Competition on bases other than cost may become more important

Low cost is the most important competitive advantage enjoyed by all of India's five companies among the Asia's top 20 most competitive ones.

(Walmart logo, used from June 30, 2008-present.)

Type	: Public
Industry	: Retailing
Founded	: 1962
Founder(s)	: Sam Walton
Headquarters	: Bentonville, Arkansas,US
Number of locations	: 8,970 (2011)
Area served	: Worldwide
Key people	: Mike Duke(CEO) H. Lee Scott(Chairman) S. Robson Walton (Chairman)
Employees	: Approx. 2.1 million (2011)
Subsidiaries	: Walmex Asda Sam's Club Seiyu Group

Wal-Mart

Wal-Mart Stores Inc. has been successful using its strategy of everyday low prices to attract customers. The idea of everyday low prices is to offer products at a cheaper rate than competitors on a consistent basis, rather than relying on sales. Wal-Mart is able to achieve this due to its large scale and efficient supply chain. They source products from cheaper domestic suppliers and from low-wage foreign markets. This allows the company to sell their items at low prices and to profit off thin margins at a high volume.

McDonald's

The restaurant industry is known for yielding low margins that can make it difficult to compete with a cost leadership marketing strategy. McDonald's has been extremely successful with this strategy by offering basic fast-food meals at low prices. They are able to keep prices low through a division of labor that allows it to hire and train inexperienced employees rather than trained cooks. It also relies on few managers who typically earn higher wages. These staff savings allow the company to offer its foods for bargain prices.

2. Differentiation

Differentiation strategies are based on offering buyers something unique or different that makes the firm's products or services distinct form that of its rivals. In a differentiation strategy a firm seeks to be unique in its industry along some dimensions that are widely valued by buyers. It selects one or more attributes that many buyers in an industry perceive as important, and uniquely positions it to meet those needs. It is rewarded for its uniqueness with a premium price.

According to porter could differentiate from the following factors:

- Product features,
- Product performance,
- Complementary services,
- Intensity of marketing activities,
- Manufacturing and design technology,
- The quality of purchased inputs,
- Procedures for checking each activity,
- The skill and experience of employees,
- Location.

When Does a Differentiation Strategy Work Best?

- There are many ways to differentiate a product that have value and please customers,
- Buyer needs and uses are diverse,
- Few rivals are following a similar differentiation approach,
- Technological change and product innovation are fast-paced,

Starbucks differentiating strategy

Starbucks also spends a lot of time and energy differentiating itself from the competition. You can see this in the design of its coffee shops, the music played there and the types of products it sells, such as coffee-brewing equipment and jazz CDs. Starbucks makes sure to keep current on the latest technology, often times being the first to introduce the newest advancements to its customers. For example, Starbucks was one of the first companies to adopt location-based promotions and mobile payments.

The differentiation strategy also involves a number of risks which include the following:

1. Limitation erodes differentiation
2. If the price difference between the differentiating firm and others is very great, it may become

   very difficult to get enough demand
3. Changes in consumer needs /tastes may make the difference in segments
4. Differentiation focuses may achieve even greater differentiating in segments

3. Focus strategy

Focus strategies aim to sell goods or services to specific customer or target market, place or segment. Focus builds competitive advantage through high specialization and concentration of resources in a given niche. The generic strategy of focus rests on the choice of a narrow competitive scope within an industry. The focuser selects a segment or group of segments in the industry and tailors its strategy to serving them to the exclusion of others. Focus strategy involves concentrating on a particular customer, product line, geographical area, channel of distribution, stage in the production process, or market niche.

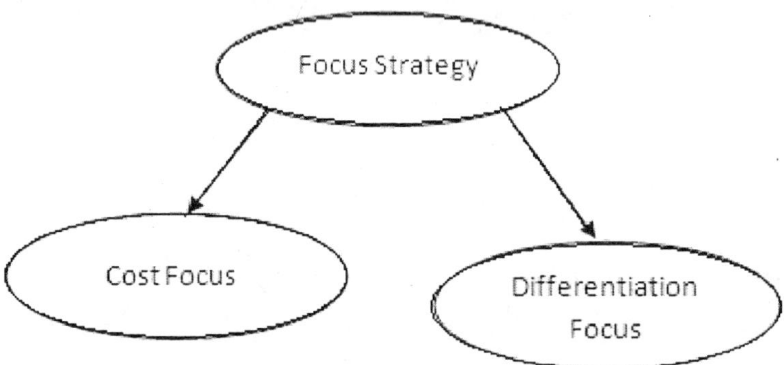

The focus strategy has two variants

(a) In cost focus a firm seeks a cost advantage in its target segment,

(b) Differentiation focus a firm seeks differentiation in its target segment. Both variants of the focus strategy rest on the differences between a foci target segment and other segments in the industry. The target segments must either have buyers with unusual needs or else the production and delivery system that best serves the target segment must differ from that of other industry segments. Cost focus exploits differences in cost behavior in some segments, while differentiation focus exploits the special needs of buyers in certain segments.

INDITEX, a European SME success story

The story of INDITEX Group from Spain demonstrates how innovative design and trademarks helped a small family-owned business grow into a solid international firm. INDITEX has introduced a kind of revolution in the fashion sector that impelled other companies to rethink their strategy.

INDITEX Group´s chairman and founder Amancio Ortega Gaona made his modest start working at the age of 14 as a gofer in a shirt store in La Coruna, Galicia. From the first venture into his own business in 1963, Mr. Ortega reached an initial milestone in 1975 with the opening of the first ZARA store in La Coruna. A decade later, he founded INDITEX as a holding company for its various subsidiaries, paving the way for the Group´s expansion outside Spain, first to Portugal in 1988, followed by the opening of outlets in New York in 1989 and in Paris in 1990. INDITEX Group launched the "Pull & Bear" chain of casual wear in 1991 and in the same year purchased 65% of the "Massimo Dutti" Group, a high-end fashion concern, which was fully acquired in 1995.

Meanwhile, it continued the drive into the international market by opening various stores in Mexico, Greece, Belgium and Sweden, respectively from 1992-1994. The Group started the "Bershka" chain targeting the younger female segment in 1998, when it also set up stores in Argentina, Japan, UK, Venezuela, Lebanon, UAE, Kuwait and Turkey.

In 1999, INDITEX acquired "Stradivarius", making it the fifth chain of the Group, and opened its stores in new countries namely the Netherlands, Germany, Poland, Saudi Arabia, Bahrain, Canada, Brazil, Chile and Uruguay. In 2000, INDITEX built its headquarters in Arteixo, A Coruna, Spain, while opening stores in four new countries. The company was listed on the Spanish stock market in May 2001 with its shares sold out the day it went public, the year when it added six more countries to its global footprint.

INDITEX has seven different firms with seven different trademarks under its umbrella. It has 1,376 stores in 42 countries across the world. INDITEX success lies in the goodwill value of the Group´s trademarks: Zara for the middle-class segment, Massimo for the high-end, and Pull & Bear for the casual clothing line. The Group does not invest a lot in advertising campaigns, but it focuses on investment in the "image" of the shops. It focuses on delivering value for money, and the capacity to adapt to the consumer´s tastes. The Group´s future looks promising, with its blueprint establishing presence worldwide, while launching a new product line: women´s underwear.

STRATEGIC ALLIANCES

Strategic alliance is the process of mutual agreement between the organizations to achieve objectives of common interest. They are obtained by the co-operation between the companies. Strategic alliance involves the individual organizations to modify its basic business activities and join in agreement with similar organizations to reduce duplication of manufacturing products and improve performance. It is stronger when the organizations involved have balancing strengths. Strategic alliances contribute in successful implementation of strategic plan because it is strategic in nature. It provides relationship between organizations to plan various strategies in achieving a common goal.

CHARACTERISTICS OF STRATEGIC ALLIANCES

1. Joint venture-based strategic alliances

Strategic alliance is often, but not always, in the form of a joint venture. A joint venture is created when two or more firms work together to form a new business entity that is separate from its "parents."

The most common kind is the joint venture through a subsidiary. In such an instance, two entities create a third separate entity with its own legal existence. For example, American Motors Corp. has formed a joint venture with government-owned Beijing Automotive Works, creating a third entity called Beijing Jeep.

Another is the joint venture by acquisition. It is created when one business purchases all or part of the shares of another. For example, in the 1990s, the Lear Corp. acquired interior components producer Masland Corp.

A third is the joint venture by merger. This is created when two or more companies are dissolved and incorporated into one surviving entity. For example, corporations A and B merge and their assets are conveyed to a newly created corporation C. After the merger, corporation C continues but corporations A and B are dissolved. It should be noted, however, that this legal mechanism is seldom used for international joint ventures.

2. Strategic alliances not based on joint ventures

In general, a strategic alliance that is not in the form of a joint venture is formed for a limited purpose and is narrower in its operations than the joint venture. Non-joint venture strategic alliances tend to be less stable and last for shorter terms than joint ventures. For example, United Airlines and British Airlines formed a strategic alliance for the purpose of marketing their North American and European routes in 1988. They did so because they were losing part of their market share to Delta and American Airlines. Within a year, however, the market shifted and they terminated the agreement.

3. Linkages that are not strategic alliances

It is important to note that not all linkages between national or international businesses are strategic alliances. Examples of arrangements that do not create strategic alliances include licensing, exporting, franchising, and foreign direct investment agreements.

NEED FOR STRATEGIC ALLIANCE

The need for strategic alliance is:

i. The new economy enables the organizations to use business policy to gain competition in market share, technologies, partner's resources etc.

ii. The fast growing organizations extensively rely on forming alliances so that it enables the organizations to add and balance resources among them. This helps the organizations to grow at a faster rate in technology and operations.

iii. Strategic alliances are required to increase productivity ratio. When two organizations involve in manufacturing the desired product, it helps in saving time for the individual organizations.

iv. An increasing desire of global operations requires strategic alliances to converge the industry in many international markets.

v. The intention for geographic expansion makes the organizations to enter into alliances for reducing the cost and manufacturing more innovative products.

BENEFITS OF STRATEGIC ALLIANCE

The organization can enter into strategic alliances for the following benefits:

i. Gaining resources and capabilities

Strategic alliance is the opportunity for the organization to achieve its objectives that lacks in the areas of knowledge, technology, and expertise. The resources and capabilities are shared among the organizations to increase the productivity. These capabilities and resources can be used by the organization for its own purposes in future.

ii. Ease of market entry

The advancements in telecommunications and computer technology have made the organizations to alliance with foreign organizations. This benefits the organization in terms of economies of scale and increment in marketing and distribution. The organizations enter into strategic alliance with international firm to reduce the cost of production. It also provides a strategic partnership to overcome many obstacles like entrenched competition and hostile government regulations.

iii. Shared risks

Risk sharing technique is another common way of a mutual arrangement that specially occurs when the market has newly launched. If there are any ambiguities or unsteadiness in a specific market, sharing risks will become a significant factor. The aggressive nature of business is to launch a new product in the market as well as, developing a well planned association is one of the processes to minimize the firm's risks.

iv. Shared knowledge and expertise

Organizations are competent in some areas and lack expertise in other areas. Such organizations form strategic alliance and gain knowledge and expertise in the lacking areas. The intangible resources gained by the organization can not only be used in joint venture but also in other projects. The knowledge gaining includes the learning to deal with government regulations, manufacturing process and methods to acquire resources.

v. Easier access to target markets

It is difficult to introduce a new manufactured product in the market since it is exposed to various obstacles. The organization experiences entrench competition, hostile government, expensiveness etc. There are risks of direct financial losses due to improper analysis of the market situation before releasing the product. Therefore the organizations choose strategic alliance as the entry mode to overcome such problems and reduce the entry cost.

Example, Flexera a software organization licensed enterprise optimization solutions, a component of strategic solution. It helped the companies and the government institutions that used applications based on management to gain continuous software compliance.

vi. Winning the political obstacle

The organizations experience difficulties in introducing a new product in other countries due to the political obstacles. Therefore the organizations form alliances with foreign organizations to introduce new products. This reduces the political factors and strict regulations imposed by the national government and also help in increasing economic standard of the country.

vii. Achieving synergy and competitive advantage

Synergy and competitive advantage act as the elements that lead businesses to greater success. Being an individual organization, it might not be strong enough to achieve these elements. Hence the organizations enter into alliance and combine individual strengths to achieve success more effectively.

The organizations indulging in strategic alliance benefits in various forms like cooperation in sharing the production facilities, sharing of knowledge, skills and technology, marketing, financing for projects etc

DIFFERENT STAGES INVOLVED IN A STRATEGIC ALLIANCE

Following are the different stages of strategic alliances:

1. Strategy development
2. Partner assessment
3. Contract negotiation
4. Alliance operation
5. Alliance termination

1. Strategy development

It is the process of identifying the objectives of forming alliances, analyzing the advantages of entering into alliances, observing the major issues, challenges and development of resource strategies for production.

2. Partner assessment

This process involves selecting the appropriate partner to join into alliance. The main elements the organization focuses in selecting the partner are; analyzing the partners strength and weakness, framing appropriate strategies, managing the partners needs and understanding the partners motives. These make the organizations under alliance to coordinate in an efficient manner to achieve effective production.

3. Contract negotiation

It is the process of determining the two parties realistic objectives such that a high caliber is formed in negotiating between the two organizations. It defines the contribution of the parties towards achieving the goal. The process also includes penalties for poor performance and highlights the negotiation procedures that are clearly stated and understood if any controversies occur between the organizations.

4. Alliance operation

This phase involves the commitment of senior management in the organization towards forming alliance. It is the process of identifying the caliber of available resources dedicated to the alliance. According to the strategic priorities the budgets are linked with resources and performance of the alliance is measured.

5. Alliance termination

It is the process of ending the alliance between the organizations when the objectives are met. All the transactions, meetings, financial venture and agreements of the organizations are terminated if both the organizations agree to terminate the alliance. This termination can either be positive or negative. If the organizations achieve its common goal, then the alliance terminates in a positive manner. But if the objective or the goals of the organizations are not met, then it ends with negative attitude.

TYPES OF STRATEGIC ALLIANCES AND BUSINESS DECISIONS

The mutual agreements between the organizations can take a number of forms and are increasing their common goals to get upper hand over their competitors.

The different types of strategic alliances are listed below:

1. Mergers and acquisitions
2. Joint venture
3. Collaborations and co-branding
4. Technological partnering
5. Contractual agreements
6. Outsourcing
7. Other Methods

MERGER AND ACQUISITION

Merger and acquisition are often known to be a single terminology defined as a process of combining two or more companies together. The fact remains that the so-called single terminologies are different terms used under different situations. Though there is a thin line difference between the two but the impact of the kind of completely different in both the cases.

The merger is considered to be a process when two or more companies come together to expand their business operations. In such a case the deal gets finalized on friendly terms and both the companies share equal profits in the newly created entity.

When one company takes over the other and rules all its business operations, it is known as acquisitions. In this process of restructuring, one company overpowers the other company and the decision is mainly taken during downturns in the economy or during declining profit margins. Among the two, the one that is financially strong and bigger in all ways establishes its power. The combined operations then run under the name of the powerful entity who also takes over the existing stocks of the other company.

Another difference is, in an acquisition usually two companies of different sizes come together to combat the challenges of downturn and in a merger two companies of same size combine to increase their strength and financial gains along with breaking the trade barriers. A deal in case of an acquisition is often done in an unfriendly manner, it is more or less a forceful or a helpless association where the powerful company either swallows the operation or a company in loss is forced to sell its entity. In case of a merger there is a friendly association where both the partners hold the same percentage of ownership and equal profit share.

REASONS FOR MERGERS

Monopoly: The nineteenth-century wave of mergers is not possible with today's laws, but mergers leading to lesser degrees of market power still possible.

Economies: Combining two firms may produce cost savings, or economies: pecuniary saving, buying goods or services more cheaply, perhaps through greater bargaining strength. Merely redistribution of income. Real economies, or economies of scope. Can be production or marketing or finance or R&D etc. Socially beneficial.

Other Motives: Financial, distress, retirement, income-tax advantages, diversification, empire building

Educing Management Inefficiencies: By replacing an inefficient management with an efficient management, savings may occur.

PROBLEMS OF MERGERS AND ACQUISTION

It's a well known fact that a good number of mergers fail because of various factors including cultural differences and flawed intentions. Most companies when signing an agreement often get to create a bigger picture of their world of expectations as they believe in the pure concept of higher capital gains when two are combined together. This belief is not always true as conditions in the market and the economy often rules the operation and functioning of any company.

The history of merger and acquisitions have revealed that almost two thirds of the mergers taking place experience failure and feel disappointed on their own terms and predefined parameters. At times even the motivation driving the mergers can prove to be intangible.

There are many factors contributing to the failure and elements that are the problems of mergers and acquisition. There are many aspects that should be understood and analyzed before signing an agreement because even one small mistake in taking a decision can completely dump both the companies with an irreversible impact.

TYPES OF MERGER

There are many types of mergers and acquisitions that redefine the business world with new strategic alliances and improved corporate philosophies. From the business structure perspective, some of the most common and significant types of mergers and acquisitions are listed below:

1. Horizontal Merger

This kind of merger exists between two companies who compete in the same industry segment. The two companies combine their operations and gains strength in terms of improved performance, increased capital, and enhanced profits. This kind substantially reduces the number of competitors in the segment and gives a higher edge over competition.

2. Vertical Merger

Vertical merger is a kind in which two or more companies in the same industry but in different fields combine together in business. In this form, the companies in merger decide to combine all the operations and productions under one shelter. It is like encompassing all the requirements and products of a single industry segment.

3. Concentric Merger

It is a combination of two or more firms somewhat related to each other in terms of customer functions, production processes, business markets, or basic required technologies. It includes the extension of the product line or acquiring components that are all the way required in the daily operations. This kind offers great opportunities to businesses as it opens a huge gateway to diversify around a common set of resources and strategic requirements.

4. Conglomerate Merger

Conglomerate merger is a kind of venture in which two or more companies belonging to different industrial sectors combine their operations. All the merged companies are no way related to their kind of business and product line rather their operations overlap that of each other. This is just a unification of businesses from different verticals under one flagship enterprise or firm.

MERGER AND ACQUISITION IN INDIA

Merger and acquisition are paying important role in the global market which increasing expanding business or profitability. After globalization, we are entering into different country that clearly indicates the strength of Indian companies. India in the recent year has shown tremendous growth in the merger and acquisition deal.

Merger and Acquisition has been actively playing in all industrial sectors. It is widely spreading far across the stretches of all industrial verticals and on all business platforms. The increasing volume is witnessed in various sectors like that of finance, pharmaceuticals, telecom, FMCG, industrial development, automotives and metals

The volume of merger and acquisition transactions in India has apparently increased to about 67.2 billion USD in 2010 from 21.3 billion USD in 2009. At present the industry is witnessing a whopping 270% increase in merger and acquisition deal in the first quarter of the financial year. This increasing percentage is mainly attributed to the increasing cross-border merger and acquisition transactions. Over that increasing interest of foreign companies in Indian companies has given a tremendous push to such transactions

Large Indian companies are going through a phase of growth as all are exploring growth potential in foreign markets and on the other end even international companies is targeting Indian companies for growth and expansion. Some of the major factors resulting in this sudden growth of merger and acquisition deal in India are favorable government policies, excess of capital flow, economic stability, corporate investments, and dynamic attitude of Indian companies.

The recent merger and acquisition 2011 made by Indian companies worldwide are those of Tata Steel acquiring Corus Group plc, UK based company with a deal of US $12,000 million and Hindalco acquiring Novelis from Canada for US $6,000 million

With these major mergers and many more on the annual chart, M&A in services India is taking a revolutionary form. Creating a niche on all platforms of corporate businesses, merger and acquisition in India is constantly rising with edge over competition.

DISTINCTION BETWEEN MERGERS AND ACQUISITIONS

Mergers	Acquisitions
1. It happens when two similar organizations proceed to become a single organization.	1. When one organization takes over another and clearly states itself as the new owner, such purchase is called acquisition.
2. Both organizations stocks are submitted and new stock is issued.	2. The acquiring organization swallows the business of acquired organization and the acquiring organization stock continues to be traded.
3. The term purchase is also called as merger when the top level managers with similar interests join together.	3. When the organizations deal is unfriendly, it leads to purchasing of the other organization. It is termed as acquisitions.
4. *Example* Transocean and Global Santa Fe, the top oil drilling companies, merged to consolidate their position in a fast-growing market.	4. *Example* Google acquired Postini to introduce services of message security, archiving, encryption, and policy enforcement.

ADVANTAGES OF AN ACQUISITION

For an entrepreneur, there are many advantages to acquiring an existing business, as indicated below:

1. ***Established business:*** The most significant advantage is that the acquired firm has an established image and track record. If the firm has been profitable, the entrepreneur would need only to continue its current strategy to be successful with the existing customer base.
2. ***Location:*** New customers are already familiar with the location
3. ***Established marketing structure:*** An acquired firm has its existing channel and sales structure. Knows suppliers, whole-sellers and manufacturers, reps are important assets to an entrepreneur. With this structure already in place, the entrepreneur can concentrate on improving or expanding the acquired business.
4. ***Cost:*** The actual cost of acquiring a business can be lower then other methods of expansion.
5. ***Existing employees:*** The employees of an existing business can be an important asset to the acquisition process. They know how to run the business and can help ensure that the

business will continue in its successful mode. They already have established relationships with customers, suppliers and channel members and can reassure these groups when a new owner takes over the business.

6. ***More opportunities to be creative:*** Since the entrepreneur does not have to be concerned with finding suppliers, channel members, hiring new employees or creating customer awareness, more time can be spent assessing opportunities to expand or strengthen the existing business and tap into potential synergies between the business.

DISADVANTAGES OF AN ACQUISITION

Although we can see that there are many advantages to acquiring an existing business, there are also disadvantages. The importance of each of the advantages and disadvantages should be weighed carefully with other expansion options.

1. ***Marginal success record:*** Most ventures that are for sale have erratic, marginally successful, or even unprofitable track record. It is important to review the records and meet with important constituents to assess that record in terms of the business's future potential. For example, if the store layout is poor, this factor can be rectified; but if the location is poor, the entrepreneur might do better using some other expansion method.

2. ***Overconfidence in ability:*** Sometimes an entrepreneur may assume that he or she succeed where others have failed. This is why a self evaluation is so important before entering into any purchase agreement. Even though the entrepreneur brings new ideas and management qualities, the venture may never be successful for reasons that are not possible to correct. Often managers are overconfident in their ability to overcome cultural differences between their current business and the one being acquired.

3. ***Key employee loss:*** Often when a business changes hands, key employees also leave. Key employee loss can be devastating to an entrepreneur who is acquiring a business since the value of the business is often a reflection of the efforts of the employees. This is particularly evident in a service business where it is difficult to separate the actual service from the person who performs it. In the acquisition negotiations, it is helpful for the entrepreneur to speak to all employees individually to get some assurance of their intentions as well as to inform them of how important they will be to the future of the business. Incentives can sometimes be used to ensure that key employees will remain with the business.

4. ***Over evaluated:*** It is possible that the actual purchase price is inflated due to the established image, customer base, channel members or suppliers. If the entrepreneur has to pay too much for a business, it is possible that the return on investment will be

unacceptable. It is important to look at the investment required in purchasing a business and at the potential profit and establish a reasonable payback to justify the investment.

After balancing the pros & cons of the acquisition, the entrepreneur needs to determine a fair for the business.

TAKEOVERS

In business, a takeover is the purchase of one company by another (the acquirer, or bidder). Indian companies, in recent times, have been using takeover or acquisition as a powerful tool to gain control over rival firms and thereby achieve rapid growth in their respective fields.

Friendly takeovers

A "friendly takeover" is an acquisition which is approved by the management. Before a bidder makes an offer for another company, it usually first informs the company's board of directors. In an ideal world, if the board feels that accepting the offer serves the shareholders better than rejecting it, it recommends the offer be accepted by the shareholders. For example, targeted companies that were making heavy loses such as Maharaja Industries Ltd, Intron Ltd, HLL's takeover of TOMCO was also a smooth one and was carried out with the consent of Tatas who wanted to divest TOMCO.

In a private company, because the shareholders and the board are usually the same people or closely connected with one another, private acquisitions are usually friendly. If the shareholders agree to sell the company, then the board is usually of the same mind or sufficiently under the orders of the equity shareholders to cooperate with the bidder.

Hostile takeovers

A "hostile takeover" allows a suitor to take over a target company whose management is unwilling to agree to a merger or takeover. A takeover is considered "hostile" if the target company's board rejects the offer, but the bidder continues to pursue it, or the bidder makes the offer directly after having announced its firm intention to make an offer. The Sheths of GE Shipping who held just 13 percent in the company had to ward off the takeover threat from the Dalmias of the Renaissance Group by paying a heavy price of Rs 54 (April 12, 2000 price was just Rs 15). In Feb 2001 N Srinivasan of Indian cements picked up controlling stakes in Raasi Cements (Rs. 320 Crore), Cement Corporation of India (Rs. 200 crore) and Visaka Cements (Rs. 320 crore) through buyouts and hostile takeovers, with a view to consolidate his position in the cement industry.

REASONS FOR TAKEOVER

1. Cost of New product Development and Increased speed to market.
2. Overcoming Entry Barriers.
3. Adequate and Easy terms working capital.
4. Access to resourceful management.
5. Increased Diversification.
6. Reshaping the firm's competitive scope.
7. Increased market power.

JOINT VENTURES

Joint venture is the most powerful business concept that has the ability to pool two or more organizations in one project to achieve a common goal. In a joint venture, both the organizations invest in the resources like money, time and skills to achieve the objectives. The joint venture has been the hallmark for most successful organizations in the world. An individual partner in a joint venture may offer time and services whereas the other focuses on investments. These pool the resources among the organizations and help each other in achieving the objectives. An agreement is formed between the two parties and the nature of the agreement is truly beneficial with huge rewards such that the profits are shared by both the organizations.

FACTORS IN JOINT VENTURE SUCCESS

Clearly, not all joint ventures succeed. An entrepreneur needs to assess this method of growth carefully and understand the factors that help ensure success as well as the problems involved before using it. The most critical factors for success are;

1. The accurate assessment of the parties and how best to manage the new entity in light of the ensuing relationships. The joint venture will be more effective if the managers can work well together. Without this chemistry, the joint venture has a low likelihood of success and may even cause the business to fail.

2. The degree of symmetry between the partners. This symmetry goes beyond chemistry to objectives and resource capabilities. When one partner feels that he or she is bringing more to the table, or when one partner wants profits and the other desires product outlet (as in the case of the Asaki-Dow international joint venture), problems arise. For a joint venture to be successful, the managers in each parent company as well as those in the new entity must concur on the objectives of the joint venture and the level of resource that will be

provided. Good relationship must be nurtured between the managers in the joint venture and those in each parent company.

3. The expectation of the results of the joint venture must be reasonable. For too often, at least one of the partners feels that a joint venture will be the cure-all for other corporate problems. Expectations of a joint venture must be realistic.

4. The timing must be right. With environments constantly, industrial conditions being modified, and markets evolving, a particular joint venture could be a success one year and a failure the next. Intense competition leads to a hostile environment and increases the risks of establishing a joint venture. Some environments are just not conducive to success. An entrepreneur must determine whether the joint venture will offer opportunities for growth or will penalize the company, for example, by preventing it from entering certain markets.

A joint venture is not a panacea for expanding the entrepreneurial venture. Rather, it should be considered one of many options for supplementing the resources of the firm and responding more quickly to competitive challenges and market opportunities. The effective use of joint ventures as a strategy for expansion requires the entrepreneur to carefully appraise the situation and the potential partner. Other strategic alternatives to the joint venture-such as acquisition, mergers and leverage buyouts-should also be considered.

COLLABORATIONS AND CO-BRANDING

Collaboration is the process of cooperative agreement of two or more organizations which may or may not have previous relationship of working together to achieve a common goal. It is the beginning to pool resources like knowledge, experience and sharing skills of team members to effectively contribute to the development of a product rather working on narrow tasks as an individual team member in support to the development. Such collaborations are the foundation for concepts like concurrent engineering or integrated product development.

Collaboration is a win-win methodology. It means that both the organizations insist upon each other to gain equal profits with no negative attitude of acquiring each other's possessions.

Effective collaboration can be obtained by the following actions:

The organizations must get involved in the process from the beginning and avail the necessary resources for collaboration.

The work culture in the organization must encourage teamwork, cooperation and collaboration.

There must be effective team work and cooperation among the employees of both the organizations to achieve the goal.

Systematic approach of product development process must be based on sharing of information, technology etc.

Co-branding involves the process of combining two or more brands into a single product or service. It is becoming a positive way to associate different brands and develop a strong brand in the market. It creates synergy among the various brands. An organized co-branding strategy leads the co brand partners to a win-win situation and helps in realizing large demands in the market.

The co-branding agreement includes the important aspects such as rights, obligations, and restrictions that are abiding to both the organizations. It also includes important provisions and the needs must be carefully drafted to provide clear guidelines to the involved organizations'. The organizations form co-branding to accomplish many goals which include expansion of customers, obtain financial benefits, respond to the needs of customers, strengthening its competitive position, introducing new product with strong image and to gain operational benefits.

It is more frequently used in the field of fashion and apparels. It can also be used for promoting campaigns, using cartoons on T-shirts, logos, distributing through branded retailer etc.

Example: The sportswear giant Nike formed co-branding agreements with Philips consumer electronic products. The Philips electronic products will contain Nikes logos and it is mainly marketed in United States since the market share of Philips is not much impressive. The newly introduced digital audio player and portable CD players of Philips will be unveiled with the Nike logo to enhance profits in the market share in United States.

TECHNOLOGICAL PARTNERING

It is the process of associating the technologies of two different companies to achieve a common goal. The two organizations work as co-owners in business and share the profits and losses. The technologies of individual organizations are shared to achieve desired outcome. The required resources like knowledge, machinery, and expertise are collaborated between the organizations.

Example: The software giant, Infosys Technologies Ltd. has entered into partnership with US based NVIDIA, GPU inventor and the world's visual technologies giant. The purpose of this partnering is to develop NVIDIA CUDA (Compute Unified Device Architecture). This technology is viewed as the next big revolution in the field of technology in lending high performance in computing. The software helps the developers of various applications to tap into the previously uncultivated power of the GPU. This will enable certain applications to achieve high performance. The capacity of CUDA is expected to multiply fifty times the performance of existing computing and reduce the run time to advance the user enterprise.

CONTRACTUAL AGREEMENTS

It is the process of agreement with specific terms between two or more organisations which guarantee in performing a specific task in return for a valuable benefit. The contractual agreement is the heart of business dealings. It is the most significant areas of legal concern and involves variations in certain situations and complexities.

The organizations require analyzing fundamental factors before involving in contractual agreements. The elements to be analyzed are:

It is necessary to identify the type of offer being laid by the organization to make an agreement.

The acceptance of the information involved in offer which results in meeting the market needs.

The organizations are required to recognize the strong commitment towards the contractual agreement.

Systematic scheduling of the process involved in manufacturing product without any hindrances to both the organizations.

Discover the terms and conditions for manufacturing the product and the guarantee of the organizations in fulfilling it.

The contract agreement includes several documents such as letters, orders, offers and counteroffers.

There are various types of contractual agreements. They are:

i. ***Conditional:*** It is based on occurrence of an event.

ii. ***Joint and several:*** The organizations promise to perform together but still they possess individual responsibilities.

iii. ***Implied:*** The judicial court will determine the contract between the organisations based on circumstances. The parties will be able to buy all manufactured products, enter into a contract to supply others requirements, or renewal of the existing contract.

OUTSOURCING

It is the process of entering into a contract with an organization or a person to perform a particular function. Most of the organizations outsource the work in numerous ways. The function being outsourced is considered as noncore to the organization.

The external firms that provide outsourcing services are called as third parties or it is commonly called as service providers. The concept of outsourcing existed from the era of work specialization. Usually organizations adopt this concept to carry out narrow functions such as payrolls, billing, and data entry. Since most organizations lack in many resources, it outsources these processes to other organizations which consists of specialized tools, facilities and trained personnel.

The four stages involved in the process of outsourcing are:

The first phase involves strategic thinking for developing the organizational philosophy about the role of business activity outsourcing.

The second phase is the process of evaluating and selecting the appropriate outsourcing projects and choosing the potential location for the work force.

Third phase is the process of contractual agreement such that the business activities are worked legally in terms of pricing and service level agreement (SLA) terms.

The final phase is to outsource management to refine the present working relationship between client and outsourcing service providers.

Example: Tatvasoft is an Indian outsourcing company that offers software development services to its clients in United States, Canada and Australia. They provide software outsourcing services and solutions with the focus on secure, scalable, and reliable business systems. The key benefits of outsourcing are cost efficiency, availability of trained staff, flexible manpower utilization, and risk minimization.

OTHER METHODS

The various other methods in forming strategic alliances can include the following:

i) ***Affiliate marketing:*** It is the process of revenue sharing between the website owner and the online merchant. This process includes the website owner to advertise the merchant's products or send the potential customers to the merchant's website. It provides added advantage to both the website owner and the merchant, since the website owner earns money in advertising and the merchants products are advertised globally instead of self marketing. Example: amazon.com was the pioneer of affiliate marketing in promoting various products of the merchants.

ii) ***Technology licensing:*** It is the contractual agreements where trademarks intellectual property and trade secrets are licensed to an external organization. The main disadvantage of licensing is the loss of control over the technology. When it belongs to other organization, there are chances of exploitation.

iii) ***Product licensing:*** This is similar to technology licensing. The only difference is that it deals with manufacturing and selling of certain products. The organizations owning the product license is provided with an opportunity to sell products within certain geographical area. The license allows selling the products within the prescribed boundary.

iv) ***Franchising:*** It is a quick process of achieving a successful objective nationwide. The organization pays certain amount of fee in setting up franchise and agrees to constant payments so that the process is financially risk-free for the organization.

v) ***Sharing R&D:*** The organizations set up strategic alliances to venture into research field. The main purpose of the organizations is to embark in the field of research and development to form a new entity.

vi) ***Distributors:*** Most of the organizations market their products by outsourcing it to various companies. These companies act as distributors where each one is located in different geographical areas. This ensures the effective distribution of products and provides employment opportunities in the various geographical areas.

INTERNATIONAL CORPORATE LEVEL STRATEGY STRATEGY

The company's expect to create value through the implementation of a business level strategy and a corporate strategy. The following three are international corporate level strategy dicuss below:

1. Multi Domestic Strategy

Multi domestic strategy and operating decisions are decentralized to strategic business units (SBU) in each country. *Examples:* One of the nations most popular hamburger chains is an example of a multi domestic strategy. The company researches each country's local customs and foods before creating its menu items and opening up a store. For example, the restaurants stores in India do not sell any sandwiches made with beef, since the Indian culture sees cows as sacred.

2. Global Strategy

Global strategy products are standardized across national markets. *Example:* GE, Apple, Sony and Gillette pursue a global strategy by competing in all markets, providing the same product for each market, strong centralized control, identifying customer needs and wants across international borders, and locating value adding activities where they can achieve the lowest cost.• Boeing's global R&D network – UK, Italy, (collobration) – Spain, Australia, Russia (FDI)

3.Transactional Strategy

Transnational strategy seeks to achieve both global efficiency and local responsiveness, Example: A very well-known cola soft drink is one example of a transnational product. This company's beverage recipe is kept secret and has not changed in many years. The product is sold in over 200 countries worldwide, and this beverage company retains exactly the same beverage formulation in each country. The bottle's label may reflect the local language, but the logo and contents remain the same.

INTERNATIONAL BUSINESS LEVELSTRATEGY

1. Factor Of Production

A country creates its own important factors such as skilled resources and technological base.The stock of factors at a given time is less important than the extent that they are upgraded and deployed. Local disadvantages in factors of production force innovation. Adverse conditions such as labor shortages or scarce raw materials force firms to develop new methods, and this innovation often leads to a national comparative advantage. *Examples:* Indian BPO sector. Japans relative lack of raw materials

2. Demand Conditions

When the market for a particular product is larger locally than in foreign markets, the local firms devote more attention to that product than do foreign firms, leading to a competitive advantage when the local firms begin exporting the product. A more demanding local market leads to national advantage. A strong, trend-setting local market helps local firms anticipate global trends.

We can take the case of Germany which has some of the worlds premier automobile companies like Mercedes, BMW, Porsche. German auto companies have dominated the world when it comes to the high-performance segment of the world automobile industry. General electric, In Indian BPO sector.

3. Related And Supporting Industries

When local supporting industries are competitive, firms enjoy more cost effective and innovative inputs. This effect is strengthened when the suppliers themselves are strong global competitors. *Example:* Silicon Valley in the USA and Silicon Glen in the UK are techno clusters of high-technology industries which includes individual computer software & semi-conductor firms. In Germany, a similar cluster exists around chemicals, synthetic dyes, textiles and textile machinery.

4. Firm Strategy Structure and Rivalry

Local conditions affect firm strategy. In Porters Five Forces model, low rivalry made an industry attractive. While at a single point in time a firm prefers less rivalry, over the long run more local rivalry is better since it puts pressure on firms to innovate and improve. In fact, high local rivalry results in less global rivalry. Local rivalry forces firms to move beyond basic advantages that the home country may enjoy, such as low factor costs.

As an example, the Japanese automobile industry with 8 major competitors (Honda, Toyota, Suzuki, Isuzu, Nissan, Mazda, Mitsubishi, and Subaru) provide intense competition in the domestic market, as well as the foreign markets in which they compete. Local rivalry have forced firms to move beyond basic advantages. examples Infosys , Wipro.

Japanese factor conditions: Japan has a relatively high number of electrical engineers per capita. Japanese demand conditions: The Japanese market was very demanding because of the written language. Large number of related and supporting industries with good technology, for example, good miniaturized components since there is less space in Japan. Domestic rivalry in the Japanese fax machine industry pushed innovation and resulted in rapid cost reductions.

CASE STUDY

Sahni Auto Industris

Sahni Auto Industries is a manufacturer and exporter of Autoparts with an annual turnover of Rupees one thousand crores. It employs about 200 persons in its factory in Punjab and its other offices in India and abroad.

The Personnel Administration and Human Resources Department of the company is headed by Mr. Amit Kapoor the Chief Personnel Manager. Mr. Amit Kapoor, an automobile Engineer joined the company 5 years ago as Product Development Manager. After a successful stint of 4 years as Product Development Manager, he was transferred to Personnel Administration and Human Resources Department as the Chief Personnel Manager as a part of Career development plan. Mr. Vikas, MBA in Human Resources from a renowned Business school, joined the company as Personnel Manager only 3 months back. He reports to Mr. Amit Kapoor the Chief Personnel Manager. He handles all routine personnel and industrial relations matters.

One day, during informal discussion with Mr. Amit Kapoor, Mr. Vikas suggested him of linking Human Resources Management with Company's strategic goals and objectives to further improve busness performance and also to develop Organisational culture that fosters more innovative ideas. He also advocated creating abundant 'Social Capital' on the ground that people tend to be more productive in an environment which has trust and goodwill embedded init rather than which is highly hierarchical and formal. Mr. Amit Kapoor disagreed with Mr, Vikas and told him that the role of Human Resources Department was only peripheral to the business and all his suggestions about its strategic role were beyond the purview of Personnel Administration and Human Resources Department. After this, Mr. Vikas started having number of arguments with Mr. Amit Kapoor in several issues relating to personnel and industrial relations since he felt that a person with a degree in Huma Resources Management was in a far better position to run Personnel Administration and Human Resources Department. Mr. Amit Kapoor the Chief Personnel Manager had often shown his displeasure on Mr. Vikas's argumentative tendency and had made it known to the General Manager.

The General Manager called Mr. Amit Kapoor in his office to inform him that he has been elected for an overseas assignment. He further told him to find a suitable person as his successor; he even suggested Mr. Vikas as a possible candidate. Mr. Amit Kapoor, however, selected Mr. Balram, who was working as Training Manager in a Multinational Company for the last 5 years. Mr. Vikas, soon started having arguments with Mr. Balram also over number of issues relating to industrial relations since he felt that he had no experience in handling industral relations matters. Mr. Balram now realised that Mr. Vikas was trying to make things difficult for him. After a series of meetings with the General Manager, Mr. Balram eventually succeeded in convincing him to transfer Mr. Vikas to an office outside Punjab. On learning about his impending transfer, Mr. Vikas wrote a letter to the General Manager giving details of various instances, when Mr. Balram had shown his incompetence in handling problematic situations. When asked for explanation by the General Manager, Mr. Balram had refuted almost all the allegations. The General Manager accepted his explanation and informed Mr. Vikas that most of his allegations against Mr. Balram were unwarranted and baseless. He further advised him to avoid confrontation with Mr. Balram. Mr. Vikas then wrote a letter to the Chairman repeating all the allegations against Mr. Balram. On investigation, the Chairman found most of the allegations true. He then called all the three the General Manager, the Chief Personnel Manager and the Personnel Manager in his office and implored them to forget the past and henceforth to work in coordination with each other in an environment of Trust and Goodwill.

Questions:

(1) Identify and discuss the major issues raised in the case.

(2) Comment on the recruitment of the two Chief Personnel Managers.

(3) Would you justify Mr. Vikas's argumentative tendency with the Chiefs? Give reasons for your answer.

(4) Do you agree with suggestion offered by Mr. Vikas to Human Resources Management with the company's strategic goals? If yes, suggest prominent areas where Human Resources Department can play role in this regard.

REVIEW QUESTIONS

Conceptual Types

1. What is Competitive Strategy?
2. What are the risks of following a best-cost provider strategy? ***(VTU, MBA, June-2010)***
3. What are strategic alliances?
4. Why do many alliances break apart?
5. What is collaborative partnership?

Analytical Types

1. Discuss the nature and significance of competitive advantage ***(VTU, MBA, June-2011)***
2. Define competitive advantage. Explain generic building blocks of competitive advantage. ***(VTU, MBA, Dec-2012)***
3. Explain the generic strategic adopted at business. ***(VTU, MBA, Dec-2012)***
4. Explain low cost provider strategy.
5. Write short notes on differentiation Strategy.
6. Discuss best cost provide strategy.
7. Explain focused strategy.
8. Write note on collaboration parnership.
9. How do mergers and acquisitions strengthen a firm's competitiveness?
10. Why do mergers fail? Why do acquisitions fail? Explain.
11. Explain Outsourcing as a strategy.
12. Explain International business level strategy.

Descriptive Types

1. Explain with example how the generic competitive strategies related to the company's.
2. Explain with example, how the firm generic competitive strategies relate to the company's quest for competitive advantage. ***(VTU, MBA, Dec-2011)***
3. Explain the risks associated with each of the three generic strategies.
4. Explain the significant differentiation strategies with examples.

5. What are different strategies for entering new business?
6. How is competitive advantage protected by using defensive strategies?
7. How do cooperative strategies lend competitive advantage to a firm? Discuss
8. What do you mean by a multicountry strategy and a global strategy Explain with examples, how a multicountry strategy differs from a global strategy.

(VTU, MBA, Jan-2010)

*****

Module-6

Business Planning in Different Environment

Unit

Syllabus

Business Planning in different environments – Entrepreneurial Level Business planning – Multi stage wealth creation model for entrepreneurs– Planning for large and diversified companies – brief overview of Innovation, integration, Diversification, Turnaround Strategies - GE nine cell planning grid and BCG matrix.

BUSINESS ENVIRONMENT

Business may be understood as the organized efforts of an enterprise to supply consumers with goods and services for a profit. Businesses vary in size, as measured by the number of employees or by sales volume etc. But, all businesses share one common purpose that is to earn profits.

The purposes of business that goes beyond earning profits are:

– an important institution in society

– for the supply of goods and services

– creating job opportunities

– offering better quality of life

– contributing to the economic growth of the country.

Hence, it is understood that the role of business is crucial from the point of view of individuals and national society as well. Society cannot do without business. Similarly, it requires no emphasis that business needs society as much. Modern business is dynamic. If there is any single word that can best describe today's business, it is 'change'. It is a 'change' that makes the companies spend substantially on research and development to survive in the market. Environment refers to all forces, which have a bearing on the functioning of business. They can be forces of economic, social, political and technological factors, apart from internal forces of the organisation. Environment factors are largely if not totally, external and beyond the control of individual industrial enterprises and their managements. The business environment poses threats to a firm or offers immense opportunities for potential market exploitation. The success of every business depends on adapting itself to the environment within which it functions. For example, when there is a change in the government polices, the business has to make the necessary changes to adapt it to the new policies. Similarly, a change in the technology may render the existing products obsolete, as we have seen that the introduction of computer has replaced the typewriters; the color television has made the black and white television out of fashion. Again a change in the fashion or customers' taste may shift the demand in the market for a particular product, e.g., the demand for jeans reduced the sale of other traditional wear. All these aspects are external factors that are beyond the control of the business. So the business units must have to adapt themselves to these changes in order to survive and succeed in business. Hence, it is very necessary to have a clear understanding of the concept of business environment and the nature of its various components.

Meaning of Business Environment

Business environment is an environment in which business is conducted. Business environment encompasses all those factors that affect a company's operations; including customers, competitors, suppliers, distributors, industry trends, substitutes, regulations, government activities, the economy, demographics, social and cultural factors, innovations, and technological developments.

An example of a business environment is a business office, such as an insurance office because they conduct the business of selling insurance to people.

FEATURES OF BUSINESS ENVIRONMENT

The main features of business environment are as follows:

1. ***Totality of external forces:*** Business environment is the sum total of all things external to business firms and, as such, is aggregated in nature.
2. ***Specific and general forces:*** Business environment includes both specific and general forces. Specific forces (such as investors, customers, competitors and suppliers) affect individual enterprises directly and immediately in their day-to-day working. General forces (such as social, political, legal and technological conditions) have impact on all business enterprises and thus may affect an individual firm only indirectly.
3. ***Dynamic nature:*** Business environment is dynamic so that it keeps on changing whether in terms of technological improvement, shifts in consumer preferences or entry of new competition in the market.
4. ***Uncertainty:*** Business environment is largely uncertain as it is very difficult to predict future happenings, especially when environment changes are taking place too frequently as in the case of information technology or fashion industries.
5. ***Relativity:*** Business environment is a relative concept since it differs from country to country and even region to region. Political conditions in the USA, for instance, differ from those in India, China or Pakistan. Similarly, demand for Sarees may be fairly high in India whereas it may be almost non-existent in France.

IMPORTANCE OF BUSINESS ENVIRONMENT

There is a close and continuous interaction between the business and its environment. This interaction helps in strengthening the business firm and using its resources more effectively. As stated above, the business environment is multifaceted, uncertain, and dynamic in nature which has a far-reaching impact on the survival and growth of the business. To be more specific, proper understanding of various aspects of business environment such as social, political, legal and economic helps the business in the following ways:

(i) First Mover Advantage

Early identification of opportunities helps an enterprise to be the first to exploit them instead of losing them to competitors. For example, Maruti Udyog became the leader in the small car market because it was the first to recognize the need of small cars in India.

(ii) Identification of Threats

Identification of possible threats helps in taking corrective and improving measures to survive the competition. For instance; if an Indian firm finds that a foreign multinational is entering the Indian market, it can meet the threat by adopting measures like, by improving the quality of the product, reducing cost of the production, engaging in aggressive advertising, and so on.

(iii) Coping with Rapid Changes

All types of enterprises are facing increasingly dynamic environment. In order to effectively cope with these significant changes, firms must understand and examine the environment and develop suitable course of action.

(iv) Improving Performance

The enterprises that continuously monitor their environment and adopt suitable business practices are the ones which not only improve their present performance but also continue to succeed in the market for a longer period.

(v) Giving Direction for Growth

The interaction with the environment leads to opening up new frontiers of growth for the business firms. It enables the business to identify the areas for growth and expansion of their activities.

(vi) Meeting Competition

It helps the firms to analyse the competitors' strategies and formulate their own strategies accordingly in order to cope with the rapidly increasing competition.

(vii) Image Building

Environmental understanding helps the business organisations in improving their image by showing their sensitivity to the environment within which they are working. For example, in view of the shortage of power, many companies have set up Captive Power Plants (CPP) in their factories to meet their own requirement of power and saving to loss of energy in transmission.

(viii) Continuous Learning

Environmental analysis makes the task of managers easier in dealing with business challenges. The managers are motivated to continuously update their knowledge, understanding and skills to meet the predicted changes in realm of business.

GOALS OF THE BUSINESS ENVIRONMENT

Following are main goals of business environment:

1. Knowledge of Information

By studying the business environment, we can know the changes of business. This information is very useful for any business. Every businessman should aware current environment of business. With this, he can think the future of his business in such environment.

2. Basis of Decisions

One of the main goals of the business environment is that it can provide all the information which is needed for taking good decisions. Suppose, you completed your internal business environment study. With this study, you can take decision relating to purchase, sale, salary and price because you know your competitor, you know your suppliers and you know your customers.

3. Helpful in making of Policies

For making good business policies, we need to know and scan business through business environment.

4. Technological Planning

Today, technology is changing very fast. So, you have to study technological environment. With this, you can make better technological planning of your business.

5. Survive in the Business

Sometime industry may face recession. Production may be unlimited but sales will be limited. Only that business will survive who estimate this entire situation in advance through business environment study.

DIMENSIONS OF BUSINESS ENVIRONMENT

The several dimensions of business environment are given below:

A. ECONOMIC ENVIRONMENT

Economic environment consists of economic factors that influence the business in a country. These factors include gross national product, corporate profits, inflation rate, employment, balance of payments, interest rates consumer income etc.

In a developing country, the low income may be the reason for the very low demand for a product.

Economic environment refers to that entire economic factor which has a bearing functioning of the business unit. Business depends on the economic environment for all the needed inputs. It also depends on the economic environment to sell the finished goods.

Components of the Economic Environment

The economic environment comprises of:

(i) ***Income and wealth:*** Income in an economy is measured by GDP, GNP and per capita income. High values of these factors show a progressive economic environment.

(ii) ***Employment levels:*** High employment represents a positive picture of the economy. However, there are many forms of unemployment, including partial employment and disguised unemployment.

(iii) ***Productivity:*** This is the output generated from a given amount of inputs. High levels of productivity support the economic environment.

Importance of Economic Environment

The competent and successful management must be capable of adapting to the economic environment. The knowledge of the economic environment helps in:

i) ***Capitalizing early opportunities:*** Environment friendly enterprise is the first movers to avail of the existing opportunities of resources to grab the market. These enterprises do not loose emerging opportunities to their competitors. For example: Asian pains have been losing their market to Good lass Nerolac because of their failure to match their technology with Cathodic Electro Deposition (CED) technology, which helped the competitor to grab the opportunity of meeting 90% paint requirement of Maruti Udyog.

ii) ***Activating management to changing needs:*** The knowledge of environmental changes sensitizes the management to make strategy to cope with the emerging problems.

For example, The turmoil in the USSR resulted in the loss of market to many companies like Hoechst. In order to meet the situation Hoechst divested its manufacturing facility in favors of IPCA Laboratories Ltd.

iii) ***Image building:*** Environmental understanding by the management builds image of the company in the minds of the people. They feel that the company is sensitive and responsive to their needs and problems. For example: G. E is said to be image conscious. It divested its computer and air-conditioning business because they could not attain 1st or 2nd position in the business as per their policy. Now they are snickering to out sourcing in India, aircraft engineering, plastic etc.

iv) ***Basis of strategy:*** Strategists can gather qualitative information regarding business environment and utilizing them in formulating effective plants. For example: ITC Hotels foresaw bright opportunities in the travel and tourism industry and started building hotels in India and abroad.

v) ***Intellectual stimulation:*** Knowledge of environment changes provides intellectual stimulation to planners and decision-making authorities. They can do it by paying more attention to people by listening to their problems and suggestion. They can also eliminate procedure complexities in a visible way. The drastic and dynamic steps will definitely keep the company better placed.

vi) ***Continuous learning:*** Environmental scanning provides continuing broad based learning to be executives. Reliance adopted the policy of decentralization and empowered their managers to close the deal themselves even regarding price. In 1993 managers were require to chat with the proprietress on alternate days for 15 minutes. The process made them so competent that now the managers are required to chat only three times in a month. It shows that continuous learning made the managers competent to take independent decision.

Impact of Economic Environment on Business

Any business organization has one goal, to maximize profit. The process of maximizing revenue is simple. Evaluate need for customers, and provide appropriate provide, within top quality and quantity. There are nevertheless many factors which affect this simple operation. These elements are often categorized as macro as well as mini, internal and external, technical as well as non-technical. All the same, the actual product sales, production and procurement of the business organizations, straight or not directly depends upon these types of elements. Therefore, it will find which entrepreneurs carefully analyze and ponder upon the economic elements impacting business companies. The impact of economic environment on business considers the following concepts:

i) Demand and offer

The need and offer are 2 primary elements that affect the working associated with a business design. The need is the will as well as capability of shoppers to buy a specific item and the provide may be the ability of the company to provide for the need for customers. It should be mentioned that all the standards which are included in this list are inter-connected. You may even study need and supply analysis.

ii) Marginal and Complete Power

Utility may be the quantity of fulfillment, that's produced by consumers from consumption of goods. This so happens that whenever continuous and successive use of units of the same goods, the fulfillment that's experienced by consumer begins decreasing. This often results into short term or even long-term fall of sales. Some organizations get ready for the actual launch of some other brand name before the fall in power and sales is experienced. The actual release of new brand, helps to ensure that the actual revenue pattern from the company does not drop. Decreasing power is among the exterior elements affecting business. You may even read more on diminishing minor utility.

iii) Cash as well as Finance

Financial allows for financial and financial policies which impact company as well as the clients from the business. Money in circulation dictates the having to pay power or rather the demand of the actual customers and also the financial facility dictates the borrowing capability of people along with the business.

iv) Financial Development and growth

Financial development dictates the quantity of finances that the society in particular is actually earning as well as improvement signifies the amount of money that's being spent in to channels associated with long-term up-gradation. Amongst all the financial elements affecting business environment, improvement is an essential one, since the company needs to focus on the actual need for a good economically dynamic society.

v) Income and Employment

An additional very important facet of the economic climate that impacts the significant from the business may be the degree of work as well as rate of earnings. The actual for each capita income as well as density of work determines the speed of need, denseness associated with need and also the purchasing power of those.

vi) Common Price Level

An additional very important facet of the actual economy, which impacts the business, is the general price levels from the goods which additionally modify the product sales from the business. Expenses of recyclable, having to pay power of individuals, price of production and fir ally, cost of transport are a few of the important components that determine the general cost level and also, the actual product sales from the firm.

vii) Industry Cycles

Industry series are the changing expenses of products as well as commodities within an economic climate. Increase, stability, a continual and drop are some of the important series which modify the costs away all goods for example uncooked materials, credit score, last products, and so on. Trade cycles additionally often modify the general cost degree.

Factors of Economic Environment

1. Growth strategy

Growth strategy is a strategy based on investing in companies and sectors which are growing faster than their peers. The benefits are usually in the form of capital gains rather than dividends.

2. Economic system

An economic system is the combination of the various agencies, entities that provide the economic structure that defines the social community. The economics system involves production, allocation of economic inputs, and distribution of economic outputs, Landlords and land availability, households, Capitalists, Banks and Government. It is a set of institutions and their various social relations.

3. Economic planning

Economic planning refers to any directing or planning of economic activity outside the mechanisms of the market, in an attempt to achieve specific economic or social outcomes. Planning is an economic mechanism for resource allocation and decision-making in contrast with the market mechanism. Most economies are mixed economies, incorporating elements of market mechanisms and planning for distributing inputs and outputs.

4. Industry

As per Section 2(j) of Industrial Disputes Act, 1947 "Industry" means any systematic activity carried on by co-operation between an employer and his workmen (whether such workmen are employed by such employer directly or by or through any agency, including a contractor) for the production, supply or distribution of goods or services with a view to satisfy human wants or wishes.

5. Agriculture

Agriculture is the cultivation of animals, plants, fungi, and other life forms for food, fiber, and other products used to sustain life. Agriculture was the key development in the rise of sedentary human civilization, whereby farming of domesticated species created food surpluses that nurtured the development of civilization. The study of agriculture is known as agricultural science. Agriculture generally speaking refers to human activities, although it is also observed in certain species of ant and termite.

6. Infrastructure

Infrastructure is basic physical and organizational structures needed for the operation of a society or enterprise or the services and facilities necessary for an economy to function. It can be generally defined as the set of interconnected structural elements that provide framework supporting an entire structure of development. It is an important term for judging a country or region's development.

7. Financial and fiscal factor

Financial factors consider the income statement is a simple and straightforward report on the proposed business's cash-generating ability. It is a score card on the financial performance of your business that reflects when sales is made and when expenses are incurred. It draws information from the various financial models developed earlier such as revenue, expenses, capital and cost of goods. Fiscal policy is the use of government expenditure and revenue collection (taxation) to influence the economy. Fiscal policy can be contrasted with the other main type of macroeconomic policy, monetary policy, which attempts to stabilize the economy by controlling interest rates and spending.

8. Removal of regional imbalance

Government had appointed a Fact Finding Committee (FFC) in August, 1983 under the Chairmanship of Dr. V.M. Dandekar for studying the problem of imbalance between different regions of the State to identify regional backlog on the basis of such a study and to suggest measures for removal of the regional backlog including long term measures to avoid such regional imbalance in the future.

9. Price and distribution control

During the ongoing post-communist economic transitions, the relative well-being of many people is changing rapidly, and governments are not well positioned to accurately measure individual living standards. Under such circumstances, continued price controls over basic consumer goods within the state sector, and the associated queuing, can form a serviceable device for targeting poor people for subsidies.

10. Economic reforms

India was a latecomer to economic reforms, embarking on the process in earnest only in 1991, in the wake of an exceptionally severe balance of payments crisis. The need for a policy shift had become evident much earlier, as many countries in East Asia achieved high growth and poverty reduction through policies which emphasized greater export orientation and encouragement of the private sector.

11. Per capita and national income

Per capita income or income per person is a measure of mean income within an economic aggregate, such as a country or city. It is calculated by taking a measure of all sources of income in the aggregate (such as GDP or Gross National Income) and dividing it by the total population. It does not attempt to reflect the distribution of income or wealth.

Global/International Economic Environment

The role of international economic environment is increasing day by day. If any business enterprise is involved in foreign trade, then it is influenced by not only its own country economic environment but also the economic environment of the country from/to which it is importing or exporting goods. There are various rules and guidelines for these trades which are issued by many organizations like World Bank, WTO, and United Nations etc.

International economics is concerned with the effects upon economic activity of international differences in productive resources and consumer preferences and the institutions that affect them. It seeks to explain the patterns and consequences of transactions and interactions between the inhabitants of different countries, including trade, investment and migration.

International trade is the exchange of capital, goods, and services across international borders or territories. In most countries, such trade represents a significant share of Gross Domestic Product (GDP). While international trade has been present throughout much of history, it's economic, social, and political importance has been on the rise in recent centuries. Industrialization, advanced transportation, globalization, multinational corporations and outsourcing are all having a major impact on the international trade system. Increasing international trade is crucial to the continuance of globalization.

The economic theory of international trade differs from the remainder of economic theory mainly because of the comparatively limited international mobility of the capital and labour. In that respect, it would appear to differ in degree rather than in principle from the trade between remote regions in one country.

Thus the methodology of international trade economics differs little from that of the remainder of economics. However, the direction of academic research on the subject has been influenced by the fact that governments have often sought to impose restrictions upon international trade, and the motive for the development of trade theory has often been a wish to determine the consequences of such restrictions. The branch of trade theory which is conventionally categorized as "classical" consists mainly of the application of deductive logic, originating with Ricardo's Theory of Comparative Advantage and developing into a range of theorems that depend for their practical value upon the realism of their postulates. "Modern" trade theory, on the other hand, depends mainly upon empirical analysis.

Economic globalization takes many forms. It may involve trade between individuals or businesses in one country with those of another. Globalization of this sort is as old as recorded history. Ancient coastal tribes traded with those in the mountains and deserts, each gaining prized goods they could not otherwise have enjoyed. Today, we take for granted the fact that much of what we consume or use originated elsewhere, often in a strange foreign land.

Businesses may decide to produce their products not only at home but also in other countries, either to evade the tariffs or quotas of countries where they wish of sells their products, or to cut their costs of production by hiring cheaper labour. Then globalization involves the bundling together of financial capital, technology, and other strategic inputs in order to transfer them as direct foreign investment in another country. Direct investment implies control over the assets transferred abroad. Foreign investments that don't involve control are called foreign portfolio equity investments. They are more likely to be made by financial institutions or investors like pension funds, insurance companies or investment trusts, which are interested only in a return on their investments commensurate with the risks they are taking. If returns fall or risks rise, portfolio investment is much less dependable than direct investment as a source of longer-term finance for a country's development.

The activities of transnational corporations are a still deeper form of globalization. They coordinate their activities with many entities throughout the world, producing in many places with complex networks of production and finance. This form of globalization has recently been named "alliance capitalism," in order to stress the growing importance of strategic alliances between business entities, as businesses search for ways to protect their competitive advantages and global market positions.

Governments also compete for economic advantage globally. They often support private research and development activities, finance worker retraining, protect the environment, and promote inter-firm alliances. When governments decide it is in their interest to cooperate rather than compete, they may form supranational organizations, like the International Monetary Fund

(IMF) and the World Trade Organization (WTO), or less formal regional bodies, in order to achieve shared objectives, e.g., stable macroeconomic conditions, more growth through trade, or "market-friendly" economies.

Globalization of economic activity describes the process of merging between domestic economies, businesses and societies. The phrase relates to economic activity that indicates that globalization involves the participation of companies and corporations actively contributing to the integration of international businesses. The features of the globalization of economic activity include an international development of trade, production, investments and flow of workforce.

International trade relates to the exchange of capital and goods in the global market. It is an essential component of the globalization of economic activity as business acts on an international level mainly to ensure benefiting from participation in the global trade system. Imports and exports are the aspects of international trade countries and corporations producing more than they can consume focus on exporting goods to countries which demand production. For example, a report by the European Central Bank indicates that through the satisfaction of foreign demand, countries like China and India have massively expanded their economies. These destinations are now a major focus for businesses looking to buy goods and import them in countries that require production, such as the U.S. and the E.U.

International production in the global economy or exported production as many economic scholars refer the term to is the occurrence where businesses start producing their goods in countries with cheaper labor and more relaxed tax systems. This allows big companies to produce more and pay less for the labor and the country housing their production facilities and activities. For example, the German car industry giants, as indicated by Turkish economist Lale Duruiz, have already exported their production in Turkey, benefiting from the economic treaty of the country with the E.U. for free movement of goods. Thus, the German producers pay no import fees when delivering their production in Europe and save up from labor costs and taxation.

Investing on an international level allows companies and financial organizations to participate in projects in different areas in the world depending on profitability and market situation. For example, where financial organizations from the developed world seek to expand their influence on an international level, they would offer to invest in the developing economies to either have a share in the production or to receive a fixed interest upon the investment they have made. This has happened in the relationships between United Arab Emirates and the United States as described by the U.A.E - U.S. Business Council. When first started investing in the developing Arab Union in the late 1990s, the U.S. input $540 million in investments. Seven years later, the U.S. investments had already grown by 724 percent, thus turning the Emirates into one of the most successful destinations American financial institutions have ever participated in. This increase in the investment value has contributed to the development of stronger ties between the countries and stable trade relations between businesses from both sides.

The globalization of economic activity includes the integration of people willing to work in foreign economies. The most advanced example of such integration is the European Union every citizen of the Union is allowed to participate and exercise a profession in all the member states of the organization through a freedom of movement legislation.

Economic Legislations

Besides the above policies, Governments of different countries frame various legislations which regulates and control the business. In India there are 20 essential economic laws, listed here in chronological order. They form the overall legal framework of the Indian business environment.

- **The Indian Contract Act (1872):** Established the framework within which contracts can be executed and enforced.
- **Negotiable Instruments Act (1881):** Set rules for promissory notes, bills of exchange, and checks.
- **Workmen's Compensation Act (1923):** Set the compensation to be paid by employers to injured workers.
- **Sale of Goods Act (1930):** A mercantile law that complemented the Contract Act (see above).
- **Payment of Wages Act (1936):** Established a minimum monthly salary for industrial and factory workers.
- **Industrial Disputes Act (1947):** Provided for the investigation and settlement of industrial disputes.
- **Minimum Wages Act (1948):** Fixed minimum pay rates for certain jobs.
- **Factories Act (1948):** Regulated labor in factories.
- **Employees Provident Fund and Miscellaneous Provisions Act (1952):** Established provident funds, family pensions, and other monetary benefits for factory employees.
- **Maternity Benefits Act (1961):** Regulated post-childbirth time off for female employees.
- **Payment of Bonus Act (1965):** Regulated bonus payments to be made to certain categories of employees on the basis of production, profit, or productivity.

- **Monopolies and Restrictive Trade Practices Act (1969):** Established rules to prevent unfair concentrations of economic power.
- **Indian Patents Act (1970):** Set rules for patent protection in India.
- **Payment of Gratuity Act (1972):** Provided for payment of gratuities to Indian employees in certain industries.
- **Copyright Act (1975):** Helped establish copyright protection in India.
- **Arbitration and Conciliation Act (1996):** Set up to govern arbitration issues.
- **Geographical Indications of Goods Act (1999):** Provided legal protection for goods originated in a particular area or region within India (examples include Darjeeling tea and Basmati rice).
- **Trademarks Act (1999):** Helped establish trademark protection in India.
- **Designs Act (2000):** Helped establish protection of designs.
- **Competition Act (2002):** Provided for the establishment of a commission that promotes competition, protects consumers, and ensures freedom of trade.

B. SOCIO-CULTURAL ENVIRONMENT

Socio-cultural environment is related to the social and cultural practices, beliefs and traditions within a particular society. It consists of language, aesthetics, education, religion and superstitions, attitudes, values, material culture, technology, social groups & organizations, business custom practices etc.

Social environment describes the characteristics of the society in which the organization exists. Literacy rate, customs, values, beliefs, life-style, demographic features and mobility of population are part of the social environment. It is important for managers to notice the direction in which the society is moving and formulate progressive policies according to the changing social scenario.

Meaning of Socio-cultural Environment

Socio-cultural Environment refers to the sum of all learned attitudes and behaviours that influence how a person thinks and behaves. For example, the way a person dresses, or feels about the need to express their individuality, is largely selected from a set of options available in that person's socio-cultural environment.

Factors of the Socio-cultural Environment

There are a number of factors that you will need to consider:

i) Language

Language is central to the expression of culture. Within each cultural group, the use of words reflects the life-style, attitudes and many of the customs of that group. Language is not only a key to understanding the group; it is the principal way of communicating within it. A language usually defines the parameters of a particular culture. Thus if several languages are spoken within the borders of a country, that country is seen to have as many cultures. In Canada, for instance, both English and French are spoken; in Belgium, French and Flemish; while in South Africa there are 11 official languages with a number of other African languages also spoken by the population. In addition, there are often variations within a language - different dialects, accents, pronunciations and terminology may distinguish one cultural group from another, e.g. English-speaking South Africans, the British, Americans and Australians.

ii) Material culture

Material culture relates to the way in which a society organizes and views its economic activities. It includes the techniques and know-how used in the creation of goods and services, the manner in which the people of the society use their capabilities, and the resulting benefits. When one refers to an 'industrialized' or a 'developing' nation, one is really referring to a material culture.

The material culture of a particular market will affect the nature and extent of demand for a product. Whereas a luxury item, such as a sophisticated piece of computer hardware, may have a ready market in a country such as France, demand for it may be non-existent in a developing country which is hampered by inadequate facilities and/or foreign exchange shortages. The material culture of a country may also necessitate modifications to the product. Electrical appliances, for example, may have to be adapted to cater for differences in voltage levels.

Material culture can also have a significant effect on the proposed marketing and distribution strategies. While highways and rail transport are the principal means of moving goods within the United States, rivers and canals are used extensively in certain European countries. If the company is planning to develop a manufacturing operation in a foreign market, aspects such as the supply of raw materials, power, transportation and financing need to be investigated.

iii) Aesthetics

A culture's aesthetics refer to its ideas concerning good taste and beauty as expressed in the fine arts - music, art, drama and dance - and in the appreciation of colour and form. Insensitivity to aesthetic values can not only lead to ineffective advertising and package design for products, it can also offend prospective customers.

iv) Social Organization

Social organization refers to the ways in which people relate to one another, form groups and organize their activities, teach acceptable behaviour and govern themselves. It thus comprises the social, educational and political systems of a society.

The exporter's ability to communicate depends to some extent, on the educational level of the foreign market. If the consumers are largely illiterate, advertising materials or package labels may have to be adapted to the needs of the market. In this regard, however, a company marketing baby food in a certain African country put the picture of a smiling child on the outside of the jar. The local resident assuming there were preserved babies inside avoided the product! In addition, there are unspoken signals which identify cultural differences, from certain taboos to less obvious practices like the time taken to answer a letter. In some societies, for instance, an important issue is dealt with immediately; in others, promptness is taken as a sign that the matter is regarded as unimportant, the time taken corresponding with the gravity of the issue.

In a culture where great importance is attached to the family unit, promotional efforts should be directed at the family rather than the individual. The size of the family unit differs from one culture to another. It can range from the nuclear family, i.e. mother, father, and children, to the extended family which includes many relatives and whose role is to provide protection, support and economic security to its members. In the extended family, characteristic of developing countries, consumption decision-making takes place in a larger unit and purchasing power patterns may be different from those evident in western cultures.

In any society, certain occupations carry more prestige, social status and monetary reward than others. In India, for example, there is a strong reluctance amongst people with university education to perform 'menial' tasks using their hands, even answering the telephone. In many countries, including France, Italy and Singapore, financial independence is considered essential for occupation-related prestige. In Japan, however, the majority of university-educated professionals tend to prefer working for large multinational firms than for themselves. Social organization is also evidenced in the operation of the class system, e.g. the Hindu caste system and the grouping of society members according to age, sex, political orientation, etc.

v) Religious beliefs, attitudes, values, space and time

Religious system refers to the spiritual side of a culture or its approach to the supernatural. Western culture is accepted as having been largely influenced by the Judeo-Christian traditions, while Eastern or Oriental cultures have been strongly influenced by Buddhism, Confucianism, Taoism and Hinduism. Although very few religions influence business activities directly, the impact of religion on human value systems and decision-making is significant. Thus, religion exerts a considerable influence on people's actions and outlook on life, as well as on the products they buy. In certain part of the world, such as Latin America, the influence of religion extends even beyond the individual or family and is manifested in a whole community's deep involvement in, and devotion to, the church.

A society's religious belief system is often dependent on its stage of human or economic development. Primitive tribesmen tend to be superstitious about life in general while people in technologically advanced cultures seem to have dismissed the notion of traditional religious worship and practice in favour of a more scientific approach to life and death.

The failure to consider specialized aspects of local religions has created a number of difficulties for firms. Companies have encountered problems in Asia when they incorporated a picture of a Buddha in their promotions. Religious ties are strong in this area, and the use of local religious symbols in advertising is strongly resented - especially when words are deliberately or even accidentally printed across the picture of a Buddha. One company was nearly burned to the ground when it ignorantly tried such a strategy. The seemingly minor incident led to a major international political conflict remembered for years.

Attitudes are psychological states that predispose people to behave in certain ways. Attitudes may relate, for example, to work, wealth, achievement, change, the role of women in the economy, etc.

Western cultures, for example, value individualism and promote the importance of autonomy and personal achievement needs. In contrast, in many eastern and developing countries, there is a strong sense of collectivism and the importance of social and security needs. For instance, the Hindu religion imparts a type of work ethic that considers work central to one's life but maintains that it must be performed as a service to others, not for one's own personal achievement.

Stereotypes are sets of attitudes in which one attributes qualities or characteristics to a person on the basis of the group to which that person belongs. An international business person's tendency to judge others by his or her personal and cultural standards instead of attempting to understand others in the context of their unique historical, political, economic and social backgrounds could, for example, be termed an undesirable attitude.

Values are judgements regarding what is valuable or important in life, and they vary greatly from one culture to another. People who are operating at a survival level will value food, shelter and clothing. Those with high security needs, on the other hand, may value job security, status, money, etc. From its value system, a culture sets norms, i.e. acceptable standards of behaviour.

Pepsodent reportedly tried to sell its toothpaste in regions of south-east Asia through a promotion which stressed that the toothpaste helped enhance white teeth. In this area, where some local people deliberately chewed betel nut in order to achieve the social prestige of darkly stained teeth, such an ad was understandably less than effective. The slogan "wonder where the yellow went" was also viewed by many as a racial slur.

The concept of space is different wherever one goes. In western corporate culture, the size and location of an executive's office is usually determined by his level of seniority in the company. The locality and size of an Arab business executive's office, on the other hand, are a poor indication of the person's importance.

Conversation distance between two people is learned early in life - almost completely unconsciously. A western business executive, conditioned to operating within a certain amount of personal space, may feel uncomfortable or alarmed at the closeness and physical contact displayed in the Middle East or Latin America, for example.

Time also has a different meaning in each country. Western cultures tend to perceive time in terms of past, present and future. They are orientated towards the future and in the process of preparing for it, they save, waste, make up or spend time. In South Africa, giving a person a deadline is a way of indicating the degree of urgency or relative importance of the work. In the Middle East, however, time does not usually include schedules and timetables. The time required to get something accomplished depends on the relationship. With South Africans, the more important an event is, the earlier it is planned, which is why last minute invitations are often regarded as an insult. In planning future events with Arab businesspersons, it is often advisable to keep the lead time to a week or less, because other factors may intervene and take precedence.

Some time ago, an American lost a major contract in Greece because he did not appreciate the Greek concept of time. The Greek executive could not understand the American's insistence on setting time limits on the length of their business meetings - he and his colleagues were prepared to spend as much time in discussion as they felt was necessary. The American also insisted that the senior managers involved in the transaction be responsible only for working out the general principles of the deal, with the actual details being left to subordinates. Suspicious that this represented a lack of commitment on the part of the American, the Greek called off the deal.

Many factors continuously produce cultural changes in a society - new technology, population shifts, availability of scarce resources and changing values regarding the role of education or women. Culture is thus dynamic, and exporters, particularly those involved in international travel and marketing, need to regularly assess what new products and service needs have been created, who the potential buyers and users are, and how best to reach them.

Impact of Socio-cultural Environment in Business

The relationship among business, culture and society involves a two-way interaction. Although we tend to think of business as operating according to a distinctive instrumental rationality of profit-and-loss and the 'bottom line' it is also influenced by the social-cultural setting in which it is embedded. At the same time business affects the wider culture and society profoundly. The impact of socio-cultural environment in business can be summarized as follows:

a) In estimating the demand for a product the consumer behaviour and their consumption pattern are to be understood apart from their purchasing power. Some latent needs of people, if understood properly, can be converted into demand. For example some products sold in sachets get good response due to the convenience and low cost.

b) The product features are designed by understanding the cultural background of consumers. The tastes and preference differ due to this aspect. For instances, products containing vegetable fats than animal fats are preferred by some groups, natural ingredients than chemical or artificial goods, are preferred by somebody, the food-stuffs also vary consumed by different groups.

c) The sales promotion techniques based on the understanding of cultural values of people usually become successful. The appeals are selected best suited to the attitude of people. We could see a number or advertisements based on the affection and importance of family relationships.

d) In developing human relations with workers, suppliers, middlemen and the public, it is necessary to understand the culture and mental make-ups of those people. For example workers in different regions behave differently. If this is understood conflicts with workers may be reduced.

e) The trade practices and services are designed based on the customs and habits of the people. This includes holidays, (Fridays, instead of Sundays in Muslim areas) working hours, consumer service, sales retail-outlets, demonstrations etc.

f) In introducing varieties, improvements and innovations in products, care should be taken to understand the social characteristics of people. Many products in cosmetics failed in Indian markets. We can also quote the hesitated acceptance of electric appliances and gas stoves in rural markets.

g) The general attitude of people towards consumption, savings and investment patterns also affect the overall business growth. Indian people usually don't prefer 'use and throw' goods. They prefer investing in gold than in shares and bonds.

h) Business is an activity undertaken by people whose values and attitudes are shaped by the culture and society of which they are a part. To some extent the roles we perform in business are quite discrete from other aspects of our lives and require that we adopt different behaviours and personas. However there is not, of course, a complete separation between 'work' and 'life'. We carry values and attitudes shaped by the wider culture and society into our roles as managers, employees and consumers.

i) It can be argued that capitalist business owes its historical origins and development in part to non-economic factors. Max Weber argued that the 'spirit of capitalism', or ethos of capitalist business, with its emphasis on accumulating wealth, can be traced to religious belief the 'Protestant ethic'. This religious belief encouraged the reinvestment of wealth in business rather than the pursuit of a life of luxury, thus fuelling economic growth and dynamism. A version of this theory persists today in the idea that economic success depends on the prevalence of a 'work ethic' in society which sees work as a morally desirable activity.

j) There may be concern that wearing a religious symbol may cause offence to others (customers or colleagues) of a different faith or none. An employer may want to keep religious conflicts out of the workplace or avoid putting off customers. If the policy was designed to protect the company's image and to attract customers, it seems to have back-fired on both counts.

k) Values are the terms on which we interact with business have a profound influence on our lives. Work is a central aspect of our lives and the vast majority of employees work in the private sector. We also depend very largely on the private sector to supply the goods and services we consume on a daily basis. It is not surprising, then, that business has major impacts on culture and society.

l) The culture industries make up a significant part of business activity, reflecting the shift from manufacturing to service industries in the wealthy economies. Culture has become increasingly big business as a growing share of consumer expenditure is dedicated to 'life-style' purchases rather than material necessities. This can be seen in the growth of the wide range of businesses concerned with leisure and tourism.

C. POLITICAL ENVIRONMENT

Political environment comprises political stability and the policies of the government. Ideological inclination of political parties, personal interest on politicians, influence of party forums etc. create political environment. For example, Bangalore established itself as the most important IT centre of India mainly because of political support.

Political and government environment has close relationship with the economic system and economic policy. For example, the communist countries had a centrally planned economic system. In most countries, apart from those laws that control investment and related matters, there are a number of laws that regulate the conduct of the business. These laws cover such matters as standards of products, packaging, promotion etc.

Meaning of Political Environment

Political environment means the set of activities of the government which include plans, policies, programs and controls which directly or indirectly involve with the business.

Impact of Political Environment on doing Business in India

As in any part of the world, political influence is highly essential to start a business in India. Especially if you are planning to start a multibillion business, some sort of political patronage is an absolute necessity. Not only for safeguarding the interest of the company but even to begin the process of getting the required sanctions, one requires hold in the high echelons of politics and administrative circles.

Indian society is highly plural. It is the biggest democracy in the world with multi party political system. In population, India is second to China, with nearly 1200 million people. This is the most important consumer market in the world. It is a fast developing world. India is the third largest economy in the world and second fast growing economy in Asia. It has the tremendous potential of development with huge intellectual human force. With all these advantages and the huge market potential, world super entrepreneurs are looking for business establishments in India. With the overcrowded population and the millions of hard working and qualified personals, India offers a very cheap work force to the world. Many have realized the business potential in India, started exploring the unique opportunities of investments.

During the last couple of decades, India has opened its market to world. It has absolutely become an open global market. Banking sector, Insurance sector and all fields of industrial and business are now open for multinational investment. Of course there are many obstructions to cross. And mostly all issues can overcome and establish business if you have the political patronage.

India has a plural political system. With numerous political parties, national level and state level, it is very difficult to get a consensus among all parties for starting any business. Also these political parties have patronage of many factors, caste, creed and ideologies.

D. LEGAL ENVIRONMENT

The government, in every country, regulates the business according to its defined priorities. Legal system of a country is framed by the government. The laws which are passed by the government for business operation is called legal environment.

The legal environment of a business refers to the relevant laws and regulations under which the business operates. Legal environment includes factors that provide rules, and penalties for violations, designed to protect society and consumers from unfair business practices and to protect businesses from unfair competitive practices. It assures uniform application of the laws by regulating the behavior and interactions of individuals against each other.

Needs for Legal Environment

i) Legal Environment maintain status quo in society ensuring stability and security of social order, enable individuals, maximum of freedom to assert themselves and determine the sphere within which the existence and activity of each individual will be secure and free.

ii) The principle of law provides uniformity and certainty to the administration of justice.

iii) The existence of fixed principles of law avoids the dangers of arbitrary, biased and dishonest decisions.

iv) The fixed principles of law protect administrators of justice from the errors of individual judgment.

Importance of Legal Environment

Legal environment is important because it incorporates the following lows:

i) ***Laws on Production or Sales:*** The production or sale of certain goods is prohibited, or at least severely restricted in many countries. This includes, among others, selling of dangerous drugs, guns and explosives, for instance. Aerosol cans containing CFCs, which are harmful to the environment, or more specifically, the ozone layer, are banned and no longer produced.

ii) ***Consumer Protection:*** Most countries have laws ensuring customers are being treated fairly by businesses. This includes the act regulating weights and measurements, ensuring that goods sold actually are the weight or size they are sold at, and the Trade Description Act, making misleading descriptions of products illegal.

Other laws include the Consumer Credit Act, ensuring consumers are aware of loan durations, interest rates etc when taking out a loan, as well as receiving copies of credit agreements, and the Sale of Goods Act, making it illegal to sell faulty or damaged goods. The return of goods and refunds, etc, is also governed by laws.

iii) ***Employee Protection:*** Laws to protect employees include laws against unfair discrimination based on race, color, religion, sex, or age; laws against unfair dismissal and sexual or other harassment; health and safety laws and laws regulating minimum wages. Many countries make written contracts between employer and employees mandatory.

iv) ***Tax and Financial Laws:*** These laws vary between countries, but generally regulate accountancy practices, interest rates on loans, taxes etc. Businesses are expected to provide sufficient documentation of income and expenditure, for instance.

Indian Legal Environment

Indian legal environment consists of the followings:

a) The Courts

Though India has a quasi-federal structure, the judiciary is unified. Broadly, there is a three tier structure. First, each administrative district (there are over 600 districts) is headed by a District Court. Then each State has a High Court. Since some States share the same High Court, there are 21 High Courts in India.

At the apex is the Supreme Court of India situated at New Delhi. The various High Courts can have very diverse characteristics. For instance, the High Court for the small State of Sikkim has strength of only two Judges, whereas the High Court for the State of Uttar Pradesh has about 100 Judges. The Supreme Court of India has about 25 Judges who sit in several divisions of varying strengths. Matters of fundamental significance are decided by a bench comprising of 5 Judges. Besides the broad three tier structure there are various specialized tribunals the more prominent ones being the Company Law Board; Monopolies and Restrictive Trade Practices Commission; Consumer Protection Forum; Debts Recovery Tribunal; Tax Tribunal. These Tribunals function under the supervisory jurisdiction of the High Court where they may be situated, though many of them (like the Monopolies Commission) allow an appeal directly to the Supreme Court.

b) Judiciary

The Indian judiciary is known for its independence and extensive powers. The High Court or the Supreme Court in exercise of their constitutionally conferred writ jurisdiction is empowered strike down legislation on the ground of unconstitutionality. They can and fairly routinely intervene with executive action as well on the ground of unreasonableness or unfairness or arbitrariness in State action.

Indeed Courts can even strike down an amendment to the Constitution on the ground that it violates the basic structure of the Constitution. Besides, the High Courts and the Supreme Court have adapted an activist mantle, which goes under the name of Public Interest Litigation, where under they can intervene with governmental policies if it may adversely impact the public at large or the public interest is such that it requires Court intervention.

c) The Bar

India has a unified all India Bar which means that an advocate enrolled with any State Bar can practice and appear in any court in the length and breadth of the country, including the Supreme Court of India.

Foreign lawyers are not permitted to appear in courts and the entry of foreign law firms into India (for non-court matters) has not yet been permitted though it is currently being debated and considered. However, they can appear in arbitrations.

d) Court Practice and Procedure

The influence of the British Judicial System which India imbibed continues in significant aspects. The official language for court proceedings in the High Court & the Supreme Court is English. Lawyers don a gown and a band as part of their uniform and address Judges as – "My Lord".

The procedural law of the land as well as most commercial and corporate laws is modeled on English laws. English case law is regularly referred to and relied upon in courts.

There is great emphasis on oral arguments. Almost all matters are heard extensively in open Court. Advocates are seldom restrained in oral arguments and complex hearings may well take days of arguments to conclude. Specialization is relatively a new phenomenon and most lawyers have a wide-ranging practice.

E. TECHNOLOGICAL ENVIRONMENT

Technological environment refers to the external factors in technology that impact business operations. Changes in technology affect how a company will do business. A business may have to dramatically change their operating strategy as a result of changes in the technological environment.

Technological environment includes the level of technology available in a country. It also indicates the pace of research and development and progress made in introducing modern technology in production. Technology provides capital intensive but cost effective alternative to traditional labor intensive methods. In a competitive business environment technology is the key to development.

Technological Environment is a systematic application of scientific knowledge to practical task is known as technology. Everyday there has been vast changes in products, services, life-styles and living conditions, these changes must be analyzed by every business unit and should adapt these changes. Business prospects depend also on the availability of certain physical facilities. Some products, like many consumer durables, have certain use facility characteristics. The sale of television sets, for example, is limited by the extent of the coverage of the telecasting. Similarly, the demand for refrigerators and other electrical appliances is affected by the extent of electrification and the reliability of power supply. The demand for LPG gas stoves is affected by the rate of growth of gas connections.

Technological factors sometimes pose problems. A firm, which is unable to cope with the technological changes, may not survive. Further, the differing technological environment of different markets or countries may call for product modifications. For example, many appliances and instruments in the U.S.A. are designed for 110 volts but this needs to be converted into 240 volts in countries which have that power system. Technological developments may increase the demand for some existing products. For example, voltage stabilizers help increase the sale of electrical appliances in markets characterized by frequent voltage fluctuations I power supply. However, the introduction of TV's, Fridges etc, within built voltage stabilizer adversely affects the demand for voltage stabilizers.

Advances in the technologies of food processing and preservation, packaging etc., have facilitated product improvements and introduction of new products and have considerably improved the marketability of products. The television has added a new dimension to product promotion. The advent of TV and VCP/VCR has, however, adversely affected the cinema theatres. The ıast changes in technologies also create problems for enterprises as they render plants and products obsolete quickly. Product-market-technology matrix generally has a much shorter life today than in the past. It is particularly so in the international marketing context. It may be interesting to note that almost half of Hindustan Lever's 1980 export business did not exist in 1987. In fact, as much as a third of the company's 1987 turnover was from products and markets, which were under three years of age.

Meaning of Technology

Technology refers to the method or technique for converting inputs to outputs in accomplishing a specific task. Thus, the terms 'method' and 'technique' refer not only to the knowledge but also to the skills and the means for accomplishing a task. It is the application of scientific knowledge for practical purposes. Technology is the usage and knowledge of tools, techniques, crafts, systems or methods of organization.

Definition of Technology

J.K. Galbraith defined technology as "A systematic application of scientific or other organized knowledge to practical tasks".

Importance of Technology

Technology plays a vital role in business. Over the years businesses have become dependent on technology so much so that if we were to take away that technology virtually all business operations around the globe would come to a grinding halt. Almost all businesses and industries around the world are using computers ranging from the most basic to the most complex of operations.

Technology played a key role in the growth of commerce and trade around the world. It is true that we have been doing business since time immemorial, long before there were computers; starting from the simple concept of barter trade when the concept of a currency was not yet introduced but trade and commerce was still slow up until the point when the computer revolution changed everything. Almost all businesses are dependent on technology on all levels from research and development, production and all the way to delivery. Small to large scale enterprises depend on computers to help them with their business needs ranging from Point of Sales systems, information management systems capable of handling all kinds of information such as employee profile, client profile, accounting and tracking, automation systems for use in large scale production of commodities, package sorting, assembly lines, all the way to marketing and communications. It doesn't end there, all these commodities also need to be transported by sea, land, and air. Just to transport your commodities by land already requires the use of multiple systems to allow for fast, efficient and safe transportation of commodities.

Without this technology the idea of globalization wouldn't have become a reality. Now all enterprises have the potential to go international through the use of the internet. If your business has a website, that marketing tool will allow your business to reach clients across thousands of miles with just a click of a button. This would not be possible without the internet. Technology allowed businesses to grow and expand in ways never thought possible.

The role that technology plays for the business sector cannot be taken for granted. If we were to take away that technology trade and commerce around the world will come to a standstill and the global economy would collapse. It is nearly impossible for one to conduct business without the aid of technology in one form or another. Almost every aspect of business is heavily influenced by technology. Technology has become very important that it has become a huge industry itself from computer hardware manufacturing, to software design and development, and robotics. Technology has become a billion dollar industry for a number of individuals.

Benefits of Technology in Business

The days when the Chief Information Officer (CIO) took implementation decisions and passed the responsibility down the line are passed. Today, the CIO is an individual who possesses business as well as technical skills, understands the new IT issues facing a business, and drives the IT changes from the top down. This is a clear indicator of the benefits businesses are enjoying through the implementation of technology. Today technology is an integral part of any business right from the purchase of computers and software to the implementation of network and security tools. This helps businesses to: i) Remain up-to-date, ii) Drive business forward iii) Sustain and survive competition.

Benefits of Technology in Communication

From hand-held computers to touch phones, technological advancements in the field of communication are endless. The means and the modes of communication are unlimited. Some of the benefits of technological advancements in the field of communication are:

i) ***Speed:*** time is no longer a constraint in communication.

ii) ***Clarity:*** With megapixel images and video, and high fidelity audio systems clarity in communication has become a never-before experience.

iii) ***Proximity:*** Technological advancements have made the world a smaller place to live in.

iv) ***Dissemination:*** whether spreading information, broadcasting news, or sharing knowledge, technology has made it faster, easier, and smarter.

Benefits of Technology in Education

Technological advancements in the field of education are fast evolving. Today, e-learning is a familiar and popular term. Some of the benefits of technology in this field are:

i) ***Personalized learning experience:*** Learners are able to take control and manage their own learning. They set their own goals, manage the process and content of learning, and communicate with peers.

ii) ***Immediate response:*** Most e-learning programs provide immediate feedbacks on learner assessments. Similarly there are features such as chat, discussion boards, e-libraries, etc that allow clarifications at a faster pace than in traditional classrooms.

iii) ***Self-paced:*** Learners can chart courses at their own pace. This ensures higher levels of motivation both in terms of completing the course as well as in performance.

iv) ***Greater access:*** Technological advancements have opened education to learners with learning disabilities and in remote locations.

Benefits of Technology in Healthcare

The marriage between medicine and technology has reshaped healthcare and revolutionized the medical profession. Some of the major benefits are:

i) ***Secure environment:*** Technology allows physicians and patients to interact in a secure and comfortable environment to discuss sensitive issues.

ii) ***Flexibility:*** Physicians can answer routine and less critical queries at a convenient time.

iii) ***Cost- and time-saving:*** Physicians can follow-up, provide advice, and re-direct patients to resources on the Internet. This saves cost and time by reducing office visits.

iv) ***Medical devices:*** Medical aids allow patients to continue recovery at home reducing their hospital stay.

v) ***Vulnerable population:*** Technology aids the very young, elderly, and patients with complex birth defects, chronic illnesses, and disabled children by alleviating their problems so that they can continue living in their homes.

Features of Technology

The main features of technology are as follows:

i) Technology continuously keeps changing. The time gap between idea and implementation is falling rapidly and the time between introduction and peak production is shortening considerably.

ii) Effects of technology are widespread and are reaching beyond the immediate point of technological impact.

iii) Technology is self-reinforcing. "Technology feeds on itself. Technology makes more technology possible". It acts as a multiplier to its own faster development.

iv) Technology has evolved and transformed our lives and society. Overall, it has brought about tremendous growth and benefit to mankind.

Meaning of Technological Environment

Technological environment refers to the firm's external environment in which changes in technology affect the firm's marketing effort. The changing technological environment may pose threats or present opportunities.

Social benefits of Technological Environment

Today technology pervades almost all aspects of our daily life from shopping, banking, making travel arrangements to university admissions. Some of the social benefits are:

i) ***Convenience:*** Provides a great deal of convenience in expediting personal and business transactions be it shopping, banking, or simply paying bills.

ii) **Speed:** From sending gifts to making payments everything gets a done with a few clicks.

iii) ***Communication:*** The world is a smaller place and technology allows everyone to keep in touch with their families and friends at a more affordable cost.

iv) ***Accuracy:*** Technology has reduced errors in mundane and monotonous chores, saving time and cost.

v) ***Development:*** Technology has brought about development in many fields such as medicine, government, business, education, etc.

F. NATURAL ENVIRONMENT

The natural environment encompasses all living and non-living things occurring naturally on Earth or some region thereof. The natural environment is contrasted with the built environment, which comprises the areas and components that are strongly influenced by humans. A geographical area is regarded as a natural environment.

A natural environment is an environment that encompasses all living and non-living things occurring naturally on Earth or some region thereof. The concept of the natural environment can be distinguished by components:

i) Complete ecological units that function as natural systems without massive human intervention, including all vegetation, microorganisms, soil, rocks, atmosphere and natural phenomena that occur within their boundaries.

ii) Universal natural resources and physical phenomena that lack clear-cut boundaries, such as air, water, and climate, as well as energy, radiation, electric charge, and magnetism, not originating from human activity.

PLANNING

Planning as a process involves the determination of the future course of action, that is why an action, what action, how to take action, and when to take action. These "why, what, how, and when" are related with different aspects of planning process. Why of action reveals that action has some objectives or the end result which an organization wants to achieve, what of action specifies the activities to be undertaken, how and when generate various policies, programs, procedures, and other related elements. Thus all these elements speak about futurity of action. Terry has defined Planning as " Planning is the selection and relating of facts and making and using of assumptions regarding the future in the visualization and formalization of proposed activities believed necessary to achieve desired results."

FEATURES OF PLANNING

On the basis of the definition of planning, its following features can be identified:

1. Planning is a process rather than behavior at a given point of time. This process determines the future course of action.

2. Planning is future oriented. It is primarily concerned with looking into the future. It requires forecasting of future situation in which the organization has to function. Therefore, correct forecasting of the future situation leads to correct decisions about the future course of actions.

3. Planning involves selection of suitable course of action. This means that there are several alternatives for achieving a particular objective or set of objectives. However, all of them are not equally feasible and suitable for the organization.

4. Planning is undertaken at all levels of the organization because all levels of management are concerned with the determination of the future course of action. However, its role increases in successively higher levels of management. Moreover,planning at different levels may be different in the context that at the top management level, managers are concerned about the totality of the organization and tries to relate it to the environment with-managers at lower levels may be involved in internal planning.

5. Planning is flexible as commitment is based on future conditions, which are always dynamic. As such, an adjustment is needed between the various factors and planning.

6. Planning is a pervasive and continuous managerial function involving complex processes of perception, analysis, conceptual thought, communication, decision, and action. The very pervasiveness of these planning elements makes it difficult to identify and observe them in detail.

IMPORTANCE OF PLANNING

1. ***Primacy of Planning:*** Planning precedes all other managerial functions. Since managerial operations in organizing, staffing, directing, and controlling are designed to support the accomplishment of organizational objectives, planning logically precedes the execution of all other managerial functions. Although all the functions intermesh in practice as a system of action, planning is unique in that it establishes the objectives necessary for all group effort. All other functions are performed to achieve the objectives set b the planning process.

2. ***To Offset Uncertainty and Change:*** There is continuous change in the environment and the organization has to work in accelerating change. This change is reflected in both tangible and intangible forms. Tangible changes are in the form of changes in technology, market forces, government regulations, etc. Intangible changes reflect in changes in attitudes, values, cultures, etc. In order to cope up with the requirements of such changes, organization must look ahead for its future course of action which is basically provided by planning process. Planning does not stop changes in the environment but gears the organization to take suitable actions so that it is successful in achieving its objectives.

3. ***To Focus Attention on Objectives:*** Planning focuses on organizational objectives and direction of action for achieving these objectives. Sometimes people in the organization may not be specific about its objectives because of lack of clarity and precise definitions. For example, often we take profit as the objective of a business organization. It is too abstract to be pursued. In order to enforce managerial actions, it should be defined more precisely. When planning action is taken, these objectives are made more concrete and tangible. The objectives are defined in more meaningful terms so that managerial actions are possible. For example, even if the organizational objective is profit earning, planning activity will specify how much profit is to be earned looking into all facilitating and constraining factors.

4. ***To Help in Coordination:*** Though all managerial functions lead to coordination in the organization, real beginning is made at the level of planning stage. The overall plans unify interdepartmental activities and consequently restrict the area of freedom in the development of purely departmental plans. Thus, various departments work in accordance with the overall plan, and harmony is achieved.

5. ***To Help in Control:*** Control involves the measurement of accomplishment of events against plans and the correction of deviations to assure the achievement of objectives as set by the plans. Thus, control is exercised in the context of planning action as standards against which actual results are to be compared are set up through planning. At the control stage, an attempt is made to monitor the performance on continuous basis so that immediate action is taken if anything goes wrong.

6. ***To Increase Organizational Effectiveness:*** Planning ensures organizational effectiveness in several ways. The concept of effectiveness is that the organization is able to achieve its objectives within the given resources. Thus, for effectiveness, it is not only necessary that resources are gut to the best of their efficiency but also that they are put in a way which ensures their maximum contribution to organizational objectives. In fact, taking appropriate planning can do this. Planning states the objectives of the organization in the context of given resources. Therefore, each resource of the organization has a specific use at a particular time. Thus, planning along with control ensures that resources are put in action in a way in which these have been specified. If this is done, organization will achieve effectiveness.

ENTREPRENEURIAL LEVEL BUSINESS PLANNING

Firm-Level Planning

A business owner has to choose a model of planning, such as strategic planning, that will guide the entire business. Planning is about setting goals that can be timed and measured to determine if a company meets the desired level of performance. Without a strategic plan, a business owner will make more reactive decisions in response to the market. With a strategic plan, all of the firm's employees will know what direction to take.

Department-Level Planning

Once a business has grown to a certain point, a business owner or manager will begin to organize employees into departments, teams or business functions. Employees will support a specific product, perform a specific function or serve customers in a defined market. At this level, regardless of business size, a department or team manager must collaborate with the owner or company manager and determine what part of the firm's goals will require his department's tactical plan. This should be a two-way process so that the staff will buy into goal setting and give their input.

Operational Planning

It used to be that middle-level managers created a tactical plan, or how the different units of the company will implement the goals in a broad sense, and that lower-level managers created operational goals. Now, many organizations do not have middle-level managers. Therefore, department-level managers end up doing tactical and operational planning. This level of planning requires that a manager consider which employee or group will be responsible for each department goal at the operational level. This will include looking at the specific activities that employees perform and how they interlace to support the department's goals.

Employee Planning

At the direction of their manager, individuals can write goals to illustrate specifically how they will help achieve operational goals. These should be as specific, measurable, achievable, relevant and timed as the goals at the other levels of planning. Individuals are also a good source of information about the product or service they support. They can suggest ways for the company to match the strengths of the business with current opportunities in the market.

BRIEF OVERVIEW OF INNOVATION

The underlying rationale of the grand strategy of innovation is to create a new product life cycle and thereby make similar existing products obsolete. Few innovative ideas prove profitable because the research, development, and premarketing costs of converting a promising idea into a profitable product are extremely high.

- Innovation is needed for both consumer and industrial markets expect periodic changes and improvements in the products offered.
- Firms seeking to make innovation as their grand strategy seek to reap the initial high profits associated with customer acceptance of a new or greatly improved product.
- As the products enters the maturity stage these companies start looking for a new innovation.
- The underlining rationale is to create a new product life cycle and thereby make similar existing products obsolete.
- This strategy is different from the product development strategy in which the product life cycle of an existing product is extended.e.g. Polaroid which heavily promotes each of its new cameras until competitors are able to match its technological innovation; by this time Polaroid normally is prepared to introduce a dramatically new or improved product.

INTEGRATION

The integration is derived from the Latin word integer, meaning whole or entire) generally means combining parts so that they work together or form a whole. A company performs a number of activities to transform an input to output. These activities include right from the procurement of raw materials to the production of finished goods and their marketing and distribution to the ultimate consumers

Horizontal Integration: When a firm's long-term strategy is based on growth through the acquisition of one or more similar firms operating at the same stage of the production-marketing chain, its grand strategy is called horizontal integration. Horizontal integration (also known as lateral integration) simply means a strategy to increase your market share by taking over a similar company. This take over / merger / buyout can be done in the same geography or probably in other countries or market segments or increasing the range of products / services to current markets, or a compination of both. Examples of Horizontal Integration are many and available in plenty. Especially in case of the technology industry, where mergers and acquisitions happen in order to increase the reach of an entity.

Vertical Integration: When a firm's grand strategy is to acquire firms that supply it with inputs (such as raw materials) or are a customer for its outputs (such as warehouses for finished products), vertical integration is involved. Backward integration is the desire to increase the dependability of the supply or quality of the raw materials used as production inputs. Forward integration is a preferred grand strategy if great advantages accrue to stable production. Some increased risks are associated with both horizontal and vertical integration. For horizontally integrated firms, the risks stem from increased commitment to one type of business. For vertically integrated firms, the risks result from the firm's expansion into areas requiring strategic managers to broaden the base of their competence and to assume additional responsibilities.

When a company expands its business into areas that are at different points on the same production path, such as when a manufacturer owns its supplier or distributor. Vertical integration can help companies reduce costs and improve efficiency by decreasing transportation expenses and reducing turnaround time, among other advantages. However, sometimes it is more effective for a company to rely on the expertise and economies of scale of other vendors rather than be vertically integrated.

Examples of vertical integration include:

A solar power company that produces photovoltaic products and also manufacturers the cells, wafers and modules to create those products would be considered vertically integrated.

The merger of Live Nation and Ticketmaster created a vertically integrated entertainment company that manages and represents artists, produces shows and sells event tickets.

TYPES OF VERTICAL INTEGRATIONS

There are basically 3 classifications of Vertical Integration namely:

Backward integration: its occur when the companies acquired to supply the firm with products, components or raw materials. Vertically integrated when it became not only a bookseller but a book publisher. As a bookseller, Amazon.com buys books from various suppliers, such as publishing companies. By becoming a publisher itself, it has integrated into its business the role of supplier and can sell books that its own publishing company publishes. Backward integration strategy is most beneficial when:

- Firm's current suppliers are unreliable, expensive or cannot supply the required inputs.
- There are only few small suppliers but many competitors in the industry.
- The industry is expanding rapidly.
- The prices of inputs are unstable.
- Suppliers earn high profit margins.
- A company has the necessary resources and capabilities to manage the new business.

Forward integration: Where the business tries to control the post production areas, namely the distribution network. Like a mobile company opening its own Mobile retail chain. If the manufacturing company engages in sales or after-sales industries it pursues a forward integration strategy. This strategy is implemented when the company wants to achieve higher economies of scale and larger market share. The forward integration strategy became very popular with the increasing internet appearance. Many manufacturing companies have built their online stores and started selling their products directly to consumers, bypassing retailers. Forward integration strategy is effective when:

- Few quality distributors are available in the industry.
- Distributors or retailers have high profit margins.
- Distributors are very expensive, unreliable or unable to meet firm's distribution needs.
- The industry is expected to grow significantly.
- There are benefits of stable production and distribution.
- The company has enough resources and capabilities to manage the new business.

Balanced integration: You guessed it right, a mix of the above two. A balanced strategy to take advantages of both the worlds.

DIVERSIFICATION

Diversification is a process of entry into a new business in the organisation either market wise or technology wise or both. Many organizations adopt a diversification strategy to minimize the risk of loss. It is also used to capitalize organizational strengths. Diversification may be the only strategy that can be used if the existing process of an organisation is discontinued due to environmental and regulatory factors.

REASONS FOR DIVERSIFICATION

- Saturation or decline of the current business.
- Additional opportunities.
- Better opportunities.
- Risk minimization.
- Better utilization of resources and strengths.
- Benefits of integration.
- Competitive strategy.
- Need related diversification.
- Consolidation.

Risks of Diversification

- No guarantee for success.
- Huge losses in new business may adversely effect the old business.
- Neglect of old business.
- Retaliation move by competitors may effect even the old business.

When to Diversify?

- Intention of extraordinary growth in assets, revenues and profits.
- Creating a large portfolio of diverse business.
- Environment helps in exploiting firm's resources.
- An uncertain environment for current products.
- Diversification more profitable than intensification.
- Firms having surplus resources to use in new ventures.

TYPES OF DIVERSIFICATION

(a) ***Concentric diversification:*** The organisation adopts concentric diversification when it takes up an activity that relates to the characteristics of its current business activity. The organisation prefers to diversify concentrically either in terms of customer group, customer functions, or alternative technologies of the organisation. It is also called as related strategy.

(b) ***Conglometric diversification:*** The organization adopts conglometric diversification when it takes up an activity that does not relate to the characteristics of its current business activity. The organisation chooses to diversify conglometrically either in terms of the customer group, customer functions, or alternative technologies of the organization. It is also called as unrelated diversification.

(ii) ***Concentration:*** Concentric expansion strategy is the first route towards growth in expanding the present lines of activities in the organisation. The present line of activities in an organisation indicates its real growth potential in the present activities, concentration of resources for present activity which means strategy for growth. The two basic concentration strategies are:

(a) ***Vertical expansion:*** The organisation adopts vertical expansion when it takes over the activity to make its own supplies. Vertical expansion reduces costs, gains control over a limited resource, obtain access to potential customers.

(b) ***Horizontal expansion:*** The organisation adopts horizontal growth when it takes over the activity to expand into other geographical locations. This increases the range of products and services offered to the current markets.

TESTS FOR JUDGING DIVERSIFICATION MOVE

Bettis, Richard and Hall (1981) say that strategists have to base diversification decisions on future expectations. Corporate strategists can make before-the-fact assessments of whether a particular diversification move is capable of increasing shareholder value by using the following tests:

Attractiveness test: The industry chosen for diversification must be attractive enough to produce consistently good returns on investment. True industry attractiveness is defined by the presence of favorable competitive conditions and a market environment conducive to long-term profitability.

Cost of entry test: The cost to enter the target industry must not be so high as to erode the potential for good profitability. The more attractive the industry, the more expensive it is to get into. Entry barriers for new start-up companies are nearly always high where barriers are low, a rush of new entrants would soon erode the potential for high profitability. And a buying company already in the business typically entails a high acquisition cost because of the industry's strong appeal. Costly entry undermines the potential for enhancing shareholder value.

Better-off test: The diversifying company must bring some potential for competitive advantage to the company's other businesses. The opportunity to create sustainable competitive advantage where none existed before, means there is also opportunity for added profitability. Diversification moves that satisfy all three tests have the greatest potential to build shareholder value over the long-term. Diversification moves that can pass only one or two tests, are highly suspect.

DIVERSIFICATION STRATEGIES

There are a number of diversification strategies and some of them are hereunder:

1. Strategies for entering new industries;
2. Related diversification strategies;
3. Unrelated diversification strategies;
4. Divestiture and liquidation strategies;
5. Corporate turnaround, retrenchment and restructuring strategies;
6. Multinational diversification.

The first three (3) involve strategies to strengthen the positions and performance of companies that have already diversified.

1. Strategies for entering new businesses

Entry into new businesses can take any of the following:

- Acquisition of an existing business is probably the most popular means of diversifying into another industry and has the advantage of much quicker entry into the target market. It also helps the diversifier overcome such entry barriers as technological inexperience, establishing suppliers relationship, being big enough to match rivals' efficiency unit costs, having to spend large sums on introductory advertising and promotion to gain market visibility and brand recognition. The cost- of-entry test requires that the expected profit stream of the acquired business provide an attractive return on the total acquisition cost and on any new capital investment needed to sustain or expand its operation.
- Internal start-up: Diversification through internal start-up involves creating a new company under the corporate umbrella to compete in the desired industry. A newly formed organization not only has it to overcome entry barriers, but also has to invest in new production capacity, develop sources of supply, grow customer base etc. Forming a start-up company to enter new industry is more attractive when:
- There is ample time to launch the business from the ground up;

- Existing firms are likely to be slow or ineffective in responding to a new entrant's efforts to crack market;
- Internal entry has Lower costs than entry via acquisition;
- The company already has most or all of the skills it needs to compete effectively;
- Adding new production capacity will not adversely impact the supply-demand balance in the industry;
- The targeted industry is populated with many relatively small firms so the new start-up does not have to compete head-to-head against large and more powerful rivals.
- *Joint ventures* these are a useful way to gain access to a new business in a number of situations. First, joint venture is a good device for doing something that is uneconomical or risky or an organization to do it alone. Second, joint ventures make sense when pooling the resources and competences of two or more independent organizations with more of the skills needed to be a strong competitor. Third, joint ventures with foreign partners are sometimes the only or best way to surmount the import quotas, tariffs and cultural roadblocks. Political realities of nationalism often require a foreign company to team up with a domestic partner in order to gain access to the national market in which the domestic partner is located. Domestic partners offer foreign companies benefits of local knowledge and access to distribution channels. However, such joint ventures often pose complicated questions about how to divide efforts among the partners and who has effective control.

2. Related diversification strategies

A related diversification strategy involves diversifying into businesses that posses some kind of strategic fit. Strategic fit exists when different businesses have sufficiently related activity-cost chains that there are important opportunities for activity sharing in one business or another. A diversified firm that exploits these activity-cost chain inter relationships and captures the benefits of strategic fit achieves a consolidated performance greater than the sum of what the businesses can earn pursuing independent strategies. The bigger the strategic fit benefits, the bigger the competitive advantage of related diversification and the more that related diversification satisfies the better-off-test for building the shareholder value. Strategic fit relationships can arise out of technology sharing, common labor skills and requirements etc. Strategic fit, relationships are important because they represent opportunities for cost-saving efficiencies, skills transfer or other benefits of activity sharing, all of which are avenues for gaining competitive advantages, over rivals that have not diversified.

3. Unrelated Diversification Strategies

A Strategy of unrelated diversification involves diversifying into whatever industries and businesses that hold the promise for attractive financial gain, pursuing strategic fit relationships that assume a back-seat role. In unrelated diversification, the corporate strategy is to diversify into any industry where top management spots a good profit opportunity. The basic premise of unrelated diversification is that any company that can be acquired on good financial terms represents a good business to diversify into. Much time and effort goes into finding and screening acquisition candidates.

The criteria used to identify suitable companies to acquire

Unrelated diversification is usually accomplished through acquisition. Corporate strategists use a variety of criteria to identify suitable companies to acquire and these are here under:

1. ***Companies whose assets are undervalued:*** Opportunities may exist to acquire such company for less than full market value and make substantial capital gains by reselling their assets and businesses for more than their acquired costs.

2. ***Companies that are financially distressed:*** Such type of business can often be purchased at a bargain price. Their operations are turned around with the aid of the parent companies' financial resources and managerial know-how and then either held as a long-term investment (because of their strong earnings potential) or sold at a profit, whichever is more attractive.

3. ***Companies with bright growth prospects but are short on investment:*** Companies that are poor in capital but opportunity rich, are usually coveted diversification candidates for a financially strong firm. Firms that pursue unrelated diversification nearly always enter new businesses by acquiring an established company rather than by forming a start-up subsidiary within its own corporate structure. Their premise is that growth by acquisition translates into enhanced shareholder value. Appeals/Attractiveness of unrelated diversification has the following appeal from several financial angles:

- Business risk is scattered over a variety of industries, making the company less dependent on any one business. While the same can be said for related diversification, unrelated diversification places no restraint on how risk is spread.

- Capital resources can be invested in whatever industries offer the best profit prospects. Cash from businesses with lower profit prospects can be diverted to acquiring and expanding business with higher growth and profit potential. Corporate financial resources are thus employed to maximum advantage.

- Company profitability is somewhat more stable because hard times in one industry may be partially offset by good times in another. Ideally, cynical downswings in some of the company's businesses are counter balanced by cynical upswings in other businesses the company has diversified into.
- To the extent that corporate managers are astute at spotting bargain-priced company with big upside profit potential, shareholders wealth can be enhanced.

While entry into an unrelated business can often pass the attractiveness and cost-of-entry test, unrelated diversification has drawbacks:

- It places on corporate-level management to make sound decisions about fundamentally different businesses operating in fundamentally different industry and competitive environments.
- The greater the number of businesses a company is in and more diverse they are, the harder it is for corporate managers to oversee each subsidiary and spot problems early.

  Hoffman and Richards (1989) say that, despite there are draw-backs, unrelated diversification can be a desirable corporate strategy. It certainly makes sense when a firm needs to diversify away from an unattractive industry and has no distinctive industry and has no distinctive skills it can transfer to related businesses. Also some owners prefer to invest in several unrelated businesses instead of family of related ones.

4. ***Divestiture and Liquidation Strategies:*** Misfits or partial fits cannot be completely avoided because it is impossible to predict precisely how getting into a new line of business will actually work out. In addition,long-term industry attractiveness changes with the time. What was once a good diversification come into a attractive industry may later turn sour. Sub-par performance by some business units is bound to occur thereby raising questions of whether to keep them or divest them. Other business units, despite adequate financial performance, may not mesh as well with the rest of the firm as originally thought. Sometimes, a business that seems sensible from a strategic fit standpoint turns out to lack the compatibility of values essential to a cultural fit. When a particular line of businesses loses its appeal, the most attractive solution usually is to sell it. Such businesses should be divested as fast as is practical, unless time is needed to get them in better shape to sell. The more business units in a diversified firm's portfolio, the more likely it will have to divest poor performance and misfits. Divestiture can take the following forms:

- Parent company can spin off a business as a financially and managerially independent company in which the parent may or may not retain partial ownership.

- Or the parent company may sell the unit out-rightly, in which case a buyer needs to be found.

5. ***Liquidation Strategies:*** Of all strategic alternatives, liquidation is the most unpleasant and painful, especially for a single business enterprise where it means the organization ceases to exist. For a multibusiness firm to liquidate one of its lines of business, is less traumatic. The hardships of lay-off, plant closing etc. still leave an ongoing organization that may be healthier after its pruning. In hopeless situations, an early liquidation usually serves owner-stockholder interests better than bankruptcy.

6. ***Multinational diversification strategies:*** The distinguishing characteristic of a multinational diversification strategy is diversity of business and diversity of national markets. Here corporate strategies must conceive and execute a substantial number of strategies atleast one for each industry, with as many multinational variations as is appropriate for the situation. At the same time, managers of diversified multinational corporations need to be alert for beneficial ways to coordinate the firm's strategic actions across industries and countries. The goal of strategic coordination at the headquarters level is to bring the full force of corporate advantage in each business and national market.

TURNAROUND

Turnaround management refers to the management measures which reverse the negative trends in the performance indicators of the company. In other words, turnaround management refers to the management measures which turn a sick company back to a healthy one or those measures which reveres the deteriorating trends of the performance indicators such as falling market share, sales ,and profitability and worsening debt-equity ratio.

A turnaround situation represents absolute and relative to industry declining performance of a sufficient magnitude to warrant explicit turnaround actions. Turnaround situations may be the result of years of gradual slowdown or months of sharp decline.

The immediacy of the resulting threat to company survival posed by the turnaround situation is known as situation severity. Severity is the governing factor in estimating the speed with which the retrenchment response will be formulated and activated.

Turnaround responses among successful firms typically include two stages of strategic activities: retrenchment and the recovery response. Retrenchment consists of cost cutting and asset reducing activities. The primary objective of the retrenchment phase is to stabilize the firm's financial condition.

The primary causes of the turnaround situation have been associated with the second phase of the turnaround process, the recovery response. Recovery is achieved when economic measures indicate that the firm has regained its pre-downturn levels of performance.

Example: XYZ bank is suffering from losses due to non-performing assets (NPA). NPA is a loan given but not, yet recovered. This bank will follow turnaround strategy and try to recover its loans by appointing recovery agents.

Manufacturing company says PQR is suffering from losses due to the excess idle time taken by labor to complete their job. The manufacturing company PQR will follow a turnaround strategy to reduce labor inactivity by installing modern machines (automation) to carry on the same work or a job.

DIVESTITURE

A divestiture strategy involves the sale of a firm or a major component of a firm. When retrenchment fails to accomplish the desired turnaround or when a non-integrated business activity achieves an unusually high market value, strategic managers often decide to sell the firm. The reasons for divestiture vary. They often arise because of partial mismatches between the acquired firm and the parent corporation, because of corporate financial needs, or because of government antitrust action.

LIQUIDATION

When liquidation is the grand strategy, the firm is typically sold in parts, only occasionally as a whole, but for its tangible asset value and not as a going concern.

BANKRUPTCY

Business failures are playing an increasingly important role in the American economy. In an average week, more than 300 companies fail. More than 75 percent of these financially desperate firms file for a "liquidation bankruptcy" they agree to a complete distribution of their assets to creditors, most of who receive a small fraction of the amount that they are owed.

The other 25 percent of these firms refuse to surrender until one final option is exhausted. Choosing a strategy to recapture its viability, such a company asks the courts for a "reorganization bankruptcy." The firm attempts to persuade its creditors to temporarily freeze their claims while it undertakes to reorganize and rebuild the company's operations more profitably.

If the judgment of the owners of a business is that its decline cannot be reversed, and the business cannot be sold as a going concern, then the alternative that is in the best interest of all may be a liquidation bankruptcy, also known as the Bankruptcy Code. The court appoints a trustee, who collects the property of the company, reduces it to cash, and distributes the proceeds proportionally to creditors on a pre rate basis as expeditiously as possible.

A proactive alternative for the endangered company is reorganization bankruptcy. Chosen for the right reasons, and implemented in the right way, reorganization bankruptcy can provide a financially, strategically, and ethically sound basis on which to advance the interests of all of a firm's stakeholders.

BCG MATRIX

It is a well-known Portfolio Management tool. It is based on product life cycle theory. It was developed in the early 70s by the Boston Consulting Group. The BCG matrix is a tool that can be used to evaluate what priorities should be given in the product portfolio of a business unit. It has 2 dimensions: market share and market growth. The basic idea behind it is that the bigger the market share a product has or the faster the product's market grows the better it is for the company.

Placing products in the BCG matrix results in 4 categories in a portfolio of a company:

Stars (high growth, high market share)

Stars are using large investment of cash. Stars are leaders in the business.Therefore they should also generate large amounts of cash. Stars are frequently roughly in balance on net cash flow. However if needed any attempt should be made to hold your market share in Stars, because the rewards will be Cash Cows if market share is kept.

Cash Cows (low growth, high market share)

Cash cows indicate generate large amounts of cash and profit but business grow rate is slow.

Cash cows require little investment and generate cash that can be utilized for investment in other business units. These SBU's are the corporation's key source of cash, and are specifically the core business. They are the base of an organization. These businesses usually follow stability strategies. When cash cows loose their appeal and move towards deterioration, then a retrenchment policy may be pursued.

Dogs (low growth, low market share)

Dogs represent businesses having weak market shares in low-growth markets. They neither generate cash nor require huge amount of cash. Due to low market share, these business units face cost disadvantages. Generally retrenchment strategies are adopted because these firms can gain market share only at the expense of competitor's/rival firms. These business firms have a weak market share because of high costs, poor quality, ineffective marketing, etc. Unless a dog has some other strategic aim, it should be liquidated if there are fewer prospects for it to gain market share. Number of dogs should be avoided and minimized in an organization.

Question Marks (high growth, low market share)

Question marks represent business units having low relative market share and located in a high growth industry. They require huge amount of cash to maintain or gain market share. They require attention to determine if the venture can be viable. Question marks are generally new goods and services which have a good commercial prospective. There is no specific strategy which can be adopted. If the firm thinks it has dominant market share, then it can adopt expansion strategy, else retrenchment strategy can be adopted. Most businesses start as question marks as the company tries to enter a high growth market in which there is already a market-share. If ignored, then question marks may become dogs, while if huge investment is made, then they have potential of becoming stars

BENEFITS OF THE BCG-MATRIX

1. The BCG-Matrix is helpful for managers to evaluate balance in the companies's current portfolio of Stars, Cash Cows, Question Marks and Dogs.
2. BCG-Matrix is applicable to large companies that seek volume and experience effects.
3. The model is simple and easy to understand.
4. It provides a base for management to decide and prepare for future actions.
5. If a company is able to use the experience curve to its advantage, it should be able to manufacture and sell new products at a price that is low enough to get early market share leadership. Once it becomes a star, it is destined to be profitable.

LIMITATIONS OF BCG MATRIX

The BCG Matrix produces a framework for allocating resources among different business units and makes it possible to compare many business units at a glance. But BCG Matrix is not free from limitations, such as:

1. BCG matrix classifies businesses as low and high, but generally businesses can be medium also. Thus, the true nature of business may not be reflected.
2. The market is not clearly defined in this model.
3. A high market share does not always leads to high profits. There are high costs also involved with high market share.
4. Growth rate and relative market share are not the only indicators of profitability. This model ignores and overlooks other indicators of profitability.
5. At times, dogs may help other businesses in gaining competitive advantage. They can earn even more than cash cows sometimes.
6. This four-celled approach is considered as to be too simplistic.

GE NINE CELL PLANNING GRID

In the late sixties and early seventies, while the Boston Consulting Group were devising the BCG or Growth Share matrix, General Electric, a leading corporation in the United States, we'are also looking at concepts and techniques for strategic planning. The firm was disappointed in the profits that they had made from their investments in the various businesses, which suggested flaws in GE's approach to investment decision-making. They became interested in the Growth-Share matrix and liked the visual approach depicting the positioning of a firm's business on the matrix. General Electric, from their own strategic planning research, objected to the two dimensional matrix which relied on market growth for industry attractiveness and relative market share for business strength. This model suggests that the long run profitability of each unit is influenced by the unit's business strength and that the ability and incentive of a firm to maintain or improve its position in a market depends on the industry attractiveness

Factors that Affect Industry Attractiveness

Whilst any assessment of Industry attractiveness is necessarily subjective, there are several factors which can help determine attractiveness. These are listed below:

- Industry size
- Industry growth
- Market profitability
- Pricing trend
- Competition intensity

- Opportunity to differentiate
- Overall risk and returns in the industry products and services
- Distribution structure

Factors that Affect Business

- Strength of assets and Competencies
- Record of technological or other innovation
- Customer loyalty Relative cost
- Market share position
- Distribution strength
- Access to finance and other investment resources
- Relative brand strength

1. The three cells at the top left hand side of the matrix are the most attractive in which to operate and require a policy of investment for growth – these are usually colored green.
2. The three cells running diagonally from left to right have a medium attractiveness, are coloured yellow and the management of businesses within this category should be more cautious and with a greater emphasis being placed on selective investment and earning retention.
3. The three cells at the bottom right hand side are the least attractive, therefore coloured red and management should follow a policy of harvesting and divesting unless the relative strengths can be improved.

Grow/Penetrate – These businesses are a target for investment, they have strong business strengths, are in attractive markets and they should therefore have high returns on investment and competitive advantage. They should receive financial and managerial support to maintain their strong position and to continue contributing to long-term profitability.

Selective Investment or Divestment - These businesses are in very attractive markets but their business strength is weak. Investment must be aimed at improving the business strengths. These businesses will probably have to be funded by other businesses in the group as they are not self-funding. Only businesses that can improve their strengths should be retained – if not they should be divested

Selective Harvest or Investment – Businesses in this box have good business strength in an industry that is losing its attractiveness. They should be supported if necessary but they may be self-supporting in cash flow terms. Selective harvesting is an option to extract cash flow but this should be done with caution so as not to run down the business prematurely.

Who Defines the Factors?

The factors are usually identified by a representative, experienced group of managers from the firm including corporate, business and functional managers.An explicit understanding of what constitutes a potentially profitable environment is essential to the formulation of strategy and for the understanding of the potential impact of competitors.A market or industry is considered to be attractive if its potential for providing a significant contribution to objectives for earnings growth and return on investment is judged to be high.

Examples of industry attractiveness factors, Different strategists and consultants have devised different sets of variables for industry or market attractiveness indicating that there is no consensus regarding the factors that make up industry attractiveness but the final factor selection is a subjective evaluation conducted by the firm.Not all of the factors have equal attractiveness to every company. They must be weighted accordingly to determine how much each factor contributes to the attractiveness of the industry to which the business belongs.The criteria or factors must be consistent for all the industries that the firm competes in so that comparisons between the various strategic businesses can be made.

CASE STUDY

SWOT ANALYSIS IN ACTION

A Skoda case study

In 1895 in Czechoslovakia, two keen cyclists, Vaclav Laurin and Vaclav Klement, designed and produced their own bicycle. Their business became Skoda in 1925. Skoda went on to manufacture cycles, cars, farm ploughs and airplanes in Eastern Europe. Skoda overcame hard times over the next 65 years. These included war, economic depression and political change

By 1990 the Czech management of Skoda was looking for a strong foreign partner. Volkswagen AG (VAG) was chosen because of its reputation for strength, quality and reliability. It is the largest car manufacturer in Europe providing an average of more than five million cars a year giving it a 12% share of the world car market.

Volkswagen AG comprises the Volkswagen, Audi, Skoda, SEAT, Volkswagen Commercial Vehicles, Lamborghini, Bentley and Bugatti brands. Each brand has its own specific character and is independent in the market. Skoda UK sells Skoda cars through its network of independent franchised dealers.

To improve its performance in the competitive car market, Skoda UK"s management needed to assess its brand positioning. Brand positioning means establishing a distinctive image for the brand compared to competing brands. Only then could it grow from being a small player. To aid its decision-making, Skoda UK obtained market research data from internal and external strategic audits. This enabled it to take advantage of new opportunities and respond to threats.

The audit provided a summary of the business's overall strategic position by using a SWOT analysis. SWOT is an acronym which stands for:

- Strengths - the internal elements of the business that contribute to improvement and growth
- Weaknesses - the attributes that will hinder a business or make it vulnerable to failure
- Opportunities - the external conditions that could enable future growth
- Threats - the external factors which could negatively affect the business.

This case study focuses on how Skoda UK's management built on all the areas of the strategic audit. The outcome of the SWOT analysis was a strategy for effective competition in the car industry.

Strengths

To identify its strengths, Skoda UK carried out research. It asked customers directly for their opinions about its cars. It also used reliable independent surveys that tested customers' feelings. For example, the annual JD Power customer satisfaction survey asks owners what they feel about cars they have owned for at least six months. JD Power surveys almost 20,000 car owners using detailed questionnaires. Skoda has been in the top five manufacturers in this survey for the past 13 years.

In Top Gear's 2007 customer satisfaction survey, 56,000 viewers gave their opinions on 152 models and voted Skoda the 'number 1 car maker'. Skoda's Octavia model has also won the 2008 *Auto Express* Driver Power 'Best Car'.

Skoda attributes these results to the business concentrating on owner experience rather than on sales. It has considered 'the human touch' from design through to sale. Skoda knows that 98% of its drivers would recommend Skoda to a friend. This is a clearly identifiable and quantifiable strength. Skoda uses this to guide its future strategic development and marketing of its brand image. Strategic management guides a business so that it can compete and grow in its market. Skoda adopted a strategy focused on building cars that their owners would enjoy. This is different from simply maximising sales of a product. As a result, Skoda's biggest strength was the satisfaction of its customers. This means the brand is associated with a quality product and happy customers.

Weaknesses

A SWOT analysis identifies areas of weakness inside the business. Skoda UK's analysis showed that in order to grow it needed to address key questions about the brand position. Skoda has only 1.7% market share. This made it a very small player in the market for cars. The main issue it needed to address was: how did Skoda fit into this highly competitive, fragmented market?

Change of direction

This understanding showed Skoda in which direction it needed to go. It needed to stop being defensive in promotional campaigns. The company had sought to correct old perceptions and demonstrate what Skoda cars were not. It realised it was now time to say what the brand does stand for. The marketing message for the change was simple: Skoda owners were known to be happy and contented with their cars. The car-buying public and the car industry as a whole were convinced that Skoda cars were great to own and drive.

Opportunities

Opportunities occur in the external environment of a business. These include for example, gaps in the market for new products or services. In analysing the external market, Skoda noted that its competitors' marketing approaches focused on the product itself. Many brands place emphasis on the machine and the driving experience:

- Audi emphasises the technology through its strapline, 'Vorsprung Durch Technik' ('advantage through technology').
- BMW promotes 'the ultimate driving machine'.

Skoda UK discovered that its customers loved their cars more than owners of competitor brands, such as Renault or Ford.

Threats

Threats come from outside of a business. These involve for example, a competitor launching cheaper products. A careful analysis of the nature, source and likelihood of these threats is a key part of the SWOT process. The UK car market includes 50 different car makers selling 200 models. Within these there are over 2,000 model derivatives. Skoda UK needed to ensure that its messages were powerful enough for customers to hear within such a crowded and competitive environment. If not, potential buyers would overlook Skoda. This posed the threat of a further loss of market share. Skoda needed a strong product range to compete in the UK and globally.

In the UK the Skoda brand is represented by seven different cars. Each one is designed to appeal to different market segments. For example:

- The Skoda Fabia is sold as a basic but quality 'city car'
- The Skoda Superb offers a more luxurious, 'up-market' appeal
- The Skoda Octavia Estate provides a family with a fun drive but also a great big boot.

Pricing reflects the competitive nature of Skoda's market. Each model range is priced to appeal to different groups within the mainstream car market. The combination of a clear range with competitive pricing has overcome the threat of the crowded market.

The challenge was how to build on this and develop the brand so that it was viewed positively. It required a whole new marketing strategy.

Think it over:

Do you think what is analysed & how things are analysed is right? If 'yes' substantiate, if 'no' give reasons.

REVIEW QUESTIONS

Conceptual Types

1. What is business planning?
2. Write note on innovation.
3. What is integration ?
4. What is vertical integration?
5. What is forward integration ?
6. What is backward integration?
7. Explain diversification as a strategy.
8. What is related or cocentric diversification?
9. Distinguish between concentric and conglomerate diversification. ***(VTU, MBA, June-2010)***
10. What do you mean by turnaround strategy? ***(VTU, MBA, Dec-2011)***

Analytical Types

1. Discuss entrepreneurial level business planning.
2. Discuss signficance of innovation.
3. Explain the integration of functional plan and policies.
4. Distinguish between related or cocentric diversification and unrelated or conglomerate diversification.
5. Explain BCG matrix for resource allocation. ***(VTU, MBA, Dec-2012)***
6. Explain innovation, integrations and diveresification. ***(VTU, MBA, Dec-2012)***
7. Explain the nature and objective of the turnaround strategy. ***(VTU, MBA, Dec-2011)***

Descriptive Types

1. Explain multi stage wealth creation model for entrepreneurs.
2. Discuss planning for large and diversified company.
3. Explain how vertical integration strategies operate across the industry value chain, with examples. Also state its strategic advantages and disadvantages. ***(VTU, MBA, Jan-2010)***
4. Give a case of any company for related diversification and unrelated diversification.

5. Describe the merits and demerits of different kinds of diversification strategies with examples. ***(VTU, MBA, Jan-2010)***
6. Which are the factors commonly employed in turnaround management.
7. Discuss long term objectives for grand strategies.
8. What is porfolio approach ? Explain the central idea behind BCG matrix.
9. Explain the GE nine-cell planning grid . ***(VTU, MBA, June-2010)***
10. What is BCG growth-shre matrix? ***(VTU, MBA, June-2010)***
11. Explain the GE 9 –cell matrix. How it can be used in practice? ***(VTU, MBA, June-2010)***
12. Explain the GE nine cell planning grid and describe its improvements over BGC matrix . ***(VTU, MBA, June-2010)***

******

Module-7

Strategy Implementation

Unit Syllabus

Strategy Implementation – Operationalizing strategy, Annual Objectives, Developing Functional Strategies, Developing and communicating concise policies. Institutionalizing the strategy. Strategy, Leadership and Culture. Ethical Process and Corporate Social Responsibility.

INTRODUCTION

In a simple way, strategy implementation can be defined as "a process through which a chosen strategy is put into action". Though this definition is very simple but does not specify what action are adopted/followed in strategy implementation. To elaborate the issues and activities involved in strategy formulation, let us consider other definitions. Steiner has defined strategy implementation as follows: "The implementation of policies and strategies is concerned with the design and management of systems to achieve the best integration of people, structures, processes, and resources, in reaching organizational purposes." McCarthy has defined Strategy implementation as follows: "Strategy implementation may be said to consist of securing resources, organizing these resources and directing the use of these resources within and outside the organizations."

FACTORS CAUSING UNSUCCESSFUL IMPLEMENTATION OF STRATEGY

Before going into the details of how a chosen strategy is implemented, it is desirable to identify the factors, which cause unsuccessful implementation of strategy so that managers can take adequate safeguard against these factors. These factors are of the following types:-

1. Unsatisfactory coupling of strategy and operational actions.
2. Insufficient attention to the negotiation of outcomes in decision situations, and
3. Defective strategy.

1. Unsatisfactory Coupling of Strategy and Actions

Unsatisfactory coupling of the strategy to the actions necessary to implement it, both within the organization and in the external decision situations with which it is concerned may cause the unsuccessful implementation of the strategy. This type of difficulty can result from a number of causes and conditions. For example, the unsatisfactory coupling of the new strategy may be due to the lack of explicit decoupling from previous strategy and commitment within the organization itself. This decoupling may be caused, in turn, by the existence of a sizable group of people within the organization who are convinced that the new strategy is not practical and that the previous ways and activities are best. Another factor responsible for this unsatisfactory coupling may be misperceptions by the strategist of the impact of the newly proposed initiatives for the organization and its people. It is sometimes assumed that the new initiatives will be accepted by the organization with a minimum of time and effort from all those who are involved. In actual practice, however, much more work is necessary to ensure that the strategy is accepted and implemented than to prepare it in the first instance. Another reason for unsuccessful coupling may be because of different perspective of strategists and implementers. In most cases, majority of people are concerned with the current operations. Their primary task is to ensure that these operations are conducted smoothly and efficiently. Their perspective is involved with the avoidance of change and of other factors that could interfere with the operations in their area of responsibility. Strategists, on the other hand, seek out changes and determine whether it can be used to the advantage of the organization. These different perspectives can result in the two groups becoming alienated from each other. For successful implementation of the strategy, a link between these two groups is necessary.

2. Insufficient Attention

Another major factor causing unsuccessful implementation of the strategy is insufficient attention to the negotiation of outcomes in the external decision situations. It is a tendency to assume, once the strategy is formulated, all that is necessary for the success of the organization is the aggressive pursuit of the strategy. However, this assumption holds well only as long as there is no change in the decision situations. If these situations change, there should be a corresponding change in the strategy also. For this, it is essential that the structure of the strategic decision situations in which the organization is involved should be kept clearly in view throughout the implementation. If this is done, changes in the conditions surrounding those decision situations can be taken in stride. Contingency strategy made during the strategy formulation process can be brought into operation when appropriate.

3. Defective Strategy

Sometimes, there may be a strategy, which cannot be implemented within the context of present and future organizational resources. Perhaps, every one of us may be aware about 'who will bell the cat'. The story goes like this. Perturbed with the sudden attack of the cat, a community of rats called a meeting to overcome this problem. At the meeting, an elder rat suggested, "bell the cat so that whenever she comes, we shall escape on hearing the sound of the bell." On this, a younger rat asked, "who will bell the cat ? Pat get the reply from the elder rat, "strategic decision making is my role , implementation is yours". Follow this pattern in their strategy formulation and implementation process. The net result is that either strategy is denounced half way or put in cold storage incurring loss in both the situations. Therefore, strategic choice should always be related with the organizational capability to implement it. While implementing a strategy, the above factors should be taken into account and various tools of strategy. Implementation should be selected carefully to ensure effective implementation

ASPECTS OF STRATEGY IMPLEMENTATION

Organizations successful at strategy implementation effectively manage six key supporting factors:

1. Action Planning
2. Organization Structure
3. Human Resources
4. The Annual Business Plan
5. Monitoring and Control
6. Linkage.

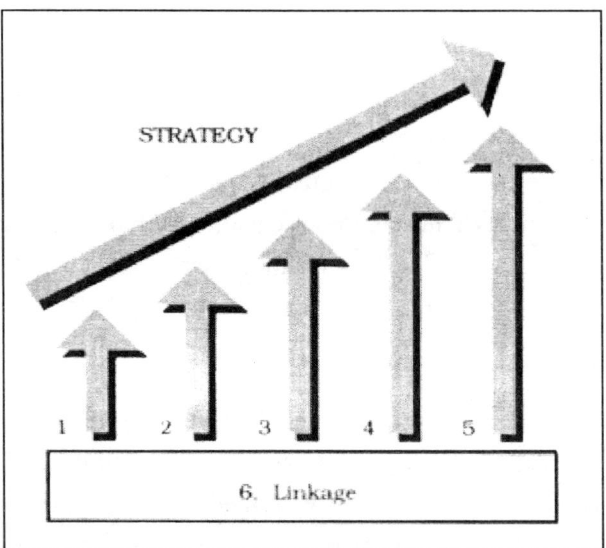

Fig: *Aspects of Strategy Implementation*

1. ***Action Planning:*** First, organizations successful at implementing strategy develop detailed action plans... chronological lists of action steps (tactics) which add the necessary detail to their strategies and assign responsibility to a specific individual for accomplishing each of those action steps. Also, they set a due date and estimate the resources required to accomplish each of their action steps. Thus they translate their broad strategy statement into a number of specific work assignments.

2. ***Organizational Structure:*** Next, those successful at implementing strategy give thought to their organizational structure. They ask if their intended strategy fits their current structure. And they ask a deeper question as well... "Is the organization's current structure appropriate to the intended strategy?"

The reason the firm had been unable to develop those products was simple... they had never organized to do so. Lacking the necessary commitment for new product development, management didn't establish an R&D group. Rather, it assigned its manufacturing engineering group the job of new product development... and hired two junior engineers for the task. Since the primary function of the manufacturing engineering group was to keep the factory humming, those engineers kept getting pulled off their "new product" projects and into the role of the manufacturing support. Result – no new products.

3. ***Human Resource Factors:*** Organizations successful at strategy implementation consider the human resource factor in making strategies happen. Further, they realize that the human resource issue is really a two part story. First, consideration of human resources requires that management think about the organization's communication needs. That they articulate the strategies so that those charged with developing the corresponding action steps (tactics) fully understand the strategy they're to implement.

   Second, managers successful at implementation are aware of the effects each new strategy will have on their human resource needs. They ask themselves the questions... "How much change does this strategy call for?" And, "How quickly must we provide for that change?" and, "What are the human resource implications of our answers to those two questions?"

   In answering these questions, they'll decide whether to allow time for employees to grow through experience, to introduce training, or to hire new employees.

4. ***The Annual Business Plan:*** Organizations successful at implementation are aware of their need to fund their intended strategies. And they begin to think about that necessary financial commitment early in the planning process. First, they "ballpark" the financial requirements when they first develop their strategy. Later when developing their action plans, they "firm up" that commitment. As a client of ours explains, they "dollarize" their strategy. That way, they link their strategic plan to their annual business plan (and their budget). And they eliminate the "surprises" they might otherwise receive at budgeting time.

5. ***Monitoring and Control:*** Monitoring and controlling the plan includes a periodic look to see if you're on course. It also includes consideration of options to get a strategy once derailed back on track. Those options (listed in order of increasing seriousness) include changing the schedule, changing the action steps (tactics), changing the strategy or (as a last resort) changing the objective.

6. ***Linkage-the Foundation for Everything Else:*** Many organizations successfully establish the above five supporting factors. They develop action plans, consider organizational

structure, take a close look at their human resource needs, fund their strategies through their annual business plan, and develop a plan to monitor and control their strategies and tactics. And yet they still fail to successfully implement those strategies and tactics. The reason, most often, is they lack linkage. Linkage is simply the tying together of all the activities of the organization...to make sure that all of the organizational resources are "rowing in the same direction."

It isn't enough to manage one, two or a few strategies supporting factors. To successfully implement your strategies, you've got to manage them all. And make sure you link them together.

Strategies require "linkage" both vertically and horizontally. Vertical linkages establish coordination and support between corporate, divisional and departmental plans. For example, a divisional strategy calling for development of a new product should be driven by a corporate objective – calling for growth, perhaps — and on knowledge of available resources — capital resources available from corporate as well as human and technological resources in the R&D department.

INTERRELATIONSHIP BETWEEN FORMULATION AND IMPLEMENTATION

Following are the main differences between Strategy Formulation and Strategy Implementation:

Strategy Formulation	***Strategy Implementation***
1. Strategy Formulation includes planning and decision-making involved in developing organization's strategic goals and plans.	1. Strategy Implementation involves all those means related to executing the strategic plans.
2. Strategy Formulation is placing the Forces before the action.	2. Strategy Implementation is managing forces during the action.
3. Strategy Formulation is an Entrepreneurial Activity based on strategic decision-making.	3. Strategic Implementation is mainly an Administrative task based on strategic and operational decisions.
4. Strategy Formulation emphasizes on effectiveness.	4. Strategy Implementation emphasizes on efficiency.
5. Strategy Formulation is a rational process.	5. Strategy Implementation is basically an operational process.

ACTIVATING STRATEGY

Activation is the process of stimulating an activity -so that it is undertaken effectively. Activation of strategy is required because only a very small group of people is involved in strategy formulation while its implementation involves a large number of people in the organization. So long if a strategy is not activated, it remains in the mind of strategists. Activation of a strategy or set of strategies requires the performance of the following activities:

1. Institutionalization of strategy,
2. Formulation of derivative-plans and programs,
3. Translation of general objectives into specific objectives and
4. Resource mobilization and allocation.

1. Institutionalization of Strategy

The first basic role of the strategist in strategy implementation is the institutionalization of the strategy. Since strategy does not become either acceptable or effective by virtue of being well designed and clearly announced, the successful implementation of strategy requires that the leader act as its promoter and defender. Often what happens is that leader's role is quite prominent in strategy formulation and his personality variables become influential factors in the strategy formulation? Thus, in practice, it becomes almost personal strategy of the top most in the organization. Therefore, there is an urgent need for the institutionalization of the strategy because without it, the strategy is subject to being undermined. Institutionalization of strategy involves two elements: Communication of strategy to organizational members and getting acceptance of strategy by these members.

a) Strategy Communication

The role of a strategist is not only to make the fundamental analytical and entrepreneurial decisions, but also to present these to the members of the organization in a way that appeals to them and brings their support. Thus, in order to get the strategy accepted and, consequently, implemented requires its communication. The form of communication may be oral through the interaction between strategist and other persons, particularly at higher level in meetings or in other ways of personal interaction. However, for a large organization with multi-location units, such a form of communication may not be adequate, and well documented written form may be required. Such a document may contain:

(i) The context in which the particular strategy has been formulated like organizational mission and objectives, environmental variables, and organizational variables.

(ii) Contents of the strategy such as the contribution of the strategy to the achievement of organizational objectives, changes required in existing organizational processes, and what is expected from personnel at different levels in the organization.

b) Strategy Acceptance

It is not just sufficient to communicate the context and content of a strategy but to get the willing acceptance of those who are responsible for its implementation. This will make organizational members to develop a positive attitude towards the strategy. This helps them to make commitment to strategy by treating their own strategy than imposed by others. Creation of such a feeling is essential for the effective implementation of the strategy. A major problem in strategy acceptance is that people often resist a strategy, particularly when it makes significant departure from the old-established practices. The basic reason of resistance emerges from the feeling that the new way of doing things will put them in some adverse situation. For example, many of the modernization strategies have been opposed by trade unions because of their perception that these would put additional work load on their members or there may be job cuts. Many of the dis-investment and divestment strategies have also been opposed by employees of all sorts and these strategies could not be implemented in many cases. Though the problem of overcoming such a resistance will be discussed in the last chapter of this part, here it may be emphasized that strategy acceptance is a pre-requisite for its effective implementation.

2. Formulation of Derivative Plans and Programs

Once the strategy is institutionalized through its communication and acceptance, the organization may proceed to formulate action plans and programs. Since these plans and programs are derived from a strategic choice (strategic plan), these are known as derivative plans and programs.

a) Action Plans

Action plans target at the most effective utilization of resources in an organization so that objectives are achieved. These action plans may be of several types like a plan for procuring a new plant, developing a new product, and so on. What types of action plans will be formulated in the organization would depend on the nature of its strategy under implementation, for example, action plans in a takeover strategy would be different from expansion through undertaking green-field projects. However, while formulating action plans, follow-questions should be put so that action plans contribute positively in strategy implementation:

1. How does the particular action plan contribute to the objectives of the strategy?
2. When will the activities devised under an action plan be undertaken?

3. Who will perform the activities?

4. What support will be needed to perform those activities?

b) Programs

A program is a single-use plan that covers relatively a large set of activities and specifies major steps, their order and timing, and responsibility for each step. There may be several programs in an organization; some of them being major, others being minor. These programs are generally supported by necessary capital and operating budgets. For example, in the case of a takeover strategy, two types of costs are involved: price to be paid for takeover and operating cost involved in takeover process. Further, the activities of takeover are identified and sequencd, timing of performance of these activities are also determined so that takeover program is completed well in time. Since there may be various programs involved in the implementation of a strategy, these should be well coordinated so that each of them contributes positively to others.

3. Translating General Objectives into Specific Objectives

Organizational objectives are of general and broad nature. They provide direction for action on continuous basis. However, these objectives are too general and, sometimes, intangible to be transformed into action. In order to make these operative, managers determine specific objectives within the framework of general objectives, which the organization and its various units will seek to achieve within a specific period. For example, growth is one of the vital objectives of every organization. This provides direction for undertaking various activities through which growth can be achieved. However, this is very general and does not provide clue about how much is the growth in what period of time. In order to overcome this problem, organizations set specific objectives to be achieved in a specified time. *For example,* Tata Group has set growth objectives in terms of doubling group turnover in four years and doubling net profit in three years. Such a specific objective provides sharp focus on the activities that may be undertaken to achieve this volume of growth. Most of the specific objectives tend to be of short range in character and have definite time limits within which the organization has to achieve these. Translation of general objectives into specific and operative objectives must fulfill two criteria.

1. Translation of general objectives into specific objectives should be tangible and meaningful. As far as possible, these objectives should be easily measurable as organizational performance is measured against these objectives.

2. Specific objectives should contribute to the achievement of general objectives. In fact, time-bound objectives are set to make the achievement of general objectives more feasible. For example, long-term objectives involving plans for the distant future may fail to make

individual objectives tangible and meaningful standards for control. This can be overcome by setting specific objectives at different stages of general long-term objectives.

4. Resource mobilization and allocation

For implementing a strategy, an organization should have commensurate resources and these resources should be committed and allocated to the various units and functions where these have optimum use. There are different types of organizational resources and each of these has specific nature and characteristics. These resources are broadly classified into two broad categories: financial and human. Financial resources are used to procure various physical resources such as land, building, plant, machinery, raw materials, etc. These resources are the means by which an organization produces goods and services of value through the conversion process. The success of the organization depends on the quality of its resources and their utilization. Therefore, the organization should feel concerned about how to mobilize resources and allocate these to various units and subunits.

a) Resources

It might be said that resources represent those assets, both tangible and intangible, with which the company has to work: its assets, including its people, and the value of its brand, a variety of individual, social, and organizational phenomena. To put it more succinctly, resources represent inputs into a company's production process, such as capital equipment, the skills of individual employees, brand names, financial resources, and talented managers. By themselves, or individually, resources generally will not enable a company to achieve a competitive advantage. They must be combined or integrated with other company resources to establish a capability. When these capabilities are identified and nurtured, they can result in core competencies, which may lead to a competitive advantage. A company's resources can be classified either as tangible or intangible.

MCKINSEY 7S MODEL APPROACH

The 7S model is a strategic model that can be used for any of the following purposes:

i. Organizational alignment or performance improvement.

ii. Understanding the core and most influential factors in an organization's strategy.

iii. Determining how best to realign an organization to a new strategy or other organization design.

iv. Examining the current workings and relations an organization exhibits.

The model, made famous by the McKinsey consulting company, is good for a thorough discussion around an organization's activities, infrastructure, and interactions.

The model and its usage-here is the 7S model that portrays seven elements of an organization.

The Seven-Ss is a framework for analyzing organizations and their effectiveness. It looks at the seven key elements that make the organizations successful, or not: strategy; structure; systems; style; skills; staff; and shared values.

Consultants at McKinsey & Company developed the 7S model in the late 1970s to help managers address the difficulties of organizational change. The model shows that organizational immune systems and the many interconnected variables involved make change complex, and that an effective change effort must address many of these issues simultaneously.

7-S Model – A Systemic Approach to Improving Organizations:

The 7-S model is a tool for managerial analysis and action that provides a structure with which to consider a company as a whole, so that the organization's problems may be diagnosed and a strategy may be developed and implemented. The 7-S diagram illustrates the multiplicity interconnectedness of elements that define an organization's ability to change. The theory helped to change the manager's thinking about how companies could be improved. It says that it is not just a matter of devising a new strategy and following it through. Nor is it a matter of setting up new systems and letting them generate improvements. There is no starting point or implied hierarchy - different factors may drive the business in any one organization.

1. Shared Values

Shared values are commonly held beliefs, mindsets, and assumptions that shape how an organization behaves – its corporate culture. Shared values are what engender trust. They are an interconnecting center of the 7Ss model. Values are the identity by which a company is known throughout its business areas, what the organization stands for and what it believes in, it central beliefs and attitudes. These values must be explicitly stated as both corporate objectives and individual values.

2. Structure

Structure is the organizational chart and associated information that shows who reports to whom and how tasks are both divided up and integrated. In other words, structures describe the hierarchy of authority and accountability in an organization, the way the organization's units relate to each other: centralized, functional divisions (top-down); decentralized (the trend in larger organizations); matrix, network, holding, etc. These relationships are frequently diagrammed in organizational charts. Most organizations use some mix of structures - pyramidal, matrix or networked ones - to accomplish their goals.

3. Strategy

Strategies are plans an organization formulates to reach identified goals, and a set of decisions and actions aimed at gaining a sustainable advantage over the competition.

4. Systems

Systems define the flow of activities involved in the daily operation of business, including its core processes and its support systems. They refer to the procedures, processes and routines that are used to manage the organization and characterize how important work is to be done. Systems include:

i. Business System

ii. Business Process Management System (BPMS)

iii. Management information system

iv. Innovation system

v. Performance management system

vi. Financial system/capital allocation system

vii. Compensation system/reward system

viii. Customer satisfaction monitoring system

5. Style

"Style" refers to the cultural style of the organization, how key managers behave in achieving the organization's goals, how managers collectively spend their time and attention, and how they use symbolic behavior. How management acts is more important that what management says.

6. Staff

"Staff" refers to the number and types of personnel within the organization and how companies develop employees and shape basic values.

7. Skills

"Skills" refer to the dominant distinctive capabilities and competencies of the personnel or of the organization as a whole.

MAKING SURE YOU HAVE THE SUPPORT FOR NEW STRATEGY IMPLEMENTATION

Often overlooked are the five key components necessary to support implementation: people, resources, structure, systems, and culture. All components must be in place in order to move from creating the plan to activating the plan.

People

The first stage of implementing your plan is to make sure to have the right people on board. The right people include those folks with required competencies and skills that are needed to support the plan. In the months following the planning process, expand employee skills through training, recruitment, or new hires to include new competencies required by the strategic plan.

Resources

It need to have sufficient funds and enough time to support implementation. Often, true costs are underestimated or not identified. True costs can include a realistic time commitment from staff to achieve a goal, a clear identification of expenses associated with a tactic, or unexpected cost overruns by a vendor. Additionally, employees must have enough time to implement what may be the additional activities that they aren't currently performing.

Structure

Set your structure of management and appropriate lines of authority, and have clear, open lines of communication with your employees. A plan owner and regular strategy meetings are the two easiest ways to put a structure in place. Meetings to review the progress should be scheduled monthly or quarterly, depending on the level of activity and time frame of the plan.

Systems

Both management and technology systems help track the progress of the plan and make it faster to adapt to changes. As part of the system, build milestones into the plan that must be achieved within a specific time frame. A scorecard is one tool used by many organizations that incorporates progress tracking and milestones. See the section "Keeping Score of Your Progress" later in this chapter for information on how to create a scorecard for your company.

Culture

Create an environment that connects employees to the organization's mission and that makes them feel comfortable. To reinforce the importance of focusing on strategy and vision, reward success. Develop some creative positive and negative consequences for achieving or not achieving the strategy. The rewards may be big or small, as long as they lift the strategy above the day-to-day so people make it a priority.

STRATEGY IMPLEMENTATION

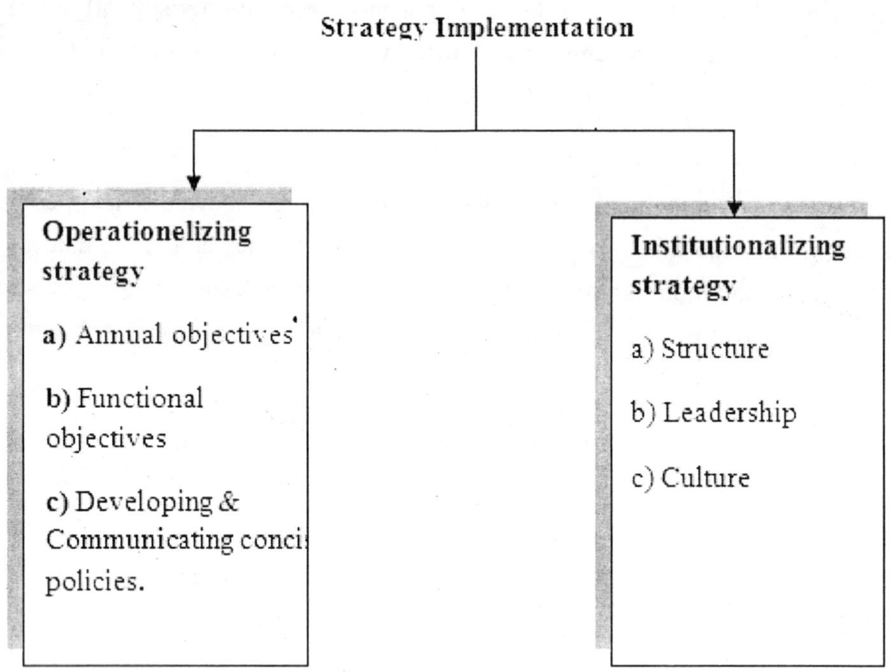

OPERATIONALIZING STRATEGY

Operationalizing strategy is the strategy which has adopted by the organization to achieve operational effectiveness. "Operational Effectiveness refers to any number of practices that allow an organization to better utilize its inputs by reducing defects in products or developing better products faster" – Michael E Porter.

The following elements are important for successful Implementation of operationlizing strategy:

a) Annual Objectives

b) Developing functional strategies

c) Developing and Communicating concise policies

a) Annual Objectives

Annual objectives serve as guidelines for action, directing and channeling efforts and activities of an organization's member. It is major instrument for monitoring progress towards achieving long term objectives. Annual objectives are essential for strategy implementation because they:

1. Serve as standards of performance.
2. The primary tool for evaluating employees.
3. Serve as a source of employee motivation and identification.
4. Provide a basis for organizational design
5. Represent basis for allocating resources.

Clearly stated and communicated objectives are critical to success in all types and sizes of firms. Annual objectives, stated in terms of profitability, growth, and market share by business segment, geographic area, customer groups, and product are common in organizations.

Annual objectives should be measurable, consistent, reasonable, challenging, clear, communicated throughout the organization, characterized by an appropriate time dimension, and accompanied by commensurate rewards and sanctions. Too often, objectives are stated in generalities, with little operational usefulness. Annual objectives such as "to improve communication" or "to improve performance" are not clear, specific, or measurable. Objectives should state quantity, quality, cost, and time and also be verifiable. Terms such as "maximize," "minimize," "as soon as possible," and "adequate" should be avoided.

Annual objectives should be compatible with employees and manager's values and should be supported by clearly stated policies. More of something is not always better! Improved quality or reduced cost may, for example, be more important than quantity. It is important to tie rewards and sanctions to the annual objectives so that employees and managers understand that achieving objectives is critical to successful strategy implementation. Clear annual objectives do not guarantee successful strategy implementation but they do increase the likelihood that personal and organizational aims can be accomplished. Over emphasis on achieving objectives can result in undesirable conduct, such as faking the numbers, distorting the records, and letting objectives become ends in themselves. Managers must be alert to these potential problems

Policies: Changes in a firm's strategic direction do not occur automatically. On a day-to-day basis, policies are needed to make a strategy work. Policies facilitate solving recurring problems and guide the implementation of strategy. Broadly defined, policy refers to specific guidelines, methods, procedures, rules, forms, and administrative practices established to support and encourage the work toward stated goals. Policies are instruments for strategy implementation. Policies set boundaries, constraints, and limits on the kinds of administrative actions that can be taken to reward and sanction behavior; they clarify what can and cannot be done in pursuit of an organization's objectives. For example, Carnival's new Paradise ship has a no-smoking policy anywhere, anytime aboard ship. It is the first cruise ship to comprehensively ban smoking. Another example of corporate policy relates to surfing the Web while at work. About 40 percent of companies today do not have a formal policy preventing employees from surfing the Internet, but software is being marketed now that allows firms to monitor how, when, where, and how long various employees use the Internet at work. Policies let both employees and managers know what is expected of them, thereby increasing the likelihood that strategies will be implemented successfully. They provide a basis for management control, allow coordination across organizational units, and reduce the amount of time managers spend making decisions. Policies also clarify what work is to be done by whom. They promote delegation of decision making to appropriate managerial levels where various problems usually arise. Many organizations have a policy manual that serves to guide and direct behavior. Policies can apply to all divisions and departments (for example, "We are an equal opportunity employer").

Some policies apply to a single department "Employees in this department must take at least one training and development course each year". Whatever their scope and form, policies serve as a mechanism for implementing strategies and obtaining objectives. Policies should be stated in writing whenever possible. They represent the means for carrying out strategic decisions.

2. Developing Functional Strategies

A functional strategy is one that dictates the task and activities of a certain business area. Owners and managers make up certain rules and guidelines for employees to follow. Each department operates by these guidelines, with all departments working together to achieve the overarching company's goals. Common areas where a company may implement a functional strategy include the production, finance, or the research and development departments. An organizational strategy may also be functional.

Functional Strategy Objectives

1. ***Profitability:*** It produce net profit in business
2. ***Market share:*** Gaining and holding a specific share of a product market.
3. ***Human talent:*** The organization can recruit and maintaining a high –quality workforce.
4. ***Financial Health:*** The organization would be acquired financial capital and earning positive returns.
5. ***Cost efficiency:*** The organization could be used the existing resource and produce a product at low cost.
6. ***Product quality:*** The organization could produce the quality of product and service through the optimal usage of organizational resources

7. ***Innovation:*** The organization can produce a new product through innovation and creativity

8. ***Social responsibility:*** Making a positive contribution to the society.

Functional Policies and Plans: The integrated strategic planning system has a significant dimension that co-ordinates the various plans from the top level of the organization down through the lower levels. Such plans are co-ordinated at different levels so that planning efforts at a lower level contribute to the higher-level efforts. Thus, integration of various functions, their plans and efforts leads to effective implementation of strategy. The integration can be achieved if various functional plans are derived directly from strategic plans and that too at the level of their formulation. However, this may not always happen, particularly in the absence of proper guidelines. An organization is a growing concern whose operational patterns have already been established which may not contribute to the type of integration needed at various levels. Further, the functional plans are prepared almost at any level of the organization. For example, the marketing manager develops overall marketing objectives, policies, action programs, budget, etc. His subordinates, in turn, develop supporting marketing plans covering each area of marketing operation-distribution, sales promotion, marketing plan-which are incorporated into overall plan of the organization. Similar exercises are done in other functional areas which are incorporated into the master plan for implementation. At all these levels, coordination is necessary which is not achieved automatically but through the development of policies. Policies are guides to action. They are in the form of specific statements or general understanding which provides guidance in decision making to members in respect of any course of action. They indicate how the task assigned to the organization might be accomplished and provide a basis for lower level managers on which to make decisions about the use of resources which have been allocated. But a policy does not tell the managers how to handle a specific activity; it is only a general guide to action. It limits the choices of managers in most cases but it does not limit them entirely

Role of Functional Policies and Plans: Functional policies play important role in strategy implementation. A functional policy is formulated basically to control and reinforce implementation of functional strategies and also the corporate strategy. Control and reinforcement of strategy implementation are facilitated by functional policies in the following ways:

1. Through the functional policies, top management can ensure that strategy is implemented by all parts of the organization as policies cover almost entire activities of the organization.

2. Policies specify the manner in which things can be done and limit discretion for managerial action. Thus, the top management of the organization can rest assured that all personnel of the organization will direct their efforts in a way relevant for strategy implementation.

3. Policies provide guidelines for managerial decisions. This aspect of the policies serves the strategy implementation in two ways. First, there will be uniformity throughout the organization in managerial action. Second, there will be considerable time savings in decision making as managers are well aware what kind of actions are required in a given situation.

4. Functional policies provide a basis for control in respective areas as policies lead to consistent patterns of behaviors. This, in turn, acts as the basis for controlling.

5. Policies provide coordination across different functions. Coordination among different functions is very important for strategy implementation. All functions of an organization are interdependent and interrelated. Therefore, what is happening in one function has its relevance for other- functions. All functions can contribute positively when they are performed in a coordinated way.

Development of Functional Policies and Plans: Managers develop policies, which are decision guides and make the strategy work. Therefore, the critical element involved in analytical exercises in policy making is the ability to factor the grand strategy into policies that are compatible, workable and just theoretically sound. It is not enough for the managers to decide to change the strategy. What comes next is equally important: How do we get there? When? and How efficiently? A manager answers these questions by preparing policies to implement the strategy. For example, if an organization chooses to go for diversification, the policy maker has to decide what to diversify into, where to diversify, how much money will be needed, from where the money will come and what changes are needed in various functions of the organization. The decisions on all these aspects are much easier if proper policies have been formulated.

The amount of policy making in the formal sense will vary with the size and complexity of the organization. If the organization is small one with simple business, only a few policies will be sufficient. Moreover, the policies are generally understood and verbal. However, in large and complex organizations, large number of policies is needed, in whatever forms, the policies are developed, and they must be judged on the following criteria:

1. Do they exist in the areas critical to the success of the organization?
2. Do they reflect present or desired organizational practices and behavior?
3. Are they clear, definite, and explicit leaving no scope for misinterpretation?
4. Are they consistent with one another and do they reflect the timing needed to accomplish the goals?
5. Are they practical in given existing or expected situations?

IMPLEMENTTION OF FUNCTIONAL POLICIES IN THE ORGNISATION

Functional policies can be separately implemented in different functional areas:

1. Financial Plans and Policies
2. Marketing Plans and policies
3. Operation Plans and Policies
4. Personnel Plans and Policies
5. Information Management Plans and Polices

1. Financial Plans and Policies

Under the financial plans and policies, focus on sources of funds , usage of funds and management of funds. Sources of funds indicate that policies related to capital structure, procurement of capital and working capital borrowings, reserves and surplus as sources of funds and the relationship with lenders, bank and financial institutions. These plans and policies are important for determining how financial resources will be made available for the implementation of strategies. Usage of funds to deal with investments or assert mix decisions. Usage of funds is important to improve the efficiency and effectiveness usage of resources in the process of strategy implementation. Management of funds can play a pivotal role in strategy implementation as it aims at the conservation and optimum utilization of funds.

2. Marketing Plans and policies

Plans and policies related to marketing have to be formulated and implanted on the basis of the 4Ps of the marketing mix that is product, pricing, place and promotion. Product plans and policies are implemented on the basis of characteristics such as quality, features, choice of models, brand names, packaging, and so on. Pricing plan and policies deal with the mode of payment, allowances, payment period, credit terms, and so on. Place plan and policies related to distribution channels of product and services such as logistic and storage inventory management, coverage of market and so on. Promotion deals with the marketing communication intended to convey the company's and its products and services image to prospective buyers.

3. Operation Plans and Policies

All these collectively influence the operation system structure and the objectives, which are used to determine the operations, plans and polices. The operations system structure and the operations system objectives both determine what operational plans and policies are to be set and implemented.

4. Personnel Plans and Policies

Personnel plans and policies relate to the manpower planning, selection, developmeɪ t, compensation, communication, appraisal, employees characteristics (quality of managers, staff and workers, perception about and the image of the organization as an employer) and Industrial relation.

5. Information Management Plans and Polices

Information capability factors relate to the design and management of the flow of information from within and outside into an organization. The value of information as a tangible resource and as a source of strategic advantage has been recognized by organizations.

INSTITUTIONALIZING THE STRATEGY

Institutionalization is the active process of establishing your initiative - not merely continuing your program, but developing relationships, practices, and procedures that become a lasting part of the organization.

It may have several different reasons for wanting to do this, depending on what kind of an initiative or organization it is. But one thing is clear: developing a plan for the institutionalization of your initiative will increase its impact. And it will certainly make your life easier, because the group members will have a better idea of what they will be doing next month and next year. In this section, we will help you lay the groundwork you need to create such a plan.

Institutionalization is a process which translates an organization's code of conduct, mission, policies, vision, and strategic plans into action guidelines applicable to the daily activities of its officers and other employees. It aims at integrating fundamental values and objectives into the organization's culture and structure.

Institutionalization is the attainment of long term viability and integration of programs within organizations, which is often characterized as the final stage in the diffusion of the new process. It is an expression of how well an organization has adopted the new process. It is an ongoing process in which a set of activities, structures and practices become an integral part of an organization for its day to day activity. Institutionalizing the strategy needs to institutionalize the strategy permeating the very day-to-day life of the company effective implementation.

Three Organizational Elements Essential:

1. Structure
2. Leadership
3. Culture

1. Structure

By structure, we mean the framework around which the group is organized, the underpinnings which keep the coalition functioning. It's the operating manual that tells members how the organization is put together and how it works. More specifically, structure describes how members are accepted, how leadership is chosen, and how decisions are made.

Why should you develop a structure for your organization?

- ***The structure gives members clear guidelines for how to proceed:*** A clearly-established structure gives the group a means to maintain order and resolve disagreements.
- ***Structure binds members together:*** It gives meaning and identity to the people who join the group, as well as to the group itself.
- ***Structure in any organization is inevitable:*** An organization, by definition, implies a structure. Your group is going to have some structure whether it chooses to or not. It might be the structure which best matches up with what kind of organization you have, what kind of people are in it, and what you see yourself doing.

RELATIONSHIP BETWEEN STRATEGY AND STRUCTURE

Strategy primarily refers to the road map laid out by an organization. The principal objective of strategy is to ensure that an organization achieves the set targets in order to sustain and grow in an increasingly competitive world. On the other hand, a structure is the manner in which the internal resources of a company get connected with each other. More specifically, structure is concerned with different groups that can be formed within an organization. For example, an organization having a functional structure will operate through the different functions such as Marketing, Finance, and Manufacturing.

Strategy is the main driver that decides the structure an organization. Also, in case the structure of a company is not synchronized with its strategy, then the company may not be able to achieve the set targets. For example, a company with a diversified product portfolio and has a functional structure (organized as per various functions such as Marketing, Finance and Operations) will not be able to compete effectively in each of the product categories. As a result, the company may start losing the market share of its products.

Evidently, structure plays a critical role in the accomplishment of an organization's overall strategy. Another notable aspect is that both strategy and structure need to be continuously interlinked in order to achieve desired results.

Organizational Structures for Strategy Implementation: An organization and its structure vary from company to company. Depending upon the objectives, an organization can be structured in different ways. The structure of an organization determines the way in which it operates and performs.

The structure in a way contributes to the achievement of common aim. Most of the organizations have structures which are hierarchical in nature, but not all. Organization structure allows for different functions and pressures to different entities, viz., departments, branches, work groups or individual. Individuals are normally employed or hired under time-limited work, contracts or work orders, or under permanent employment contracts. Organizational structure can be formal or informal.

Organization structure types:

Pre-bureaucratic Structure: Centralized, seen in small companies, lacks standardization of tasks, and suits new organizations for the owner to have total control.

Bureaucratic Structure: Some standardization is seen, ideal for complex and large organizations, suits hierarchical organizations.

Post-bureaucratic Structure: Not bureaucratic in functions, Decisions are taken by consensus, and dialogue than an authority, more a network than hierarchy, horizontal decision making process, more of participation and empowerment.

Functional Structure: Each division/employees function for specialized tasks, could lead to lack of communication and being slow.

Divisional Structure: Divisions can be geographical or product/service basis. Each division within a divisional set-up contains all resources and functions within.

Matrix Structure: These group employees by both function and product, uses groups of employees for the strengths and to make up for the weaknesses, matrix structure is one of the best form of an organization.

Flat Structure: Common in entrepreneurial startups. Later becomes hierarchical; becomes bureaucratic.

Team Structure: This is flexible type, and as a team performs designated tasks. The team defines the entire organization. Even large bureaucratic structure use team structures to benefit

Network Structure: Contracts are out-sourced, and the business functions can be done better and more cheaply. Electronic means are used for coordination and control of external relations.

Virtual Structure: Internet is used for boundary less organization. A small organization can operate globally to be a market leader in a niche. A number of niche markets make the company highly profitable and the cost of reaching the customers and clients is dramatically cheaper.

Strategy Implementation: Structure is the design of the organization through which strategy is administered. Sometimes, a change in the organization strategy leads to new administrative problems which in turn require a new or re-fashioned structure for the successful implementation of the new strategy. Organizational structure has to align with organizational strategies and must integrate strategy formulation and implementation.

Organizations use strategy implementation model, strategic change, human resources and strategy implementation, strategy and structured incentives control, for effective implementation of strategy through organizational structure. Strategy affects structure, and the choice of structure affects efficiency and effectiveness.

STRATEGY AND LEADERSHIP

Strategic Leadership: Strategic leadership is the process of transforming an organization with the help of its people so -as to put it in a unique position. Thus, two aspects are involved in strategic leadership. First, it transforms the organization which involves changing all faces such as size, management practices, culture and values, and people in such a way that the organization becomes unique. Second, the strategic leadership process emphasizes people because they are the source for transforming various physical and financial resources of the organization into outputs that are meaningful to the society. Thus, strategic leadership proceeds as follows:

1. Strategic leadership deals with vision-keeping the mission in sight-and with effectiveness and results. It is less oriented to organizational efficiency in-terms of cost-benefit analysis.
2. Strategic leadership emphasises transformational aspect and, therefore transformational leaders emerge in the organization. Transformational leadership is the set of abilities that allow a leader to recognize the need for change. To create a vision to guide that change and to execute that change effectively.
3. Strategic leadership inspires and motivates people to work together with a common vision and purpose.
4. Strategic leadership has an external focus rather internal focus.

This external focus helps the organization to relate itself with its environment.

LEADERSHIP ROLE IN IMPLEMNTATION

Strategic leadership plays an important role in strategy implementation. The role of effective leadership in strategy implementation can be explained as follows:

1. Introducing Change

Change is a must for organizational growth and development. Without changes, an organization would lead to doom. Therefore, introducing changes in the organization is one of the prime responsibilities of the leadership. Organizational changes takes place as a result of changes in technology, consumer's tastes, likes and dislikes, changes in competitors' strategy, political changes, etc. Organizations have to respond and adjust to the changes in the environment. Failure to do so would result in poor performance of the organization and ultimately closure. Changes affect the existing equilibrium in the organization, and therefore, leadership should ensure that changes do not generate resistance on the part of the people in the organization. For this purpose, the leadership should consider the following aspects while introducing a change, there should be concern for the people as well as for the objectives of the organization.

- Employees should be encouraged to participate in the process of change right from the initiation stage.
- Change should be introduced with objective explanation.
- Leadership should create a psychological climate suitable for change.
- Change should be introduced on impersonal requirements rather than on personal grounds.

2. Integrating Conflicting Interests

Organization consists of various people, groups, departments or sub-units. Every person on group may have certain interests, which may clash with those of others in the organization. For instance, there can be conflict of interest between the superior and subordinates, top level and the lower level, between the production department and marketing department, and so on. Therefore, an important role of leadership at various levels is to integrate the conflicting interests of people and groups in the organization. It is to be noted that some amount of conflicts is desirable in the organization. This is because; some conflicts facilitate change in the organization. Conflicts may arise due to problems in the functioning in the organization. Conflicts bring to surface dormant or latent problems and help the organization in solving it. The solution to the problem often requires changes in the organization. It is also true that conflict s can create problems in the organization. Among other things, conflicts affect interpersonal relations. This is because; each person or group tries to find fault with others rather than trying to sort out the conflict. People involved in the conflict may spread false information. There is loss of trust and faith in each other. In general, conflicts can adversely affect the performance of the organization. Therefore, effective leadership is required in sorting out conflicts in the organization.

3. Developing Leadership Ability of Managers

Managers need to be effective leaders. This is because; managers need to influence and inspire the subordinates in order to accomplish the organizational goals. For this purpose, there is a need to develop leadership abilities in the managers. There are several measures, which can be used for developing leadership ability of the managers

- Leadership training – in which training programs can be undertaken to expose managers to various leadership problems and situations.
- Internal exposure – where managers can be exposed to various situations in the organization such as solving of conflicts.
- Challenging tasks can be set by top management to be achieved by managers within a certain time frame.
- Autonomy and accountability – where managers can be provided with enough autonomy to handle certain situations and they should be held accountable for their actions.

4. Developing Appropriate Organizational Climate

Effective leadership is required for developing an appropriate organizational climate in the organization. Organizational climate refers to a set of values, beliefs and norms that are shared by an organization's members. The organizational climate gives a distinct identity to an organization.

- It influences the morale, motivation and performance of its members. Some of the important features of organizational climate are:
- It is a combination of social, cultural, physical, psychological, and other conditions within an organization.
- It evolves over a fairly long period of time.
- It can be relatively stable over a period of time. However, there may be changes in organizational climate, with a change in top management, or management's philosophy.
- It gives a separate identity to the organization as compared to other organizations, as each organization has its own set of values, beliefs, practices, emotions, etc. To adopt appropriate

organizational climate, the leadership, especially at the top management level must adopt certain policies and practices:

- High standards of excellence in every area of operations and evaluation.
- High standards of moral character, especially at the top management level.
- Encouragement for innovation with the consequent freedom to act upon the ideas.
- Proper delegation of authority throughout the organization.
- Matching rewards with performance rather than on subjective grounds.
- Situational leadership style with high concern both for people, and objectives of the organization.

5. Developing Motivational System

One of the important roles of leadership is to motivate, people in the organization. Motivation is vital for better performance on the part of the people. The leadership must be a dynamic force in motivating people involved in strategy implementation. The leadership must understand the process of motivation, which involves:

- *Presence of needs:* Every person has a certain amount of needs, which can range from physiological needs to self-actualization needs.
- *Efforts:* An individual puts in his efforts in order to satisfy such needs. The more the needs, the more are the efforts.
- *Performance:* The effort of a person leads him/her into certain work performance.
- *Rewards:* Good performance is rewarded with monetary and/or non-monetary incentives. The leadership should note that motivation is a continuous process. This is because; human needs and desires are never ending. When one need is satisfied, another need emerges that needs to be satisfied. Therefore, leadership must identify the emerging needs of the people and strive to satisfy such needs at regular intervals through a proper mix of monetary and non-monetary incentives

6. Clarity in Goals

The leader must set clear and well defined goals and objectives. Before setting goals, the leader must analyse the internal and external environment. The leader may consult his subordinates before finalizing the goals. A leader can be effective when there is clarity in goals and roles to be performed to achieve those goals. In the absence of clear goals, the leader may not be able to get the support and commitment from the subordinates in the performance of the activities.

7. Relations

The leader must maintain excellent relations with his subordinates, and also with the other departmental heads. The leader on his own may develop good relations with his subordinates, but he also needs excellent support from the organization to develop and maintain good relations with the subordinates. Good relations facilitate interpersonal relations between the leader and his subordinates. Therefore, the leader should have a substantial hold over the resources and authority required to manage the subordinates and to get the work done for them.

8. Leadership Styles

A leader would be effective, if he adopts the right leadership style depending upon the situation. He can be autocratic, especially, when the situation is quite demanding and there is little time to consult subordinates. He may adopt consultative leadership style, especially when subordinates views and suggestions are important in decision-making. He may also follow participative leadership style, especially, when the participation of the subordinates is vital in decision-making.

LEADERSHIP STYLES

Every manager develops a style in managing the activities. Such styles vary from leader to leader, from situation to situation, and from organization to organization. "Leadership style is a pattern of behavior designed to integrate organizational and personal interest in pursuit of some objective". Edwin Flippo. The main types of leadership styles are as follows:

1. Autocratic style

An autocrat is the one who takes all decisions by himself and expects to be obeyed by his subordinates. The subordinates have no scope to question the superior. Certain points to be noted in this respect:

- The superior makes the decision.
- The superior does not consult the subordinates in decision making.
- The superior is responsible for the decision.
- The relations between superior and subordinates are formal his style is suitable when:

  - Quick decisions are to be made.
  - Subordinates are inexperienced and it does not make any sense to consult them.
  - Subordinates are not affected by the decisions.

2. Bureaucratic style

This type of leadership style is more followed in government departments. The bureaucrats often follow rules and regulations in totality. They do not use their discretion; even do away w th more formalities. They strictly follow the scalar chain principle, even in the case of urgency. The following points to be noted:

- The bureaucrat takes the decisions by strictly following the formalities, or rules and regulations.
- The subordinates are often not consulted.
- The bureaucrat may avoid responsibility.
- The relations between superior and subordinates are formal.
- This style results in delay and red tapism, and unwanted paper work.

3. Consultative Style

In this type, the leader consults his subordinates before taking a decision. The leader feels that it is always advisable to consult the subordinates. This type of leader is open minded and would welcome suggestions from the subordinates before making a decision. The following points to be noted:

- The superior consults the subordinates before making a decision.
- The subordinates may give their suggestions or comments, which the superior may or may not accept.
- The superior makes the decision.
- The superior is responsible for the decision.
- The relations between the superior and subordinates are informal. This type style is suitable when:
- There is no urgency of the decision, which allows the leader to consult subordinates.
- The suggestions and the comments of the subordinates are vital in making a decision.
- The subordinates are experienced and matured and can provide suggestion and comments.

4. Participative style

The latter not only consults the subordinates, but allows them to take part in decision making. The following points are to be noted:

- The superior consults his subordinates before making his decision.

- The leader along with the group takes part in decision making.
- Both the leader and the group share the responsibility for making the decision.
- The relations are informal. This type style is suitable when:
- Group decision making is required.
- There is an immediate possibility of opposition from a group of followers.
- There are experienced and matured followers.

5. Laissez-faire style

This style aims at creating a family atmosphere within the organization. The leader is respected and treated as a father figure by the subordinates. The following points to be noted:

- This style is mostly followed in Japanese organizations.
- The leader considers him as a parent figure.
- The leader may consult his subordinates; mostly the leader takes the decision.
- The relations are very homely. This type of style is more suitable in small organizations, where there are handfuls of employees, and just one leader or boss. The letter advises, guides, and helps the subordinates even during their personal hardships.

6. Sociocratic Style

Sociocratic attempt to run their organizations like a social club. They believe that good fellowship or friendship is more important than productivity. They keep people happy even at the cost of the organization. They believe in a warm and pleasant atmosphere. For them, the interest of the subordinates comes first, and then that of the organization. The following points are to be noted:

- The superior take the decision by keeping the interest of the subordinates. The interest of the organization may be secondary.
- The superior consults the subordinates for decision making.

7. Neurocratic Style

A Neurocratic leader is highly task oriented and wants to get the things done at any cost. He is highly sensitive and gets quickly upset at failures. The following points are to be noted:

- The leader may be eccentric and emotional.
- The leader may not consult the subordinates in decision making.

- The leader is responsible for decision making, but he may shift the responsibility on to his subordinates.

8.Situational Style

Now-a-days, in most well managed organization, the managers follow situational leadership style. This means, the leadership style varies depending upon the situation. In other words, the leader may be autocratic at times, consultative at times, and participative at times, depending upon the decision and the situation.

ORGANIZATIONAL CULTURE

Organizational culture is another element which affects strategy implementation as it provides a framework within, which the behavior of the members takes place. Though there are differing Views on what constitute an organizational culture, generally, it is defined as a set of assumptions the members of an organization share in common. For example, organizational culture has been defined as follows.

"Organizational culture is the set of assumptions, like Beliefs, values and norms that are shared by an organization's members. Thus, there are two types of elements, which define the culture of an organization: abstract elements and material elements. Abstract - elements are internally oriented and include values, beliefs, attitudes, and feelings. Material elements are externally focused and include building, personnel dresses, products, etc. Vijay Sathe has exemplified some common things to demonstrate the components of organizational culture:

Shared things (e.g.. the way people dress)

Shared saying (e.g.., let's go down to work)

Shared actions (e.g., a service-oriented approach)

Shared feelings (e.g., hard work is not rewarded here)

IMPACT OF ORGANIZATIONAL CULTURE

Organizational culture is very important factor, which affects the different organizational processes including implementation of strategy; strategy implementation involves completion of different processes. In particular, corporate culture affects the following aspects of the organization.

1. ***Objective Setting:*** Culture molds people and people are the basic building blocks of the organization. The objectives of the organization must reflect, at least in part, the objectives

of its members, particularly those who are the key decision makers. Thus for one organization, the objective may be profit maximization but the same objective may be unworthy; mean, and petty for another organization.

2. ***Work Ethics:*** Ethics relating to conformity to the principles of human conduct. According to common usage, moral. good, right, honest, etc. are more or less used as synonymous to ethical act. Work ethics in an organization are derived from its 'culture. Thus, corporate culture-determines the ethical standards for the organization' as a whole and its individual members.

3. ***Motivational Pattern:*** Culture interacts 'to develop in each person' a motivational pattern. Culture determines the way people approach their jobs and even life in general. If organizational culture is geared towards achievement, people will find it quite motivating and put their utmost energies for the work. In its absence, high achievement-oriented people develop frustration and desert the organization Therefore; for implementing strategies, particularly growth strategies. Organizational culture should be achievable-oriented.

4. ***Organizational Processes:*** Various organizational - processes like planning, decision making, controlling, etc. are determined by the organizational Culture because these processes are carried out by the people, intlle organization. Bhattacharya has analyzed the cultures of various professionally managed companies including' multinationals as well as family-managed companies in India to find out how cultures affect organizational processes.

RELATING CULTURE AND STRATEGY

We have seen that strategy and culture are interlinked; culture affects how-a strategy may be implemented though it has a role in strategy formulation too. Our emphasis here is to analyze how organizational culture can be made. a facilitating factor in 'strategy implementation. In relating strategy and culture strategists have four alternatives:

1. To ignore corporate culture
2. To adapt' strategy implementation to suit corporate culture
3. To change corporate culture to suit strategic requirements
4. To change the' strategy to 'fit the corporate culture.

Each of these alternatives has different implications for the total strategic management. Now let us see how a particular alternative is relevant.

1. Strategists can simply ignore the corporate culture while implementing a strategy especially when it is not possible to change corporate culture. In fact, corporate culture is built over a period of time and therefore cannot be changed over night; cultural change is a slow process and is time-consuming. Ignoring culture in strategic management is not a better alternative because it may be dysfunctional.
2. Another alternative to the above is to change strategy implementation to suit corporate culture. Strategists may have flexibility in organizational design, organizational systems and processes for strategy implementation. These variables can be manipulated to serve the interests of 'corporate culture. However in such a case, each specific situation in the organization calls for an innovative solution.
3. The third alternative is to change the strategy itself if it does not fit with the corporate culture. However, changing strategy midway is- not a very desirable proposition. Therefore, corporate culture should -be considered as a determinant of strategic choice.
4. The last alternative in relating strategy is to change corporate culture to suit strategic requirements. This is the optimum choice in the present prevailing Indian business environment, which is becoming more and more competitive day-by-day necessitating change in old methods.

In fact many companies have failed simply because they were not able to adopt suitable strategies due to corporate cultural constraints. Though the cultural change process is a slow attempt can be made to change the culture. This transition may be brought by making strategic task explicit, enhancing managerial capability to imbibe changes, arid exhibiting a strong and assertive leadership.

CASE STUDY

BUILDING A JOINT VENTURE IN AN EMERGING MARKET

A Burmah Castrol case study

Burmah Castrol is a leading internal marketer of specialized lubricant and chemical products and services. With operations in over 50 countries, Burmah Castrol employs some 20,000 people world-wide. Burmah Castrol's organization is based on a number of business streams which operate in the lubricants and chemicals sectors. The lubricants business, which operates under the name Castrol, supplies specialist products and services to the Consumer, Industrial, Commercial and Marine markets. Castrol is the world's leading independent marketer of specialised lubricants and lubrication services.

The chemicals businesses are involved in the marketing of high value added speciality chemicals to industrial end-users. There are five principal businesses - Foundry, Construction, Printing Inks, Releasants, Steel – and a Specialities Group. Once again, the chemicals businesses are highly international with operations in over 40 countries world-wide.

Emerging Markets

In recent years we have seen the development of a truly global economy. We have moved forward from the days when the world was seen as being made up of First World (capitalist), Second World (communist) and Third World (less developed countries). Clearly, divisions continue to exist between the nations, particularly in terms of income per head, but new markets are developing and strengthening all the time.

The development of new market models in former communist strongholds in Eastern Europe and parts of South East Asia provides a tremendous opportunity to well-established companies in the West. There is great demand in these countries for the sorts of goods that we have taken for granted for so long, as well as a demand for advanced technology which will enable them to improve home-based production techniques greatly.

In order to take advantage of new market opportunities, many large Western companies are developing joint ventures with enterprises in the new emerging markets. This case study focuses on a joint venture between Castrol, Burmah Castrol's lubricants business, and Vietnam's Saigon Petroleum. It sets out the rationale for the joint venture and examines the benefits to the two parties.

Positioned at the centre of the fastest growing economic zone in the world, Vietnam offers a unique opportunity for Burmah Castrol to continue geographic expansion of its heartland business. Vietnam is situated on the eastern seaboard of the Indo-chinese peninsula. Neighboring countries are China to the north and Laos and Cambodia to the west. Vietnam has a land area approximately one third larger than the UK. The population of Vietnam is 75 million people. The two major cities are Hanoi in the north and Ho Chi Minh City (formerly Saigon) in the sou h. The majority of the population lives in rural areas and is evenly spread through the countryside.

Vietnam is ruled along classic Marxist-Leninist lines where the Communist Party of Vietnam and the Government are totally fused. Following the much publicized period of Doi Moi (Renewal) in Vietnam, it now appears likely that pursuit of a free market economy through stage by stage reform is the aim of the Vietnamese Government. Doi Moi has opened up Vietnamese markets to foreign investors and companies.

In 1990, the Soviet Union cut back heavily on direct aid in the form of subsidies to Vietnam. The resultant loss of cheap lubricants, previously supplied by the Soviet Union, has led the Government to liberalize the lubricants industry and elevate it to a priority investment category. Market reforms, therefore, are taking place but the Government is not prepared to engage in the sort of widespread reforms that would threaten the existing political system.

Economic Background

Prior to the Vietnam war in the 1960s and early 1970s, Vietnam was at a similar stage of economic development to Singapore, Thailand and Malaysia, which are all now highly profitable economies for Burmah Castrol. There is little reason to doubt that following reform of the economy, Vietnam will enter an accelerated growth period and offer similar significant opportunities for the sale of Castrol lubricants, even though Vietnam is currently one of the poorest nations in the world.

Economic problems increased when Vietnam invaded Cambodia in 1979 and became involved in conflict with the Khmer Rouge and other resistance movements within Cambodia. This invasion brought further political isolation from Western countries and a US-led trade and investment embargo, which was maintained until 1994. Until recently, the maintenance of a 1.3 million strong army was also a considerable drain on Vietnam's economic resources. However, economic reforms since 1987 have helped lead to a turnaround in the economy. By allowing peasants once again to own land and sell their produce at market prices, Vietnam has been transformed from a net rice importer to the world's third largest rice exporting nation. Like other South East Asian economies, Vietnam has been experiencing rates of growth which are the envy of the West. Vietnam possesses enormous mineral resources and recent foreign investment in offshore oil exploration activities has finally borne fruit. Successful processing of these finds will provide much-needed US dollars and a catalyst for economic growth.

Whilst the foreign investment law of Vietnam allows foreign companies to invest at 100% equity, the preferred investment route of the State Investment authority is through a joint venture with a local partner. This makes good sense - a well-connected, established local partner with access to foreign currency can help the foreign investor greatly, making a joint venture the most appropriate strategy.

1. Is it making a joint venture the most appropriate strategy ? Discuss the issues of advantage and challenges.

2. Do you think the steps adopted were of strategic nature? What would be your assessment & analysis of things in the given context?

REVIEW QUESTIONS

Conceptual Types

1. What is strategy implementation?
2. What is project implementation?
3. What is procedural implementation?
4. What is organisational analysis?
5. How do you match organisation structure to strategy?
6. What is functional strategy?
7. Explain the term “leadership style”?
8. Give the meaning of “leadership implementation?”
9. What do you mean by “corporate culture?”
10. What do you mean by the term “social responsibilities”?
11. What is Corporate Social responsibility?

Analytical Types

1. Explain various aspects of strategy implementation.
2. Write a note on project implementation.
3. What are the principal strategy implementation tasks?
4. Explain strategic groups and its implications.
5. Write note on operationalizing strategy.
6. Explain annual objectives of strategy implementation.
7. Explain various aspects of functional strategy.
8. What is the marketing strategy? Explain its characteristics.
9. How do you developing and communicating concise policy.
10. Explain the importance of leadership implementation in an organisation.
11. What is corporate culture? Explain various policies of corporate culture.
12. Where does Corporate Culture originate from?
13. Explain Social Responsibility for economic growth.

14. Why is leadership an important element in strategy implementation ?

(VTU, MBA, Dec-2011)

15. Explain how the leadership and structure of affirm affect implementing the strategy

(VTU, MBA, June-2010)

Descriptive Types

1. Explain importance of strategic implementation. Discuss the inter relationship between formulation and implementation.
2. Discuss the role of strategy implementation.
3. Discuss the process of strategy implementation.
4. What are functional level strategies? How it enhances the competitive advantage?
5. Explain the dimensions of effective leadership of the strategy execution process.

(VTU, MBA, June-2010)

6. Critically evaluate the different types of organizational structures ad their relevance in effective strategy implementation. ***(VTU, MBA, June-2010)***

*****

Module-8

Strategic Evaluation and Control

Unit

Syllabus

Strategic Control, guiding and evaluating strategies. Establishing Strategic Controls. Operational Control Systems. Monitoring performance and evaluating deviations, challenges of Strategy Implementation. Role of Corporate Governance.

INTRODUCTION

Strategic control and evaluation is concerned with tracking a strategy as it is being implemented, detecting problems or changes in its underlying premises, and making necessary adjustments. In contrast to post action control, strategic control is concerned with guiding action in behalf of the strategy as that action is taking place and when the end result is still several years off. Managers responsible for the success of a strategy typically are concerned with two sets of questions:

1. Are we moving in the proper direction?
2. How are we performing?

Strategic evaluation and control relates to that aspect of strategic management through which an organization ensures whether it is achieving its objectives Contemplated in the strategic action. If not, what corrective actions are required for Strategic effectiveness. Glueck and Jauch have defined strategic evaluation as follows: "Evaluation of the strategy is that phase of the strategic management process in which the top managers determine whether their strategic choice as implemented is meeting the objectives of the enterprise. There are two aspects in this phase of strategic management: evaluation which emphasizes measurement of the results of a strategic action and control which emphasizes on taking necessary actions in the light of the gap that exists between intended results and actual results in the strategic action.

However, because of the on-going nature of strategy evaluation and control process both these are intertwined. In practice, the term control is used in a broad sense which includes the evaluative aspect too because unless the results of an action are known, control actions cannot be taken.

IMPORTANCE OF STRATEGY EVALUATION

1. The strategic-management process results in decisions that can have significant, long-lasting consequences. Erroneous strategic decisions can inflict severe penalties and can be exceedingly difficult, if not impossible, to reverse.

2. Most strategists agree, therefore, that strategy evaluation is vital to an organization's well-being; timely evaluations can alert management to problems or potential problems before a situation becomes critical.

3. Strategy evaluation includes three basic activities:

   a. Examining the underlying bases of a firm's strategy.

   b. Comparing expected results with actual results.

   c. Taking corrective actions to ensure that performance conforms to plans.

4. The strategy-evaluation stage of the strategic-management process.

5. Strategy evaluation can be a complex and sensitive undertaking. Too much emphasis on evaluating strategies may be expensive and counterproductive. Yet, too little or no evaluation can create even worse problems. Strategy evaluation is essential to ensure that stated objectives are being achieved.

6. It is impossible to demonstrate conclusively that a particular strategy is optimal, but it can be evaluated for critical flaws. Here are four criteria to use in evaluating a strategy:

   a. Consistency

   b. Consonance

   c. Feasibility

   d. Advantage

7. These trends make strategy evaluation difficult:

   a. Dramatic increase in environmental complexity

   b. Difficulties in predicting future

   c. Increasing number of variables

   d. Rapid rate of obsolescence

   e. Increase in the number of world events affecting organizations

   f. Decreasing time spans for planning

8. Strategy evaluation is necessary for all sizes and kinds of organizations. Strategy evaluation should initiate managerial questioning of expectations and assumptions, trigger a review of objectives and values, and stimulate creativity in generating alternatives and formulating criteria of evaluation.
9. Evaluating strategies on a continuous rather than a periodic basis allows benchmarks of progress to be established and more effectively monitored.
10. Managers and employees of the firm should continually be aware of progress being made toward achieving the firm's objectives. As critical success factors change, organizational members should be involved in determining appropriate corrective actions.

BARRIERS IN STRATEGIC EVALUATION AND CONTROL

Strategic evaluation and control being an appraisal process for the organisation as a whole and people who are involved in strategic management process either at the stage of strategy formulation or strategy implementation or both, is not free from certain barriers and problems. These barriers and problems center around two factors: motivational and operational. Let us see what these problems are and how these problems may be overcome.

1. MOTIVATIONAL PROBLEMS

The first problem in strategic evaluation is the motivation of managers (strategists) to evaluate whether they have chosen correct strategy after its results are available. Often two problem; are involved in motivation to evaluate the strategy: psychological problem and lack of direct relationship between performance and rewards.

a. Psychological Barriers

Managers are seldom motivated to evaluate their strategies because of the psychological barriers of accepting their mistakes. Top management formulates the strategy, which is very conscious about its sense of achievement. It hardly appreciates any mistake it may commit at the level of strategy formulation. Even if something goes wrong at the level of strategy formulation, it may put the blame on the operating management and tries to find out the faults at the level of strategy implementation. This over-conscious approach of top management may prevent the objective review of whether correct strategy has been chosen and implemented. This may result into delay in taking correct alterative action and bringing the organisation back at satisfactory level. This happens more in the case of retrenchment strategy, particularly divestment strategy where a particular business has failed because of strategic mistake and in order to save the organization from further damage, the business has to be sold.

b. Lack of Direct Relationship between Performance and Rewards

Another problem in motivation to review strategy is' the lack of direct relationship between performance achievement and incentives. It is true that performance achievement itself is a source of motivation but this cannot always happen. Such a situation hardly motivates the managers to review their strategy correctly. This happens more in the case of family-managed businesses where professional managers are treated as outsiders and top positions, particularly at the board level, are reserved for insiders. Naturally very bright managers are not' motivated to review correctness or otherwise of their strategy. The family managers of such organizations are even more prone to psychological problem of not reviewing their strategy and admit their mistakes. Thus, what is required for motivating managers to evaluate their performance and strategy is the right type of motivational climate in the organisation. Linking performance and rewards as closely as possible can set this climate. This linking is required not only for the top level but for the lower down in the organisation too. Many forward-looking companies though few in number, have taken this step when they have adopted the policy of taking board members from outside their families and friend groups. These companies have taken this- step not only to satisfy the requirements of financial institutions of broad basing the directorship but they have taken this step to motivate their top level managers. Naturally top managers in such companies can take any step to fulfill the organizational requirements including the evaluation of their strategy.

2. OPERATIONAL PROBLEMS

Even if managers agree to evaluate the strategy, the problem of strategic evaluation is not over, though a beginning has been made. This is so because strategic evaluation is a nebulous process; many factors are not as clear as the managers would like these to be. These factors are in the areas of determination of evaluative criteria, performance measurement, and taking suitable corrective actions. All these are involved in strategic evaluation and control. However, nebulousness nature is not unique to strategic evaluation and control only but it is unique to the entire strategic management process. We shall make an attempt later in this chapter as to how these operational problems may be overcome.

ESTABLISHING STRATEGIC CONTROLS

The four basic types of strategic control are described below:

1. Premise Control

Every strategy is based on certain planning premises-assumptions or predictions. Premise control is designed to check systematically and continuously whether the premises on which the strategy is based are still valid.

Key questions for management are:

* Which premises should be monitored: environmental factors-those over which the firm has no control but those that can influence strategy and industry factors-that influence success in a particular industry.

* How are premise controls enacted: the strategy's key premises should be identified and recorded during the planning process and responsibilities for monitoring those premises should be assigned to those with qualified sources of information.

2. Special Alert Control

A special alert control is the thorough, and often rapid, reconsideration of the firm's strategy because of a sudden, unexpected event.

3. Strategic Surveillance

Strategic surveillance is designed to monitor a broad range of events inside and outside the firm that are likely to affect the course of its strategy. The basic idea behind strategic surveillance is that important yet unanticipated information may be uncovered by a general monitoring of multiple information sources.

4. Implementation Control

Implementation control is designed to assess whether the overall strategy should be changed in light of results. Two types of implementation controls are:

* *Monitoring strategic thrusts:* projects that need to be done if the strategy is to be accomplished and information on the strategy's progress.

* *Milestone reviews:* critical events and resource allocations through time, and full-scale assessment to scrutinize the strategy.

Implementation control is also enabled through operational control systems like budgets, schedules and key success factors. To be effective, operational control systems must take four steps common to all post action controls:

- Set standards of performance
- Measure actual performance
- Identify deviations from standards set
- Initiate corrective action

OPERATIONAL CONTROL

Operational controls provide post-action evaluation and control over short periods. They require systematic evaluation of performance against predetermined standards. An important issue here is identification and evaluation of performance deviations, with careful attention paid to find the underlying causes for and strategic implications of observed deviations before management react. Firms generally employ trigger points and contingency plans for this purpose.

DIFFERENCES BETWEEN STRATEGIC CONTROL AND OPERATIONAL CONTROL

Attribute	Strategic control	Operational control
Basic question	Are we moving in the right direction?	How are we performing?
Aim	Proactive, continuous questioning of the basic direction of strategy	Allocation and use of resources organizational resources
Main Concern	Steering the future direction of the Organization	Action control
Focus	External environment	Internal organization
Time horizon	Long-term	Short-term
Exercise of control	Exclusively by top management, may be through lower-level support	Mainly by executive or middle management or the direction of top management
Main techniques	Environmental scanning, information gathering, questioning and review	Budgets, schedules and MBO

CONTROL PROCESS /STEPS OF OPERTIONAL CONTROL SYSTEMS

Control particularly a process consisting of four major steps as shown in Figure exercises operational control:

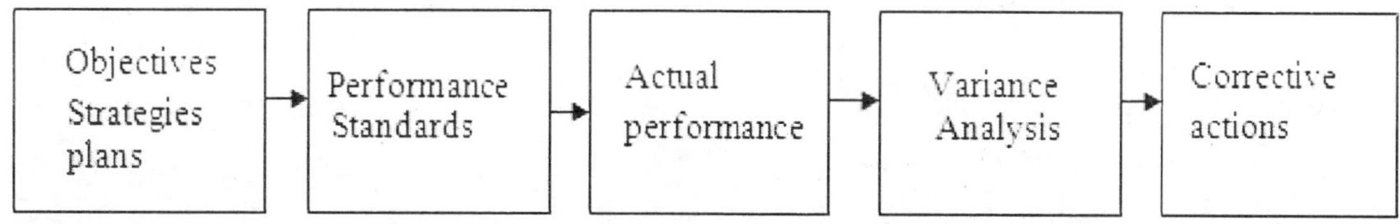

The Control Process

In order to exercise control, managers have to take four steps as indicated in Figure These steps are as follows:

1. Setting performance standards
2. Measuring actual performance
3. Analyzing variance
4. Taking corrective actions.

1. Setting Performance Standards

Every function in the organizations begins with plans, which are goals, objectives, or targets to be achieved. In the light of these, standards are established which are criteria against which actual results are measured. For setting standards for control purposes, it is important to identify clearly and precisely the results which are desired. Precision in the statement of these standards is important. In many areas, great precision is possible. However, in some areas, standards are less precise. Standards may be precise if they are set in quantities-physical, such as volume of products, man-hour or monetary, such as costs, revenues, investment. They may also be in qualitative terms, which measure performance. After setting the standards, it is also important to decide about the level of achievement or performance, which will be regarded as good or satisfactory. There are several characteristics of a particular work that determine best performance. Important characteristics, which should be considered while determining any level of performance as well for some operations are:

i. Output

ii. Expense

iii. Resources.

Expense refers to services or functions, which may be expressed in quantity, for achieving a particular level of output. Resources refer to capital expenditure, human resources, etc. after identifying these characteristics; the desired level of each characteristic is determined. The desired level of performance should be reasonable and feasible. The level should have some amount of flexibility also, and should be stated in terms of range-maximum and minimum.

Control standards are most effective when they are related to the performance of a specific individual because a particular individual can be made responsible for specific results. However, sometimes accountability for a desired result is not so simply assigned; for example, the decision regarding investment in inventory- is affected by purchase, rate of production, and sales. In such a situation, where no one person is accountable for the levels of inventories, standards may be set for each step that is being performed by a person.

2. Measuring Actual Performance

The second major step in control process is the measurement of performance. The step involves measuring the performance in respect of a work in terms of control standards. The presence of standard implies a corresponding ability to observe and comprehend the nature of existing conditions and to ascertain the degree of control being achieved. The measurement of performance against standards should be on a future basis, so that deviations may be detected in advance of their actual occurrence and avoided by appropriate actions. Appraisal of actual or expected performance becomes an easy task, if standards are properly determined and methods of measuring performance which can be expressed in physical and monetary terms, such as production units, sales volume, profits, etc. can be easily and precisely measurable. The performance, which is qualitative and intangible such as human relations, employee morale, etc., cannot be measured precisely. For such purposes, techniques like psychological tests and opinion surveys may be applied. Such techniques draw heavily from intuitive judgment and experience, and these tools are fat" from exact. According to Peter Drucker, it is very much desirable to have clear and common measurements in all key areas of business. It is not necessary that measurements are rigidly quantitative. In his opinion, for measuring tangible and intangible performance, measurement must be:

i. Clear, simple, and rational,

ii. Relevant,

iii. Direct attention and efforts, and

iv. Reliable, self-announcing, and understandable without complicated interpretation or philosophical discussions.

3. Analyzing Variance

The third major step in control process is the comparison of actual and standard performance. It involves two steps:

i) Finding out the extent of deviations, and

ii) Identifying the causes of such deviations.

When adequate standards are developed and actual performance is measured accurately, any variation will be clearly revealed.. Management may have information relating to work performance, data, charts, graphs and written reports, besides personal observation to keep itself informed about performance in different segments of the organisation. Such performance is compared with the standard to find out whether the various segments and individuals of the organisation are progressing in the right direction. When the standards are achieved, no further managerial action is necessary and control process is complete. However, standards may not be achieved in all cases and the extent of variations may differ from case to case. Naturally, management is required to determine whether strict compliance with standards is required or there should be a permissible limit of variation. In fact, there cannot be any uniform practice for determining such variations. Such variations depend upon the type of activity. For example, a very minute variation in engineering products may be significant than a wide variation in other activities. When the deviation between standard and actual performance is beyond the prescribed limit, an analysis is made of the causes of such deviations. For controlling and planning purposes, ascertaining the causes of variations along with computation of variations is important because such analysis helps management in taking up proper control action. The analysis will pinpoint the causes, which ate controllable by the person re-possible. In such a case, person concerned will take necessary corrective action. However,If the variation is caused by uncontrollable factors the person concerned cannot be held responsible and he cannot take any action. Measurement of performance.' analysis of deviations and their causes may be of no use unless these are communicated to the person who can take corrective action. Such communication is presented generally in the form of a report showing performance standard actual performance deviations between those two, tolerance limits, and causes for deviations. As soon as possible reports containing control information should be sent to the person whose performance is being measured and controlled. The underlying philosophy is that the person who is responsible for a job can have a better influence on final results by his own action. A summary of the control report should be given to the superior concerned because the person on the job may either need help of his superior in improving the performance or may need warning for his failure. In addition, other people who may be interested in control reports are (i) executives engaged in formulating new plans: and (ii) staff personnel who are expected to be familiar with control information for giving any advice about the activity under control when approached.

4. Taking Corrective Actions

This is the last step in the control process, which requires that actions should be taken to maintain the desired degree of control in the system or operation. An organisation is not a self-regulating system such as thermostat, which operates in a state of equilibrium put there by engineering design. In a business organisation, this type of automatic control cannot be established because the state of affairs that exists is the result of so many factors in the total environment. Thus some additional actions are required to maintain the control. Such actions may be on the following lines:

1. Improvement in the performance by taking suitable actions if the performance is not up to the mark:

2. Resetting the performance standards if these are too high and unrealistic; or
3. Change the objectives, strategies and plans if these are not workable.

MONITORING PERFORMANCE AND EVALUATING DEVIATIONS

Operating control system require the establishment of performance standards. In addition, progress must be monitored and deviations from standards evaluated as the strategy is implemented. Timely information must be obtained so that deviations can be identified, the underlying cause determined, and actions taken to correct or exploit them. Below illustrates a simplified report on the current status of key performance indicators linked to the firm.s strategy. These performance indicators represent progress after two years of a five-year plan intended to differentiate the firm as a customer service- oriented provider of high-quality products.

Key success factors	Objective, Assumption Or budget	Forecast Performance at this time	Current Performance	Current deviation Analysis	Analysis
Cost control : Ratio of indirect overhead to direct field and labor costs	10%	15%	12%	+3 (ahead	Are we moving too fast or is there more unnecessary overhead than originally thought?
Gross profit Customer service:	39%	40%	40%	0%	
Installation cycle in days	2.5 days	3 days	2.7 days	0.5 (ahead)	Can this progress be maintained?
Ratio of service to sales personnel	3.2	2.7	2.1	-0.6 (behind)	Why are we behind here? How can we maintain the installation cycle progress?
Product quality: Percentage of products returned	1.0%	2.0	2.1%	-0.1% (behind)	Why are we behind here? Ramifications for other operations?
Product performance	100%	92%	80%	-12% (behind)	

versus specification					
Marketing: Sales per employee monthly	12500	1500	Rs. 12,100	+Rs 600 (ahead)	Good progress. Is it creating any problems to support?
Expansion of product line	6	3	5	+2 product (ahead)	Are the products ready? Are the perfect standards met?
Employee morale in service area: Absenteeism rate	2.5%	3.0%	3.0%	(on target)	
Turnover rate	5%	0	15%	-8% (behind)	Looks like a problem! Why are we so far behind?
Competition: New product introductions (average number)	6	3	6	-3 (behind)	Did we underestimate timing? Implications for our basic assumptions?

Exhibit 1: Monitoring and Evaluating Performance Deviations

Management's concern is comparing progress to date with expected progress at this point in the plan. Of particular interest is the current deviation because it provides a basis for examining suggested actions (usually from subordinate managers) and for finalizing decisions on any necessary changes or adjustments in the company's operations. In Above, the company appears to be maintaining control of its cost structure. Indeed, it is ahead of schedule on reducing overhead. The company is well ahead of its delivery cycle target, while slightly below its service/sales personnel ratio objective. Product returns look OK, although product performance against specification is below standard. Sales per employee and expansion of the product line are ahead of schedule. Absenteeism in the service area is meeting projections, but turnover is higher than planned. Competitors appear to be introducing products more rapidly than expected. After deviations and the underlying reasons for them are identified, the implications of these deviations for the ultimate success of the strategy must be seriously considered. For example, the rapid product line expansion indicated in the above may be in response to competitors. Increased rate of product expansion. At the same time, product performance is still low and, while the installation cycle is slightly above standard (improving customer service), the ratio of service to sales personnel is below its target. Contributing to this substandard ratio (and perhaps reflecting a lack of organization commitment to customer service) is the exceptionally high turnover in customer service personnel. The rapid reduction in indirect overhead costs might mean that administrative integration of customer service and product development requirements had been reduced too quickly.

As a result of this information, operations managers face several options. The deviations observed may be attributed primarily to internal factors or discrepancies. In this case, priorities can be scaled up or down. For example, greater emphasis might be placed on retaining customer service personnel while de-emphasizing overhead reduction and new product development. On the other hand, the management team could decide to continue as planned in the face of increasing competition and decide to accept or gradually improve the customer service situation. Another possibility is reformulating the strategy or a component of the strategy in the face of rapidly increasing competition. For example, the firm might decide to shift emphasis toward more standardized or lower priced products to overcome customer service problems and take advantage of an apparently ambitious sales force. This interpretation of the above illustrates is but one of many possible explanations. The important point is the critical need to monitor progress against standards and give serious, in depth attention to both the reasons underlying observed deviations and the most appropriate responses to them. Evaluations such as this are appropriate for organizational subunits, product groups, and operating units in a firm. Budgets, schedules, and other operating control systems with performance targets and standards linked to the strategic plan deserve this type of attention in detecting and evaluating deviations. The time frame is more compressed usually quarterly or even monthly during the budgeted year. The operating manager typically reviews year-to-date progress against budgeted figures. After deviations are evaluated, slight adjustments may be necessary to keep progress, expenditures, or other factors in line with programmed needs of the strategy. In the unusual event that deviations are extreme-usually because of unforeseen change- management is alerted to the possible need for revising the budget, reconsidering certain functional plans related to budgeted expenditures, or examining the units and effectiveness of the managers responsible. An acceptable level of deviation should be allowed before action is taken; if not, the control process will become an administrative overload. Standards should not be regarded as absolute because the estimates used to formulate them are typically based on historical data, which, by definition, are .after the fact.. Furthermore, absolute standards (keep equipment busy 100 percent of the time, or meet 100 percent of quota) are often used with no provision for variability. Standards are also often derived from Strategic Evaluation and Control 393 averages, which, by definition, ignore variability. These difficulties suggest the need for definition acceptable ranges of deviation in budgetary figures or key indicators of strategic success. This approach helps in avoiding administrative difficulties, recognizing measurement variability, delegating more realistic authority to operating managers in making short-term decisions, and hopefully improves motivation.

Some companies use trigger point for clarification of standards, particularly in monitoring key success factors. A trigger point is a level of deviation of a key indicator or figure (such as a competitor's actions or a critical cost category) that management identifies in the planning process as representing either a major threat or an unusual opportunity. When that point is .hit,. Management is immediately alerted (triggered.) to consider necessary adjustments in the firm.s strategy. Some companies take this idea a major step forward and develop one or more contingency plans to be implemented once predetermined trigger points are reached. These contingency plans redirect priorities and actions rapidly so that valuable reaction time is not wasted on administrative assessment and deliberation of the extreme deviation. Correcting deviations in performance brings the entire management task into focus. Managers can correct performance by changing measures. Perhaps deviations can be resolved by changing plans. Management can eliminate poor performance by changing how things are done, by hiring new people, by retaining present workers, by changing job assignments, and so on. Correcting deviations from plans, therefore, can involve all of the functions, tasks, and responsibilities of operations managers. Operational control systems are intended to provide essential feedback so that company managers can make the necessary decisions and adjustments to implement the current strategy.

EVALUATION TECHNIQUES FOR OPERATIONAL CONTROL

The classification of evaluation techniques in the three parts: internal analysis, comparative analysis, and comprehensive analysis.

Internal analysis

Internal analysis, which consists of value-chain analysis, quantitative (financial and non-financial) analysis, and qualitative analysis, deals with the identification of the strengths and weaknesses of a firm in absolute terms.

1. Value chain analysis focuses on a set of interrelated activities performed in a value-chain analysis for the purpose of operational evaluation lies in its ability to Strategic Evaluation and Control segregate the total tasks of a firm into identifiable activities which can then be evaluated for effectiveness.

2. Quantitative analysis takes up the financial parameters and the non-financial quantitative parameters, such as, physical units or time, in order to assess performance. The obvious benefit of using quantitative factors (either financial or physical parameters) is the ease of evaluation

and the verifiability of the assessment done. These are probably the most- used methods for evaluation for operational control. Among the scores of financial techniques described in all standard texts in the area of finance are traditional techniques, such as, ratio analysis, or newer Techniques, such as, economic value-added (EVA) and its variations, and activity based costing (ABC). These are proven methods so far as their efficacy for evaluating operational effectiveness is concerned. Apart from the financial quantitative techniques, there are several non-financial quantitative techniques available for the evaluation for operational control, such as: computation of absenteeism, market ranking, rate of advertising recall, total cycle time of production, service call rate, or number of patents registered per period. Many more techniques can be evolved by firms to suit their specific requirement.

3. Qualitative analysis supplements the quantitative analysis by including those aspects which is not feasible to measure on the basis of figures and numbers. The methods that could be used for qualitative analysis are based on intuition, judgement, and informed opinion. Techniques like surveys and experimentation can be used for the evaluation of performance for exercising operational control.

Comparative analysis

This consists of historical analysis, industry norms, and benchmarking. It compares the performance of a firm with its own past performance, or with other firms.

1. Historical analysis is a frequently used method for comparing the performance of a firm over a given period of time. This method has the added benefit of enabling a firm to note how the performance has taken place over a period of time and to analyse the trend or pattern. Such an analysis can offer the firm a better perception of its performance as compared to an absolute assessment.
2. Industry norms is a comparative method for analyzing performance that has the advantage of making a firm competitive in comparison to its peers in the same industry. Being a comparative assessment, evaluation on the basis of industry norms enables a firm to bring its performance at least up to the level of other firms and then attempt to surpass it.
3. Benchmarking is a comparative method where a firm finds practices in an area and then attempts to bring its own performance in that area in line with the best Practice. Best practices are the benchmarks that should be adopted by a firm as the standards to exercise operational control. Through this method, performance can be evaluated continually till it reaches the best practice level. In order to excel, a firm shall have to exceed the benchmarks. In this manner, benchmarking offers firms a tangible method to evaluate performance.

Comprehensive analysis

This includes balanced scorecard and key factor rating. This analysis adopts a total approach rather than focusing on one area of activity, or a function or department.

STRATEGIC MANAGEMENT

1. Balanced scorecard method is based on the identification of four key performance measures of customer perspective, internal business perspective, innovation and learning perspective, and the financial perspective. This method is a balanced approach to performance measurement as a range of parameters is taken into account for evaluation.
2. Key factor rating is a method that takes into account the key factors in several areas and then sets out to evaluate performance on the basis of these. This is quite a comprehensive method as it takes a holistic view of the performance areas in an organization besides the several techniques referred to above, we could mention four other techniques that are used by some companies to assess performance. These are the network techniques, parta system, management by objectives, and the memorandum of understanding.
3. The parta system is an indigenous system adopted usually by Marwadi firms to keep track of daily cash generation. Parta is the pre-determined budget of the net cash inflows from operation before tax and dividend. The parta is decided in between the family group and company head, and actual performance is compared to this budgeted parta on a daily basis, thus making parta an effective operational control device.
4. path method (CPM), and their variants, are used extensively for the operational controls of scheduling and resource allocation in projects. When network techniques are modified for use as a cost accounting system, they become highly effective operational controls for project costs and performance.
5. Management by Objectives (MBO) is a system, proposed by Drucker, which is based on a regular evaluation of performance against objectives which are decided upon mutually by the superior and the subordinate. By the process of consultation, objective-setting leads to the establishment of a control system that operates on the basis of commitment and self-control. Thus, the scope of MBO to be used as an operational control is quite extensive.
6. Memorandum of understanding Just like MBO is a commitment to objectives between individuals, a memorandum of understanding (MOU) is an agreement between a public enterprise and the Government, represented by the administrative ministry in which both parties clearly specify their commitments and responsibilities. Having done that, the enterprises are evaluated on the basis of the MOU. Though an MOU is usually thought of

as a technique used solely in the context of public enterprises, its use can be extended to any situation where an external agency is required to evaluate a firm's performance. Thus, a multinational company can set an MoU with its subsidiary and a family business group council can use an MoU to evaluate its constituent companies. With the greater professionalization of private firms, especially in the family business sector, the use of MoUs can be helpful. But in India the usage of MoU is traditionally confined to the evaluation of performance in a public enterprise. Operational control systems guide, monitor, and evaluate progress in meeting annual objectives. While strategic controls attempt to steer the company over an extended Strategic Evaluation and Control time period (usually five years or more), operational controls provide post-action evaluation and control over short time periods ¾usually from one month to one year. To be effective, operational control systems must take four steps common to all post action controls:

1. Set standards of performance.
2. Measure actual performance.
3. Identify deviations from standards.
4. Initiate corrective action or adjustment.

CHALLENGES IN STRATEGY IMPLEMENTATION

The strategy implementation is an important part of the strategic management process because the instance of proper implementation, we won't get good results from the business. We will face the some of the challenges in the strategy implementation. The following challenges are below.

- Insufficient partner buy-in: In conducting strategic planning, firm leaders and partners involved in the process develop a strong understanding of the business imperative behind the chosen strategy and the need for change in order to achieve partner goals. However, partners removed from the process may struggle to identify with the goals and strategies outlined by firm leaders. These partners may not see a need for change, and without understanding the background and rationale for the chosen strategy, these partners may never buy-in to strategic plan and, as a result, will passively or actively interfere with the implementation process.
- Insufficient leadership attention: Too often, law firm leaders view the strategy development process as a linear or finite initiative. After undergoing a resource intensive strategic planning process, the firm's Managing Partner and Executive Committee members may

find themselves jumping back into billable work or immersing themselves in other firm matters, mistakenly believing that writing the plan was the majority of the work involved. Within weeks of finalizing the plan, strategies start to collect dust, partners lose interest, and eventually, months pass with little or no reference to the plan or real action from firm leaders to move forward with implementation.

- Ineffective leadership: Leading strategy implementation requires a balancing act - the ability to work closely with partners in order to build cohesion and support for the firm's strategy, while maintaining the objectivity required in order to make difficult decisions. Strategy implementation frequently fails due to weak leadership, evidenced by firm leaders unable or unwilling to carry out the difficult decisions agreed upon in the plan. To compound the problem, partners within the firm often fail to hold leaders accountable for driving implementation, which ultimately leads to a loss of both the firm's investment in the strategy development process as well as the opportunities associated with establishing differentiation in the market and gaining a competitive advantage.
- Weak or inappropriate strategy: During the course of strategic planning, the lack of a realistic and honest assessment of the firm will lead to the development of a weak, inappropriate or potentially unachievable strategy. A weak strategy may also result from overly aspirational or unrealistic firm leaders or partners who adopt an ill-fitting strategy with respect to the firm's current position or market competition. Without a viable strategy, firms struggle to take actions to effectively implement the plan identified.
- Resistance to change: The difficulty of driving significant change in an industry rooted in autonomy and individual lawyer behaviors is not to be underestimated. More often than not, executing on strategy requires adopting a change in approach and new ways of doing things. In the context of law firms, this translates to convincing members of the firm, and in particular partners, that change is needed and that the chosen approach is the right one.

ROLE OF CORPORATE GOVERNANCE

The Organization for Economic Cooperation and Development (OECD) defines corporate Governance as “a set of relationships between a company’s management, its board, its shareholders, and other stakeholders. Corporate governance also provides the structure through which the objectives of the company are set, and the means of attaining those objectives and monitoring performance are determined. Good corporate governance should provide proper incentives for the board and management to pursue objectives that are in the interests of the company and its shareholders and should facilitate effective monitoring.”

Appropriate organizational structures, policies and other controls help promote, but do not ensure, good corporate governance. Governance lapses can still occur through undesirable behavior and corporate values. Effective corporate governance is not only the result of "hard" structural elements, but also "soft" behavioral factors driven by dedicated directors and management performing faithfully their duty of care to the institution.

What makes organizational structures and policies effective, in practice, are knowledgeable and competent individuals with a clear understanding of their role and a strong commitment to carrying out their respective responsibilities.

CASE STUDY

AIR TRAFFIC

Finnair established in 1923, and it is the sixth oldest scheduled airline in the world. The Four main sectors of the company are flight operations, travel agencies, tour operations, and hotel and restaurant operations. Flight operations constitute about 80 % of the net sales of the company. All the operations are closely connected with marketing the services of the parent company and producing support services for flight operations. State ownership of the case company has gradually been reduced. At the end of March 1996, the Finnish State owned 60.7 % of the company's shares.

The case company is an international medium-sized airline. In 1995/1996, the consolidated net sales amounted to FIM 7,182 million and the company employed about 10,000 people. The net profit for the accounting period 1995/1996 was FIM 372 million. The flight operations are focused in international route traffic, consisting mainly of European traffic. In 1995/1996, the share of international route traffic was approximately 70% of air transport revenues.

Previously, Finn air's cost level has been quite high compared with other European airlines, but its costs have gradually been cut down, being today below the average level of European airlines (Expanding Horizons 1994). Personnel costs, constituting one third of the total costs of the company, are the largest cost item. Additionally, the largest cost items consist of fuel purchases for flight operations, purchases of materials and supplies for passenger services, and ground service costs.

Air traffic is a very capital-intensive industry, and during the last few decades there have been rapid innovations in aviation technology. Therefore, airlines need to finance major capital investments. In 1996, Finnair decided to modernize its holiday traffic fleet, and a new aircraft family for European traffic has quite recently been chosen.

During the last few years, the organizational structure of Finnair has often been changed.

At the beginning of the 1990's, the organization was decentralized but, a few years later, increasing competition led to a centralization of the organizational structure again. In 1990, the separate group management was suppressed and three operational groups,flight operations group, a technical group and a commercial group were formed of the prior seven departments of the parent company. The commercial group was divided into four route sectors responsible for their results. In 1992, the Supervisory Board of Finnair decided to change the organizational structure in order to improve the market position of the company, to increase the efficiency of planning operations and to reduce organizational levels. The four route sectors at the commercial department were united into two groups: Finnair North and Finnair International.

In order to improve the profitability of the company a strategic action programme was approved by the Supervisory Board of Finnair in February 1993. Thereafter, further organizational restructuring actions have been implemented, and the number of employees has been reduced. In April 1993, Finnair North and Finnair International were united into Marketing Group. The Marketing Group was made responsible for marketing functions, traffic planning and route profitability.

In November 1993, an extraordinary general meeting approved an Amendment to the Articles of Association in order to increase the authority of the Board of Directors, and correspondingly reduce the authority of the Supervisory Board. In April 1994, a new administrative body, the internal Board of Management, was formed to replace the prior Management Group.

The members of the body are appointed by the Board of Directors. Thereafter, further organizational changes have been implemented in the Group structure. During the financial year 1995/1996, a single administrative unit, Finnair Travel Service, was established in order to eliminate overlapping in package tours, and Finnair's ten travel agencies operating abroad were combined into a single organization called Norvista. In addition, the subsidiary companies Finnaviation and Karair were merged with the parent company in 1996. The financial management functions of the subsidiaries were integrated and a common accounting system was introduced.

The planning system of the company is decentralized. Thus, planning operations are performed separately at the marketing department, the technical department and the operational department. Calculations for route planning are made at the marketing department. The company has regarded the lack of a long-term and extensive traffic planning system as a problem. The budgeting process is entrusted to the financing department, but the budget proposals concerning personnel, expenses and investments are made by the functional groups. Budget objectives are defined and their achievement is controlled by the Board of Directors. The objectives are tight and the budget cannot be revised during the year.

In the 1990's, the control system of the company has been under a development process.

According to the interviews at the financing department, the objective of the reform has been to increase the flexibility and diversity of the reporting and the performance measurement systems. The reform aims at reducing the amount of information the top management has to deal with. Therefore, the control system will be coordinated so that top management receives only the most important information. Furthermore, the management group has been trained in activity-based management, and a few experimental activity-based costing projects have been carried out in the case company.

Starting from the spring of 1997, a new action programme has been prepared in order to improve the structural profitability of the company by FIM 500 million by the end of 1999.

The objective of the programme is to attain sustainable structural changes by increasing revenues and cutting costs, since in the competitive markets the company has to be agile and capable of quickly reacting to environmental changes. Thus, work processes have to be reorganized and co-operation has to be increased. In addition, the company has invested heavily in its service concept. The company aims at becoming the best European airline measured by punctuality.

The airline industry environment at the moment, European airlines are undergoing a process of radical change. On the one hand, deregulation has increased competition and the environment has turned dynamic and turbulent. On the other hand, the economic recession reduced demand for air traffic at the beginning of the 1990's. However, in the middle of the decade demand started to recover and the profitability of European airlines has improved. International air traffic has traditionally been regulated by a group of bilateral and multilateral agreements and by the rules of the International Air Transport Association (IATA). The regulations have affected entry to routes, capacity and fares. The basis of these regulations is the Chicago Convention concluded in 1944, which covers both regular route traffic and irregular charter traffic. In the 1980's, the provisions of bilateral agreements were loosened in the European air traffic. At the same time, the European Commission has gradually liberalized air traffic regulations. The first liberalization package was accepted in December 1987. The second package was accepted in June 1990, and the third package was implemented at the beginning of 1993. Thereafter, the whole area of the European Community has been a home market for Community air carriers. The final cabotage restrictions on air traffic in Europe were removed in 1997. Analogous to the United States, deregulation has led to significant structural and operational changes within the European airline industry (Doganis 1991, 95). Airlines have restructured their operations and increased cooperation. In the last few years, airlines providing worldwide services have built up alliances through holdings and agreements. Moreover, some national flag carriers have been privatized.

Finnair has had cooperation negotiations with several airlines. At the beginning of the 1990's, the establishment of the Quality Alliance with SAS, Swissair and Austrian Airlines did not materialize. Thereafter, Finnair has concluded cooperation and code sharing agreements for example with Lufthansa, Delta Air Lines, Swissair, Sabena, Alitalia and Transwede. Recently, cooperation negotiations with British Airways about route structure, development of customer service and marketing have been opened.

There has been another structural change in airline markets as airlines are forming huband-spoke route structures. The reason for this development trend is that it offers economies of scale and scope in air traffic. On the one hand, economies of scale mainly consist of economies of density in different routes (e.g. McGowan & Seabright 1989, Cronshaw & Thompson 1991). Economies of density arise as the unit costs of operation decrease at the same time the amount of traffic increases on a route. Hub-and-spoke networks allow carriers to increase average traffic levels on all routes. Higher traffic density on a route allows the airline to use larger, more efficient aircraft and to operate this equipment more intensively (Brueckner & Spiller 1994). On the other hand, economies of scope are attainable through a hub-and-spoke routestructure as load factors of aircrafts increase and unit costs decrease. In the last few years, Finnair has established a new hub in Stockholm.

After liberalizing bilateral agreements, a number of charter airlines have started to operate scheduled services, since scheduled operations permit charter airlines to charge higher fares, to increase their revenues and to improve aircraft and crew utilization. In addition, several new small airlines have entered the scheduled routes. Most of the revenue-pooling agreements between European carriers have also been abolished (Doganis 1991, 100–103). At the beginning of the 1980's, air traffic markets were regarded as a case example of contestable markets (Bailey & Panzar 1981, Bailey & Friedlaender 1982). The entry of new airlines was considered easy because of the homogeneity of airline services and the transferability of air traffic fleet into other markets. In contrast, later studies (e.g. Graham et al. 1983, Call & Keeler 1985, Moore 1986) have suggested that air traffic markets do not perfectly fulfill the conditions of contestable markets. In spite of deregulation, there still remain some entry barriers restricting competition in air traffic. For example, computer reservation systems and the allocation of slots may erect entry barriers (McGowan & Seabright 1989).

Competitive strategy and strategic positioning of the case company -The competitive strategy of the case company is to develop a profitable and competitive route structure, taking into consideration the needs of customers travelling from Finland, to Finland and through Finland. Thus, the aim of the company is to focus its services on a geographical market segment. The focus or niche strategy is based on differentiation by offering services of superior quality. In addition, gateway traffic by arranging further connections from Finland to other continents has been increasingly emphasized. Typically, the main stages of a value chain of an airline are as follows (Shank & Govindarajan 1992):

1. Providing information about seat reservation and ticket services;
2. Flight from point A to point B; and
3. Providing other services to customers before, during and after the flight.

The sources of competitive advantage and strategic cost drivers are different at each stage of the value chain. Although the air service part of the product is fairly homogeneous, the chain of services can be differentiated from that of the competitors more easily than single services.

Economies of scope between different stages of the value chain are attainable through vertical Integration. Thus, airlines have been keen on expanding their operations vertically into other areas of the travel industry in order to gain greater control over the total travel product .A value chain has not been formed and used in the strategic planning of the case company. However, the operations have been classified into basic services, support services, additional services and special services. Traffic sectors have been grouped into European, Atlantic, Far Eastern and domestic sectors. Furthermore, at the business unit level, the markets have been segmented into five segments: business travel, holiday travel, travelling for special events, or for meeting relatives and friends, and special group travel.

Scale and scope are important structural cost drivers in the case company. In addition, executional cost drivers, for example capacity utilization, total quality management, and linkages with suppliers and/or customers, have been increasingly emphasized. Planning information of the route decision The case route was opened for traffic at the end of March 1992. According to the management of the case company, the establishment of the route was a strategic decision to take advantage of the opportunities of the liberalized air traffic markets. In order to be prepared for the deregulated environment, the case company tried to get economies of scope by expanding its route network in Europe.

Airline planning is a dynamic and iterative process (Doganis 1991, 202). During the planning process, calculations were made of expected revenues and costs, and the profitability of the route was anticipated. In addition, the revenues and costs of alternative routes were analyzed. Revenue calculations were based on demand forecasts of alternative routes in different price categories. The preferences of customers in various geographical segments were discovered with the assistance of local organizations placed near the markets. Price information was acquired through IATA, and information about competitors' time schedules through CRS-systems. Revenue and cost calculations are usually made for one year at a time. In broad outline, calculations for route planning are similar for all routes. The costs of the routes are calculated both for one return flight and for each flight period.

Ex ante cost calculations are, as a rule, quite detailed. The total cost consists of traffic costs, technical costs, operation costs, and commercial costs. Traffic costs consist of direct variable costs, for instance fuel, landing fees, and ground handling. Technical costs include line maintenance, overhauls, and spare parts. Operation costs include cockpit, cabin service, and in flight service costs. Commercial costs are in most cases indirect fixed costs. They include costs of the foreign sales offices and costs of the marketing department of the company. The establishment of the new route did not entail considerable incremental costs. No new air traffic fleet was acquired for the route. Due to a new airport office established in Barcelona, there was a slight increase in the labor costs and marketing costs in Spain compared with the previous year. The decision to establish the route was a multi-stage process in the organization. As the organization has been frequently changed, planning calculations are made by several persons in different parts of the organization. Therefore, practical calculatory applications by various departments may differ. Ultimately, the marketing department is responsible for the route planning calculations. The final decision on the establishment of the route was made by the Management Group. Furthermore, route scenario calculations envision long-run growth possibilities for 15 years, including alternative air traffic fleet choices, and projecting possible demand, cost and profitability. Control information of the route decision Profitability in air traffic depends on the unit cost, the unit revenue and the load factors achieved (Doganis 1991, 282). In the case company, there is a control system measuring route profitability. The system controls unit cost and revenues, results by route, by air traffic type and by traffic segment, load factors and freight revenues etc. The system is partly based on actual, partly on budgeted figures.

Route profitability is assessed by contribution margins. As a general rule, both variable and fixed costs should be covered by all established routes. At the latest, the routes have to be profitable within three years. It may suffice, for instance in case of excess capacity that a positive margin over variable costs is earned. Every route is also considered a part of the whole route network value.

By means of the case firm's cost accounting system, it is not possible to monitor customer profitability, as the costs caused by one customer cannot be identified. Neither can the profitability of each customer segment be determined. In particular, the marketing managers regarded this insufficiency of information as a problem. It would be possible to use activity-based costing to examine customer or customer segment profitability. However, according to the Financial Director, customer profitability calculations were considered too expensive to make, even if an activity-based costing system was established.

As a rule, the control system of the case company does not gather benchmark information about competitors. In spite of that, information about competitors' market shares can be achieved. Some non-financial performance measures are used in the case company, for example passenger and overall load factors, flight hours and kilometers, available seat and tonne kilometers, revenue passenger and tonne kilometers and number of passengers, cargo and mail.

It seems, however, that the non-financial measures are not systematically consonant to the strategy of the company.

In the case company, route planning and control calculations are made at different departments. The marketing department is responsible for route planning calculations, whereas route profitability calculations are carried out at the department of internal relations and traffic planning. This decentralization appears to cause problems in the flow of information. Budget reports are produced monthly, and exact reports on budget deviations are obtained from quarterly accounts. However, especially at the marketing department, information about budget deviations was not received quickly enough on the lower organizational levels. The level of detail in planning and route profitability calculations has increased during the last few years. This seems, at least partly, to result from economic deregulation, since increasing competition calls for detailed information about costs even at the establishment stage of a route. The established case route has reached its short-run and long-run objectives quite well. In the spring of 1995, two years after its establishment, the profitability of the route was better than the budgeted profitability figures. In addition, the traffic frequency on the route has been increasing. Analysis of strategic control information of the route decision Planning and control information assisting the management in the route decision of the case company was analyzed by the theoretical model of strategic control information developed in the study. Furthermore, the applicability of information to the deregulated environment and to the service sector was investigated.

According to the Executive Vice President of the marketing division, the establishment of the route was a strategic long-run investment. In the long run, high profitability and a large market share were the principal objectives of the route. These objectives are similar to the objectives of build units in the portfolio models of strategic planning. The market environment of build units is often uncertain, and products are at a growth stage of their life cycles. In contrast, the objective of budgets in the case company was to control the achievement of targets. Therefore, this budget objective seems to be unsuitable for the business environment of the case company. In the uncertain and turbulent competitive environment, companies following a build strategy would rather need budgets to support their planning functions. The case company has not decisively changed its competitive strategy in order to be prepared for economic deregulation in the environment. However, the company has actively begun to take advantage of the opportunities of deregulation in its route planning. Finnair has been one of the first airlines in Europe that has actively expanded its route structure due to deregulation. Deregulation is regarded as an opportunity for the company. The established route gave Finnair cost advantages, and assisted in following the differentiation strategy Traditional methods were emphasized in generating information for the strategic planning of the case route. Moreover, the information gathered was short-run information for the most part. A value chain for the route was not identified, and therefore the strategic objectives for each value activity could not be specified. Lack of a value chain was found a drawback in the planning and control system of the case company. However, it would have been difficult to identify the value chain, as the responsibility centers of the functional organization were not analogous to value activities. The planning information of the route, for instance the SWOT analysis, was mostly based on internal information of the company. Moreover, internal performance measures were emphasized in the control information of the route. Profitability, service level, and load factors were measured by traditional management accounting variance analyses. Measurement of the cost, profitability and load factors of the route was principally considered to support the cost leadership strategy. In contrast, measurement of the quality of services was connected to the customer-oriented differentiation strategy. Gaining a sustainable competitive advantage calls for continuous improvement. Increasing competition has gradually led the case company to changing its control systems so that they are more agile and detailed than before. The use of historical data has been considered a drawback in the present control system of the case firm. More future-oriented information would be needed. Moreover, the control system did not systematically report benchmarking information. More information especially about competitors was considered to be expedient in the decision making process of the company. The organizational structure of the case company has frequently been changed. Due to the formal and rigid organizational structure and a strong corporate culture, the changes have resulted in much resistance within the organization, gradually, however, in a less degree. As deficient coordination between different service functions was considered a problem in the organization, the organizational structure of the case company was recently centralized. However, centralization may restrict the flow of market information to each part of the organization, and it may hamper the progress of a service culture. Most of the characteristics typical of service companies could be found in the strategic control information of the case company. Customer-driven planning and control information was emphasized. Information about demand factors was gathered, in particular, as revenues were considered critical in the budgeting process. Customer needs were examined by the local organizations of the company. In the last few years, customer focus has been increasingly emphasized in the case company. As the preferences and the quantity of resources used by each customer vary, it would be important for management to be aware of customer and customer segment costs and profitability.

CONCLUSIONS AND DISCUSSION

The purpose of the study was to analyze how airlines use their management control systems in order to gain a sustainable competitive advantage in a situation of environmental change resulting from economic deregulation. Moreover, the distinct characteristics of strategic control information in the service sector were studied.

First, a general model for strategic control information applicable to various industries and environments was developed. Second, in the empirical case study, the strategic control information in an air traffic route decision was investigated. An airline was chosen as the case company, on the one hand, because it is a service company, and on the other hand, because the environment of air traffic is rapidly changing resulting from the deregulation process. Strategic control information was defined as the information generated by management control systems to assist management at all stages of a strategic decision process, and which emphasizes long-run external information. The objective of strategic control information is to contribute to management decision making in order to gain a sustainable competitive advantage. The competitive strategy affects the characteristics of accounting information needed at the planning stage. The achievement of strategic objectives is measured by control information.

In conclusion, producing planning and control information for strategic decision making in the case company was mainly based on traditional methods, and the control systems did not generate a great deal of information in accordance with the theoretical model developed in the study. Contribution margins were used to assist strategic planning, although they may not be considered particularly suitable for strategic long-run planning purposes. The information assisting decision making was short-run information for the most part. The control information of the case company was concentrated on internal performance measurement, and the control system did not systematically collect benchmarking information about customers and competitors.

Strategic control information could have been used more in order to aid decision making in the case company. Nevertheless, it is obvious that strategic viewpoints were, at least in part, taken into account in management decision making, in spite of the shortcomings of the control system. An indication of this is that the route decision supported the competitive strategy, and it seemed to be possible to achieve a sustainable competitive advantage by the established route.

Entry and prices have been strictly regulated in air traffic. During the past ten years, a gradual deregulation has taken place and a significant change in the competitive environment cawas not able to produce information applicable to the deregulated environment. Especially the flexibility of the control system had not fulfilled, up to the end of the 2-year interview period, the requirements of the deregulated environment.

In the 1990's, however, the management control systems of the case company have been under a development process, and the company has gradually begun to adjust its competitive strategy and organizational structure to the deregulated environment. The characteristics of strategic control information were not clearly found in the route decision investigated in the study. Recently, the agility and flexibility of the control system have been increased and customer focus has been emphasized.

In the case company, the development process of the control system aims at limiting the amount of information the top management has to deal with. In response to the increasingly competitive environment, the control system will be changed to be more interactive. This finding supports the dynamic process model developed by Simons (1990, 1991, 1995). On the basis of his model, interactive management control systems are used in order to give top management information about strategic uncertainties that arise as the firm aims at gaining competitive advantage.

In addition, this study provides support to the results for other strategic management accounting research. First, the study suggests that the control information of the case company has increasingly emphasized customer focus. This supports Bromwich's (1990) point that products are a package of characteristics offered to consumers. In order to survive in a competitive market, a firm must offer the cheapest way for the consumer to obtain the bundle of characteristics being offered. There is therefore a need for market-oriented information for decision making.

Second, the need to develop planning and control systems has been realized especially at the marketing department of the company. This conclusion is consistent with the results of Cunningham (1990, 1992). He found that companies in highly competitive environments have management control and accounting systems that are dominated by marketing considerations. As marketing functions pull information through the system, they are considered to be accounting crafts.

Moreover, the studies of strategic change processes in organizations (e.g. Scapens & Roberts 1993, Scapens, Burns & Ezzamel 1996, Kloot 1997) suggest that management accounting practices tend to change slowly. In the last few years, the planning and control systems of the case company have been gradually developed to be compatible with the changing competitive environment. The change process continues to be in progress.

The model of strategic control information developed in this study will be useful for further studies. The characteristics of strategic control information can, at least, be generalized to apply to other traffic companies producing mass services. Furthermore, future work could extend the analysis of one strategic decision to the examination of planning and control systems at the company leveln be identified. According to the empirical analysis, the control system in the case company.

REVIEW QUESTIONS

Conceptual Types

1. What is strategic control?
2. What is strategy evaluation?
3. What do you mean by strategy evaluation and control?
4. Mention the various levels of strategy.
5. What is operational level strategy?
6. What is management control?
7. State the various evaluation techniques for operational control.
8. What is corporate governance?
9. Explain the need for Corporate Governance.
10. State the external corporate governance controls.
11. Give any two problems of corporate governance.
12. What do you mean by corporate governance philosophy?

Analytical Types

1. Explain different types of strategy control. ***(VTU, MBA, Dec-2011)***
2. What are the features of an effective control system?
3. What is control system? Explain the different type of control systems. ***(VTU, MBA, Dec-2012)***
4. Explain the strategy evaluation and control process.
5. Explain steps involved in designing effective control systems. ***(VTU, MBA, Dec-2012)***
6. Explain the different criteria for evaluating strategy.
7. Explain control model of Corporate Governance.
8. What are benefits of good corporate governance?
9. What are the principal constituents of corporate governance?

Descriptive Types

1. Explain the nature and importance of strategic evaluation.
2. Explain different types of strategic controls. Give examples for each type.
   (VTU, MBA, Dec-2011)
3. Discuss the types of strategic control. ***(VTU, MBA, June-2010)***
4. Discuss establishing strategic control.
5. Explain management control and its features.
6. What do you mean by operational control system ?
7. Explain various financial control techniques of evaluation.
8. Discuss challenges of strategic implementation.
9. Explain Corporate Governance in historical perspective.
10. State the objectives of corporate governance.
11. Explain various issues in corporate governance.
12. Explain various role of corporate governance.

******